THE HILL

The Hill

A MEMOIR OF WAR IN HELMAND PROVINCE

Aaron Kirk

The Second Mission Foundation

The Hill

A Memoir of War in Helmand Province
by Aaron Kirk

First Edition
Hardcover

Copyright © Aaron Kirk, 2020

Published in the United States of America in 2021 by
The Second Mission Foundation.

Edited by Linda Seme
Cover art by Eliyana Beitler
Cover design by David Provolo
ISBN (hardcover): 978173200926
ISBN: (paperback): 9781736200902
ISBN: (epub): 9781736200919
Library of Congress Control Number: 2021906256

The Second Mission Foundation
Charles Faint, Executive Director
1001 Bishop Street
Honolulu, HI 96813
www.secondmissionfoundation.org

This book is dedicated to R.D.,
and to the lower enlisted, who shoulder the heaviest burdens
in all of America's wars.

AUTHOR'S NOTE

This is a work of creative nonfiction. It reflects my interpretation of events that occurred when I was a Marine infantryman a decade ago.

In the interest of privacy I have changed names and details. At times I have combined several people into one person or eliminated people altogether. Some events were relayed to me. Dialogue is re-created from a faulty and ever-worsening memory. I write to the best of my recollection and cannot promise anything more.

This is a highly personal account of my experience during four years in the Marine Corps. A story about wild unwasted youth. About a windswept hill in a desolate field deep in southern Helmand province. About disappointment, adolescence, misery, courage, failure, and redemption. About ordinary men—boys, some of us—in extraordinary circumstances.

This is a story about grunts.

Part One

*There was nothing to
do but fight the war we
were given, even when it
didn't live up to
our expectations*

1

Step by Step

Garmsir District, Helmand Province, Afghanistan
2011

I am scraping furrows in the ground, searching for a bomb. The device in my hands is called a sickle. Some call it a Holley stick, after the Gunny who invented it. It's a six-foot-long piece of bamboo with a dull iron hook on the end. An opium farmer sold us the hook. We found the bamboo by the river. We used duct tape and nails to attach the sickle part to the bamboo part. We used a rock to grind the edge off the sickle blade. Now the sickle pulls up wires but doesn't cut them.

You don't want to cut the wires.

I draw two-foot by two-foot X's. I make sure the X's intersect. I pull from far to near, left to right, then right to left. I make sure not to drop the sickle blade too heavily in the soft dirt. I move forward slowly. I step only where the X's cross.

"Clear," I say to the guy behind me.

I backtrack through the cleared path. He takes my place. He carries a metal detector, and as he starts off in an uncleared direction, he swings the metal detector's head back and forth, back and forth, rhythmically, stepping with each swing. His eyes scan not just the ground in front of him but also the path ahead, which is not a path at all but open field.

We don't walk paths.

His pace is measured but not slow. He misses very little.

I remain stationary as his team leader, my number two, walks up and grabs the Holley stick from me. Wordlessly, routinely, he takes his place five yards behind the sweeper. He guides the sweeper. He nudges him this way and that, grunting rather than speaking. Another Marine passes, a medium machine gun on his shoulder, belts of ammunition across his chest. Tribal tattoos. He carries the Animal Mother vibe. Full Metal Jacket. Except, unlike Vietnam, he also carries thirty pounds of ceramic body armor and Oakley sunglasses.

Ten yards later a wiry, hairy man with a backpack trudges by. I hear the hum of the electronic Thor device he's carrying. The hum means it's working. The fact that we haven't been blown up with a radio-con-trolled bomb also means it's working. His neck is bright red, burned by the device's signal-blocking radiation. He'll get cancer someday, we're all sure of it, but at least we know the Thor is working. I also know it's working because it blocked my radio check with the Hill a few minutes ago, before we cleared the goat-trail intersection. We don't walk trails, but sometimes we clear the intersections. Usually the sickle-man does it. Sometimes I do it so he doesn't have to. Sometimes the Thor isn't working.

Ten yards after the Thor-man I fall in line. Number five. Four men in front of me, three behind. Sometimes more behind me, but never more in front, unless I'm clearing or walking up to investigate some-thing. Five is the best place to control. Six is my interpreter, Jack, walk-ing a little too close, but I let it go. Seven carries the big radio that can reach our platoon back at Patrol Base Durzay. Eight is an Afghan Na-tional Army soldier in green camouflage.

I pull my knees up a bit more as my boots sink into the mud. I step on furrows. I ruin the work of whoever plowed the field.

The movement would have tired me a thousand fields and a hun-dred patrols ago, but now it is routine. My head moves side to side, noting walled compounds in the distance, rows of planted trees between every three or four fields, a motorcycle driving along a dirt road.

I turn and walk backwards for a moment. Though I am burdened by body armor and kit I move with agility, like a jungle cat, choosing my steps carefully. I shrug my shoulders against the weight of my plate carrier. Check my radios, black and green. Rifle, safety on. Night vision monocle in its pouch. Casio on my left wrist, Garmin GPS on my right. Map and notebook in the slim kangaroo pocket for easy access.

There are four men in front of me.
I am a walking casevac nineline.
Any moment now.
I am a bundle of nerve endings.
I won't hear it. One step, two step, one step, two step.
I expect explosions.

We do not walk where others walk. We do not walk trails. We do not walk paths. And yet with every step I expect blinding flames and deafening noise. I brace for ringing ears. I think about the instant I will be blown up. I am certain it will happen. I fear the earth erupting, and I know it is inevitable. In some ways, I long for it. Every second of every patrol, I wait for the ground to move. It doesn't matter how many bombs we find safely. There's always another one.

Four men, four chances to step on something before I do.

Our ranger-file formation stops. Nobody speaks. We take a knee and alternate facing left and right as the sickle-man pulls at something up ahead. I check my map. We're two hundred meters from the third village of the day. I need to speak with the village elder before we can return to the Hill. I like him. He's not as bad as the one I met an hour ago.

I check the position of the sun. Mid-day. There will be *naan* bread and chai tea for us.

We rise. We walk.

We near the edge of the village. There are children playing outside of a house with tall brown mud walls and a blue door. They run to us and as they do they cross a footbridge and I begin to relax.

One less canal to ford.

A bridge is the perfect place to die. But today, because seven or eight children cross this bridge, it means we can cross it too. As we cross, children surround the four-man. One grabs his arm, tugging at his sleeve, trying to hold his hand. Four-man obliges. They walk the bridge together, and as they do, the child looks up at him and extends his other hand. Four-man smiles and pulls a blue pen out of his drop pouch. The child's mascara eyes light up. He grabs the pen with orange, henna-dyed fingernails. We are safely across the bridge.

On the other side we walk toward a small town square. There are people—men—around. People mean we can walk on the road without sweeping. So that's what we do, being careful to stay on hard-pack. Old men and young men in brown *dishdashas* and sparkling skullcaps smoke Pine cigarettes and smile at us from under a single metal awning. The mosque in the square is just another smooth-sided mud house with a red-and-yellow door and a megaphone-speaker mounted on a twenty-foot stick. The outdoor prayer area is a raised mud bowl with edges. We don't sit on it.

Instead, my men flop down in a ditch and on walls around the square and on the edge of a well. They take off their helmets and their backpacks and rest their rifles against their legs or the ground. The machine gunner casually relaxes into a position with a clear field of fire down the road.

"Jack, Nate, let's go inside," I say. I look at the Corpsman. "Doc?"

He's a few feet from a cozy-looking wall with shade. He turns back to look at me. It's his turn for tea.

"You want to come inside?" I ask.

"Nah, I'm...I'm good," he says. He reaches the wall and turns around. He pulls his bulky medical backpack off one strap at a time and lays it at his feet. Following the rest of the squad's example, he leans against the wall and slumps down slowly, haltingly, until he is seated on a ledge, his rifle buttstock-down in the dirt, his hands inside his flak jacket, chin in the air, breathing in heat that permeates even the shadows.

Jack, my interpreter, and Nate, the Marine who was carrying the Thor, join me in walking toward the house with the blue door. Nate leaves the Thor by the sickle-man. He turns it off to save the battery. I hope it works when we leave.

The village elder prefers to meet me in this small outer house. A few kids linger by the door. I nod to Jack. He speaks to them in Pashto. They speak back. He gives one of them a pen. The kid runs toward a compound at the edge of town. We wait by the door, smoking cigarettes.

I spend the time it takes for the village elder to arrive thinking about the relative danger of sitting in a village versus walking in fields. I reassure myself that we're perfectly safe relaxing in this mud town. Nobody is going to shoot at us here. Nobody can blow us up inside the village. The edges of this little hamlet should be part of the safe zone, too. They *have* to be. These farmers would know if there were a bomb nearby. How could they not? After what happened before? After all their promises?

I would know if someone planted a bomb in my backyard.

Or would I?

I am not dead yet.
But I will be soon.
Not yet.

The village elder appears from around the corner of the building. I take off my right glove to shake his withered hand. He is white beard and leathered skin and decades of war and a pilgrimage to Mecca. I am a twenty-one-year-old from Colorado with a Blink-182 tattoo on my calf.

I say hello about four different ways in Pashto and he reciprocates. I make sure to smile. He motions to the house. We walk together, slowly, my interpreter on his other side, another Afghan leading us, Nate behind me, smoking a cigarette. The door to the house is small and creaks when we open it. The sole window holds no glass, but there are two metal bars crossed in the middle. I can't tell if they're for decoration. A child rushes past me to grab some pillows from the corner and spread them on the floor. As the child runs out we sit across from the elder, Jack to my left, Nate to my right. I keep my body armor on and lay my rifle across my lap. I reach for the pack of smokes I keep in my left shirt pocket but find it empty. The village elder offers me one and I accept.

I tell him *thank you* in Pashto.

He nods and smiles. What a pair of souls we are.

"It doesn't matter what I say to you," I say in English, smiling and waving around the room. Jack translates something into Pashto. It's probably not what I said, because the village elder responds kindly.

"I really wish you would tell me who put that bomb on the road over by The Hill," I remark. I sigh. "It really bums me out that none of you guys will tell me that."

Jack looks at me quizzically. I give him a certain expression and he translates something into Pashto. The village elder talks this time. He goes on for some time. I turn to Jack.

"He says he likes the American patrols. He says there are no Taliban here."

"Great," I say. "That's great." I wonder if we should get smokes at the bazaar on the way back.

"He wants to know when you are going to leave."

"Why? Tell him I asked why he wants to know that."

Jack translates. The elder speaks for even longer this time.

"He says the land around The Hill belongs to him."

"So?"

"He says he can't farm it while you are there."

"Why not?"

Jack says something in Pashto. The elder responds.

"He says people are afraid to go near the base. There is a lot of noise during the night."

I think for a long moment.

"Tell him we'll be gone in like, four months," I finally say.

"Are we supposed to tell him that?" Nate asks.

I shrug. "I don't know. Maybe not."

Jack relays my message. The elder's face seems to brighten.

There is a light knock at the door and two children enter, one carrying a plate of bread, the other a teapot and hard candies.

"Jack, tell him I said thanks for the tea."

Jack is drinking tea. He hasn't taken off his sunglasses. He tells the kid. Another smile. Another hand wave.

We sit in silence for a few moments and enjoy the respite from the sun.

Why am I here?

I am here because I have to be. Because of counterinsurgency. Because presence patrols and key leader engagements. I think the elder is here because I have a gun.

He's not a bad guy. I don't think he's Taliban. But I couldn't really say he's on my side, either. Not after what happened.

Speaking of which.

"Jack," I say. "Does he have any more information about who put that bomb by the bridge when we first got here? Did he ever find anything out about that?"

Jack asks. The elder, as expected, shakes his head no.

"Of course he doesn't know anything," Nate says. "Why would he? He just runs the place."

I concur with Nate's assessment.

"Well, thanks anyway," I say.

I place my tea back down on the saucer. "Jack, tell him we're leaving."

We get up and gather our gear. After we exit the house, I shake the elder's hand. I shake the hand of the other Afghan man who was in our meeting and didn't say a word. He is black-haired. He, too, has orange fingernails.

"I just want you to know," I say, pulling him close, placing my other hand on top of the hand I'm shaking, smiling broadly. "I don't blame you. I blame your leadership."

Nate snorts. The politely confused Afghan thanks me and does the Pashtun hand-flip. We wave goodbye and walk toward the men. I point my finger in the air and make a few circles as the squad stands up and gathers its gear. I pull out my green radio.

"KT-4, Two-Three Actual, over."

"This is KT-4, over."

"Roger, Two-Three is moving, returning to base."

"Roger, copy Two-Three RTB en route to the Hill, over."

"Roger, solid. Out."

We walk out of the village the opposite way we came in, single file, an expanding Slinky, ten yards of dispersion between each of us. We avoid the bridge we don't cross anymore and instead walk through the canal a few dozen meters downstream. The canal is too wide to jump and has water in it. I sigh as I slide down the embankment and land in murky water. I am soaked to my knees. My boots pull mud from the canal bed. I pull on sawgrass and haul myself up the opposite side. I kick the mud from my boots and hope they dry before we get back. I'm not optimistic.

The way back to the Hill is more of the same. Rugged micro-terrain, dirt-piles to trip on. Date trees and field after field of poppies. The occasional wild dog. The spaces between the fields are covered in a knee-high yellow grass that turns green as it approaches canals that have water.

As I swing wide around the corner of a crumbling compound wall, I get a clear view of a great tan mound of dirt rising from the flatness around it. Even at a mile's distance I can make out its features: sheer cliff on one side, gentle slope on the other. On top, sagging Hesco barrier walls, camouflage netting, fire from the burn pit. My pulse quickens, the way it does every time I see it. My palms sweat as I think about all the steps I still must take before I get there. And as quickly as it appears, the landmark recedes, hidden behind compound walls, leaving in its place only a burning mental image and a familiar name:

Patrol Base KT-4.

The Hill.

Home.

2

Real Problems

My friend Rob told me a story once. He said that when he was a boot some Classic Marine Corps Shit happened. It's his first trip to Afghanistan, right as he's getting ready to leave. Rob's got two weeks left before he's on a plane home. There's a new battalion on deck, taking over all the positions. A fresh platoon arrives at Rob's patrol base. For a short time the two units do patrols and stand post together. One day Rob gets paired up with this kid, Schmidt.

Schmidt's a classic screwup. Whole platoon hates him. Easy to see why. Standing post with him is a complete drag. Complains about his wife. Complains about his platoon sergeant. Complains about his squad leader, the chow, the post schedule. Wants to go home. Doesn't know why he joined the Marine Corps.

He vocalizes things that everyone thinks but doesn't say, at least not often. You let it slip every once in a while: *fuck the Marine Corps.* You say it while you're standing around freezing, or when the chow's cold, or when you're on day four of a five-day field op. But you don't make a big deal of it. You don't let it become part of your character. If it's part of your character, you're done for. Nobody wants to be here, but if everyone knows you don't want to be here, they start to doubt your reliability. They start to think you won't run toward the sound of the guns. Maybe you'll just lay down in a canal. Wish things were different, instead of facing things head on.

They think you'll fall asleep on post. Shoot in the wrong direction. Get people killed.

They start to think you have Real Problems. Things are All About You and you are Somehow Special and your problems are More Important Than Everyone Else's. Then—and maybe this is the real problem—instead of helping you, really helping you, professionally helping you, they make it worse.

Schmidt's seniors had his number. Rob says he never saw anyone get fucked with the way they fucked with Schmidt. They hated him. They didn't want to go to war with him, yet here he was, at war. He didn't want to be there, and nobody seemed to want him there.

All they'd let Schmidt do was stand post. Eight hours in a box behind a machine gun, him and his thoughts. During the handover period, Schmidt had another Marine to share these thoughts with. And share them he did.

After one shift, Rob came off while Schmidt stayed there for another eight hours. Sixteen hours standing in the same spot. Rob didn't know why. Probably Schmidt's seniors made him do it. Rob didn't care. He was going home.

Nobody knows exactly how the next part went. They know Schmidt was outside the tiny base. Nobody knows exactly why he was out there, but you can guess. Maybe he was trying to get away from his squad. Maybe he felt trapped and alone. Maybe he felt worthless. Maybe he wanted privacy.

Maybe he was sitting on a sandbag, staring into the fields. No way to know for sure, but maybe he stood up with a weary, resigned look on his face, the kind of look you first see in bootcamp, when a kid's had enough incentive training, enough smoking, enough of the back-and-forth to the shower, enough of the quarterdeck, enough of isolation and loneliness and not fitting in. The look a man gets when nothing's getting through except his own thoughts, thoughts that lead him in dangerous directions. Maybe Schmidt was fighting some internal battle.

Maybe he was thinking about his family or his finances or his place in Afghanistan as a Marine. Maybe he didn't want to be a Shock Troop, Devil Dog, Blood Sucking War Machine anymore.

All anybody knows for sure is that Schmidt decided to suck on the barrel of his rifle and pull the trigger. In doing so he blew his head wide open and landed awkwardly in soft dirt. His brains splattered onto the Hesco barrier.

Not long after this, his platoon finds him. They call in a routine medevac. Maybe they think: already? The deployment's just started. Maybe somebody wins a bet.

Rob, on patrol with his squad, comes around the corner as the helicopter lands. He sees Schmidt's squad mates load the body onto a Blackhawk. He sees them grind Schmidt's bloody brain matter into the moondust with the toes of their boots, kicking skull fragments and gore until there's nothing left to remind anyone that Schmidt was ever there.

Later that day he watches Schmidt's squad rifle through his kit. They grab issued equipment, clothing, magazine pouches. They send back a fraction of the gear Schmidt is supposed to have. They joke about the Ghost of Schmidt, haunting and malingering. There is little sympathy for his weakness, and they are happy to be rid of him. Now they don't have to worry about going to war with someone who has Real Problems.

3

Semper Fidelis

When I joined the Marine Corps in 2008, I didn't know there was a war going on.

My father deployed to Iraq during the initial invasion. Five years later, I was mostly oblivious. I didn't know that anyone was still fighting that war. Or that Afghanistan was still churning, now in its seventh year. Or that American soldiers rotated overseas on seven, twelve, fourteen-month deployments. Or that troops were killed and maimed and disfigured almost every day.

As a teenager I was obstinate and self-centered and lacked work ethic. I changed my mind often. When I was fourteen I told my father that I would never, under any circumstances, join the military. Four years later I was standing on the yellow footprints of Marine Corps Recruit Depot San Diego.

I don't think anyone has just one reason to join. I watched a lot of war movies. I didn't play team sports, which seemed to be a prerequisite for Marines. I spent my teenage years doing squats and deadlifts and pullups and early functional fitness workouts. I had a brief fling with parkour. I delivered cheesesteak sandwiches in my late-eighties Volvo. I loved punk rock and skateboarding but gave it all up one year because

I wanted a girlfriend. I wore Aeropostale because I couldn't afford Hollister.

I joined the Marine Corps because I was immature. I joined the Marine Corps because I didn't belong anywhere, because I desperately wanted people to include me. I wanted to be part of something, anything—a brotherhood, a clan, a tribe. I wanted the true "military experience." I wanted someone to slam my head into a chalkboard, like in the movie *Jarhead*. I wanted to give out a Code Red on a poorly performing fellow grunt, like in *A Few Good Men*.

I wanted attention. I wanted people in my high school to ask: where have you been? And I'd say: the Marines.

I did not join to go to war. I didn't even know war was a possibility.

I was the type of kid who wore Tapout t-shirts but would do anything to avoid a fight. The kid who loved playing *Magic: The Gathering* and *World of Warcraft* but never told anyone. The type of teenager who borrowed his dad's car to take a girl out on a date because he was embarrassed of the car he bought himself, with his own money, just because it was old.

I joined to posture. I joined because I fucked up high school so bad that by the time I got to senior year I had no way of getting admitted to any reputable college. I joined because I was too afraid to face the rest of my life.

First I met with Army recruiters, because my father was in the Army. I was immediately turned off, unimpressed by their gray uniforms and their sunken eyes. Even so, I entertained the idea. I worked with them at first, passing the entrance exam with a high enough score to obtain any military occupational specialty. They offered me a large signing bonus, told me they could guarantee whatever job I wanted. I was noncommittal.

One morning out of curiosity I walked next door to the Marines, where I spoke with an enormous Dominican Staff Sergeant. He was a far cry from the Army recruiters next door. He was muscular, intense, focused. He wore civilian clothes. The first time he saw me, he looked me up and down with disdain and nodded to a pullup bar in the corner.

"Do as many as you can," he said.

I hopped up and squeaked out sixteen. I dropped heavily off the bar and looked to him, desperate for approval.

"Hmm. You *might* have what it takes to be a Marine. Come back tomorrow."

That was all I needed to sign my life away.

I was eager for bootcamp because I believed—really believed—in the idea of the Marine Corps. I bought into my recruiter's pitch. I was onboard with the brochures and the cards he showed me. The concept that Marines never lie, cheat, or steal. I believed that I would be a part of an elite group of fighting men that adheres to a set of principles, a code of honor, courage and commitment. I assumed the recruiting commercials were true.

I found that part of the Marine Corps, for a time. I found it on the parade field at MCRD San Diego, standing at attention for hours while our platoon waited on the Senior Drill Instructor to inspect us. I found it in my nightly firewatch and physical training and getting smoked on the quarterdeck and being too sick to hike. I found it in memorizing the names of famous Marine Corps battles: Khe Sanh, Saigon, Tarawa, Fallujah. Heroes: John Basilone and Smedley Butler and Chesty Puller. I found it every morning at the sound of reveille.

I found out things about myself I'd never even wondered. For example, I could go three months without masturbating. I could stop shitting for two weeks. I could run three miles in twenty minutes and fifty seconds and I could do thirty-five strict pullups unbroken. I could stand in one spot without moving for four hours.

Somewhere in between pissing in the same urinal as three other men and getting your ass beat during pugil stick training you realize the Marine Corps isn't made up of perfect people. You notice the Drill Instructors are not invincible. They suck down Monster energy drinks and have alcohol problems and make phone calls to angry spouses and sometimes they even sleep. And many of them are not very smart, and many of them are mean, and they are often bullies, and some of them can't turn it off.

But all of them are role models. They take the job of making new Marines very seriously. The perfect Marine is an obedient killing machine who executes orders with violence and unrelenting aggression. Drill Instructors are there to facilitate the transformation from the old harmless you to the new murderous you.

In order to be a Marine, you must, at least temporarily, give up the part of you which identifies as "I." You become something else, a person in flux, an accelerated creature of habit, instantaneous in your reactions. You are loud. You dart toward things until you are told to stop. You move to the sound of the (simulated) shooting. You exercise speed, surprise and violence of action. You try not to give up. You fail. You succeed.

Drill Instructors are there to make sure you won't think twice when you're told to hop off a landing craft and charge ashore, knowing you'll die. To make sure you don't ask *why* the order was given, only *what* the order is. The core of their curriculum is instant obedience to orders. They teach you to take initiative, so when the person in charge of you gets killed, you can take his or her place.

They teach you that Marines are interchangeable. Standard-issue. Equally worthless.

Some of the things you learn in recruit training you carry with you. Some things you don't. I tied a dogtag in my sneaker-laces for months after I left, because I thought that was a rule. I shaved on weekends, even when I didn't have to. I changed the way I spoke, interspersing "oohrah" and "kill" into everyday conversations. One thing I didn't do was tuck my t-shirt into my shorts, like some devil dogs I saw on base. I always thought that looked pretty fucking stupid.

Some of the lessons I learned at recruit training were important: to always take initiative. To fix problems as soon as you saw them. To correct others. To be first. To never lie, cheat or steal.

Other lessons were not as important. To kill with a bayonet. To tie your boots left lace over right. To wear Bulldog aftershave. To stomp a man's head into the ground while maintaining a proper combat stance.

You follow. You lead. You learn to be loud, louder than you've ever been, louder than anyone should ever be. Your voice goes away in the first month and comes back in the third.

You learn history. Every battle the Marine Corps ever fought. Every important year. Every hero. You learn tradition and slang and jargon. You learn about combat from Drill Instructors who were there and also from those who weren't. Portholes for glasses, deck for floor, moonbeam for flashlight. You learn that infantry is the only job that matters, and that every Marine is a rifleman, and you believe that until later, when you learn it's not true.

One day, near the end, they give you a metal Eagle, Globe and Anchor. You cry because it's expected.

The day I graduate, I ask one of my Drill Instructors if I can wear contact lenses instead of the ugly "birth control goggles" they issue the near-sighted. Sergeant Jackson. Arms so huge he has to modify the sleeves of his dress uniform to fit them. Gruff and battle-hardened. "I was eighteen, leading a fireteam in the graveyard in Nasiryah," he would say to us every couple of days during our time on the depot. He tells me no, I am not allowed to wear contacts. I do it anyway. He finds out. I pay for it in sweat. I leave bootcamp and head to my next duty station, the School of Infantry. I never see him again.

The School of Infantry is where you become a grunt. It is where basic Marines gain their first introduction to the gritty world of field soldiering. You don't know it when you're there, but you're learning things that grunts throughout history have spent entire wars learning, unlearning and relearning.

In SOI you don't have to yell as much. You get more time to eat. You don't do close-order drill. You have free time in the evening, on the weekends. You can grow your hair out just a little bit. The Sergeants teaching you infantry skills have long haircuts and don't wear Smokey

Bear hats. They strike you as authentic, far more real than the spit-and-polish Drill Instructors of your first three months in the Corps.

Bootcamp is theater. It's spectacular and over-the-top and designed to beat you down and build you back up into something teachable. The Drill Instructors themselves come from all over. Some of them have seen real combat. Some of them are infantry, but you find out later that most aren't. Drill Instructor, by and large, is not a job that attracts many grunts. It's too regimented, too precise, too unforgiving. Grunts don't become Drill Instructors because it's too much work. It's as intense as being in a fleet unit about to deploy, maybe more so. You need a break after being in the fleet too long, so most grunts become embassy guards or SOI instructors or recruiters. Or so I'm told. I never stay in long enough to do any of this.

The instructors at SOI, on the other hand, are infantrymen. Grunts. They take their jobs seriously, although they joke and fool around and let you go off base. They teach the real skills you need to kill the enemy and stay alive as a foot-mobile light infantryman. You learn to dig and to endure and to smoke and to eat and to sit and to watch. From their example you learn to lead. Perhaps most importantly, you start to learn about The Marine Corps Way.

The Marine Corps Way guides you, hinders you, changes you during your time in the Corps. Only parts of the Marine Corps Way are written down. You learn about it in classes: always wear a belt with belt loops. Once a Marine, Always a Marine. But most of it isn't inscribed anywhere. It's not recorded, either, at least not formally. It's passed down from one Marine to another. Most Marines don't even know they're following the Way. They certainly don't call it The Way. More likely, they'll say "this is just how it's done," or "this is how we did it in when I was a boot" or "because you're a United States Marine." If bootcamp is doctrine, then the Marine Corps Way is something like operational art. It is interpreted differently everywhere you go, but it has principles, underpinnings, maybe even rules. You can apply it to almost anything.

It's like a philosophy with physical repercussions. It's a religion where the doomsday passages actually happen.

Let me give you an example.

A young Marine, fresh out of recruit training, lets his hair grow out on his ten-day leave before reporting to SOI. He lives near a military base, so on the last day of leave he goes to the barber. He's tired of shaving his head. He doesn't like the high-and-tight haircut he got before graduating, so he opts for something with a little more fluff: a medium-regulation haircut. Medium reg, as they call it. Comes out looking good. Professional. Marine-like. Or so he thinks.

He flies, checks in to the school. He's wearing his Alphas, the classic green Marine Corps uniform. A business suit with a belt and one ribbon. His single ribbon is perfectly aligned over his breast pocket, his belt is the exact length proscribed in the uniform manual. Even so, as soon as he walks to the check-in table he feels a cold anger directed at him. He realizes he's fucked up. He sees the Corporal checking him in and quickly realizes this salty Marine is on the verge of spontaneous combustion.

"What the fuck is that?" the Corporal asks, pointing to the young Marine's head.

"A medium reg, Corporal," says the Marine.

"Who said you could get that?"

"Nobody, Corporal."

"Fix it," says the Corporal.

"But the barbershop is closed, Corporal," says the boot.

"Do I look like I give a fuck?"

"No, Corporal."

So that night the Marine shaves his head with a Bic razor. And he receives a lesson in the Marine Corps Way.

The Marine Corps Way exists both inside and outside the official narrative. It is a subplot, an essential undercurrent to the experience of being a Marine. It seems to be felt most keenly in the units that see close combat, though all Marines find themselves touched by it sooner or later.

It ebbs and flows like the current in a river. Sometimes it is strong and overpowers you. Sometimes you can fight it. But you never leave the river, not until you've made it all the way to the sea. Then you're free, if you choose to be.

In the School of Infantry you're split into sub-categories of grunt. The bigger, stronger, duller Marines become machine gunners. The miscreants and skateboarders become mortarmen. The Mormons become anti-tank missilemen and the computer geeks and college dropouts become assaultmen. The majority of new Marine infantrymen become regular grunts. Riflemen. Oh-three-eleven.

They make me an assaultman. Designator oh-three-fifty-one. They choose you by your ASVAB score, the standardized test you take before you go into the military. If it's high enough you can be an assaultman.

You don't have to become a machine gunner or a mortarman or an assaultman. You can fight it, stay with the rest, be a rifleman. There is pride in the occupation. History. Oh-three-eleven infantry: the number you yell at the Drill Instructors when you're in line for chow. It's what every Marine aspires to be, and most never are. Riflemen do what everyone who joins the Corps wanted to do when they first saw the recruiting commercials. Oh-three-eleven infantry is the heart and soul of the Marine Corps.

I become an assaultman. As an oh-three-fifty-one they teach you basic infantry skills, and then specialized skills. They teach you to shoot rockets from a shoulder-mounted launcher, the SMAW. You learn demolitions: water charges, claymores, bangalores, C-4, TNT. You learn to make a little loop of detonation cord with a blasting cap on the end, hang it on a door handle, and blow it, destroying the door handle and allowing the guys behind you to clear the room. You learn to yell "breach" when you hit a door with a big metal ram. You learn to prime and use a C-4 satchel charge that, were it to explode in your hands, would blow your head all the way back to the barracks.

The SMAW, the Shoulder-Fired, Multipurpose Assault Weapon, is your bread and butter. It is your burden. Your extra weight on the hike. Your badge of honor. It's got a shitty little nine-millimeter gun on the side that mimics the flight path of the smoothbore rocket it fires, a "spotting gun" of sorts. On a live-fire range, when you see the spotting round hit the target, you yell at your assistant gunner:

"On target!"

Your buddy looks behind you, makes sure nobody will get waxed when you fire.

"Backblast area all clear!" he shouts.

"Rocket!" you scream. You depress the firing lever and the trigger at the same time. The launcher explodes next to your head, inundates you with concussive waves that take your breath away. You watch the rocket sail, a flying tube of death reaching for the husk of some torn-up metal tank silhouette.

The Marine Corps Way: everything's a competition. So you count your rocket shots, how many hits and misses you have. I leave the range twelve out of twelve.

Later, when we're throwing grenades, I barely make it over the wall. My instructor berates me for having an arm "like a girl."

Toward the end of your time at SOI you learn where you're going to be assigned. Most of us go to the same three states: Hawaii, California, North Carolina. A few go to Washington, D.C., to be part of the unit at the 8th and I barracks. Bodybearers, Silent Drill Team, White House guard. Some go to a school to become a kind of close-quarters security forces detachment.

A few who signed a particular contract jump into the pipeline to become an oh-three-twenty-one Reconnaissance Man, a kind of special operations job. Being Recon means you have to run fast and hump a lot of weight and swim well. Our class at SOI already knows who these recon contracts are. Most of them are standouts, physical studs, the best of the best. One of them is a lump of putty. Nobody knows why he signed up for it, not even him. Nobody thinks he'll make it. I never learn if he did.

I'm with twenty or thirty guys who get Hawaii orders. Most of them I know. Some I even went to bootcamp with. Over the next four years I will come to know these men better, as we travel together to Marine Corps Base Kaneohe Bay and then, later, a place far more treacherous:

Helmand Province, Afghanistan.

4

Boot

There is no such thing as a "boot."

There is no such thing as a "senior Lance Corporal."

There is no requirement to keep your hair high and tight if you have never deployed.

There is no requirement to shave your head on your first day in Afghanistan or Iraq, if you have never been before.

You will never be made to conduct physical training as a punishment.

You will never be physically or verbally abused by those in charge of you.

There is no hazing in the Marine Corps.

I'm standing near the basketball courts, outside the Charlie Company, First Battalion, Third Marines office, my hands behind my back at parade rest. I'm watching a fellow boot, a tall African-American guy named Terrance, get screamed at by two or three senior Marines for having an unsatisfactory haircut. We've just met Charlie company, a hundred and fifty or so Marine infantrymen and Navy Corpsmen, who have returned from a month of leave following a deployment to Iraq.

As an assaultman, I fall into Weapons Platoon, along with Terrance and a few others I know from the School of Infantry.

We'd spent the last few weeks living in a mold-infested squad bay with no privacy and bathrooms whose lights would flicker and spark while we took ice-cold showers. A couple of hundred boots, the entire battalion's new blood, slept together in close quarters, our personal effects unsecured because the wall lockers did not lock. We were the replacements for men who would be getting out of the Marine Corps in the next six to twelve months.

We, the new guys, came from both coasts. There was a School of Infantry in North Carolina in addition to the one in California, for those unfortunate enough to live east of the Mississippi.

For a couple of months we were on our own. We did odd jobs, directed by the broke-dicks who stayed back from deployment and the Sergeants who had just moved to the unit. Some of us were promoted to Lance Corporal. Others stayed Privates First Class and a couple were just plain Privates. There was a sort of bullshit pecking order, the blind leading the blind. Boot Lance Corporals would yell at boot Privates to clean hallways or take out trash.

After a few weeks of this our fellow boots realized they had no authority and no idea how to lead. Our only examples to that point had been the shouting Drill Instructors in bootcamp and the sarcastic Combat Instructors at SOI. These boot Lances thought it was all about being loud and, every once in a while, getting physical. It didn't work.

During this time, before Charlie Company returned from Iraq, I bought a car. A white V-6 Camaro, 1996 vintage. I used my five-thousand dollar enlistment bonus to buy it off a guy who was leaving the island and needed it gone fast. I could fit four guys in it, uncomfortably, so we didn't have to pay for a fifty-dollar cab to Waikiki Beach in Honolulu. During this period of calm before the storm, I swam in the ocean and ran along the flightline. I lifted weights in the small annex gym by our squad bay, doing deadlifts and back squats, building my legs, taking every powder, pill and liquid available in the base's GNC supplement shop. I got drunk. I had my first hangover. I explored the beaches of Kailua and Pyramid Rock and the North Shore.

For a while, life in the fleet wasn't so bad.

And then all of a sudden, after we met Charlie Company on those basketball courts, it was.

A guy I knew, a real stud, honor graduate from bootcamp and the School of Infantry, got bitten by a spider, a brown recluse maybe, in that mold-infested squad bay. Right on his face. His cheek swelled up so bad he looked like the Elephant Man. He went to the hospital. I didn't see him for months.

Finally I run into him outside the barracks. He's gaunt, faint, a shadow of his former self. Twenty or thirty pounds lighter, but wearing the same old clothes, so he's got a belt cinched tight around sagging cargo shorts while his polo shirt droops on thin shoulders. You can see where the venom had eaten away at his face, a mess of mangled scar tissue, still healing. I ask him what he's up to. He says he's in the Wounded Warrior battalion now. Medical issues are keeping him from the upcoming deployment. He really wishes he could go, but the docs won't let him. I say don't sweat it, there's always another deployment, and I mean it. I feel for him. He wishes me luck, says stay safe, watch out for IED's. I tell him to watch out for spiders. We chuckle. I notice he hasn't shaved the decrepit skin around his spider bite. I wonder how long it will be before somebody comes along and screams at him about it.

Another lesson in the Marine Corps Way: being a boot means that even though a guy is the same rank as you, you call him by his rank, and not by his name. It's "yes, Lance Corporal, no Lance Corporal, aye aye Lance Corporal," even though you're a Lance Corporal too. The difference is, he's a "senior" Lance Corporal. And if he tells you to do something, you'd better hurry up and do it.

The "fleet," as we call it, is a catch-all term for the operational units that deploy. It comprises infantry, aviation, engineers, tanks, the units needed to project power the world over. It does not include ceremonial units like the Silent Drill Team, or the Recruit Depots, or the school-houses that teach advanced courses. In the fleet, Sergeants and Corporals are in short supply. The infantry doesn't seem to get promoted as much as othr jobs. It's a system thing; the Marine Corps uses "cutting scores" to determine promotion rates. You hit the cutting score, you get the next rank. Your score is based on your physical fitness test, rifle score and a couple of other components. But the biggest factor is how long you've been in.

Each military occupational specialty has a different score for promotion. On average it takes between three and four years for a grunt to get promoted, sometimes longer. This means that a three-year infantryman can still be a Lance Corporal, while a three-year admin Marine has already made Sergeant. As a grunt, you deploy as a Lance Corporal and return as a Lance Corporal. Maybe at the end of your enlistment you become a full Corporal, right when it doesn't mean anything. Only a very select few skip the line with a meritorious promotion. Chances are, no matter how awesome you are, you won't pick up meritoriously. This isn't 1944.

So I'm a Lance Corporal, with senior Lance Corporals in charge of me. I am the bottom rung of the shit ladder. I bear the brunt of collective adherence to the Marine Corps Way. The unwritten doctrine of Doing Things the Way They Have Always Been Done.

My seniors are like the fathers who perpetuate the domestic abuse of their own fathers. They know no other way to teach.

I spend my time as a boot learning. Observing. Trying. Failing. I try to fit in. But it's difficult to relate to a group of guys who just came back from Iraq.

Iraq. As if the deployment itself was enough. No more training needed. The boots can do it all. We are going to war again, but that only seems to matter for us who have never been. Those who have been to war once are already prepared.

"I've done my share of firewatch," the senior Lance Corporals say. So you only sleep a couple of hours.

"I've done plenty of gun drills," they say. So you run back and forth across the field, pretending to shoot a SMAW, shouting *backblast area all clear* until you're hoarse, conducting buddy rushes and tourniquet drills and fireman's carries and casevac nineline evacuations. You run with another boot, seniors on the sidelines, smoking Marlboro's.

Connection eludes. It's hard to connect with men who seem to harbor a built-up resentment toward their Iraq experience, an anger which pours over and onto you, the boot. These seniors, young men still, did not get the war they wanted, the one with gunfights and dead checks and bill drills and door-kicking. Few of them earned combat action ribbons, the coveted piece of cloth that says you were actually shot at or blown up. And yet they lost a man to the enemy; I cannot imagine how this must feel. The pain of that loss and their inability to do anything about it seems to color their relationship with the boots.

For Marines, the early years of Iraq were legendary. In bootcamp and the School of Infantry I would listen raptly as my instructors recounted combat stories: sniping from bombed-out buildings in Ramadi, clearing houses in Fallujah, cyclic-rate machine guns in cities whose names I couldn't pronounce. When I joined I didn't know there was a war going on. I thought Iraq was over. When I found out it wasn't, I searched YouTube for combat footage. I watched and rewatched the same Operation Phantom Fury videos over and over, taking in every detail: the mismatched green flak jackets, the tanks rumbling down narrow streets, the dust rising from mosque minarets shot by high-caliber machine guns. Iraq always intrigued me.

My seniors didn't get that kind of Iraq war. They spent their deployment patrolling mostly-pacified Iraqi streets, manning machineguns they never fired, riding in armored vehicles, wearing cumbersome flak jackets. The inane regulations of the garrison Marine Corps followed them to a war in its final act. Jetting out of forward operating bases and Iraqi police stations with nobody to shoot at, nothing to destroy, and no way to avenge a man they lost.

If I were wiser, I might think that perhaps their anger is not with me, or my fellow boots. Perhaps they are still fighting their own personal wars, and I am just one more ancillary casualty.

But I am not that wise. I am just miserable, and tired of hearing about Iraq.

Go to the field, come back. In the train-up to Afghanistan all you do is sweat and drink and bullshit and complain. You shoot rockets and endure a nitpicking room inspection every Thursday. You try to run as fast as you can, you try not to fall out of the hikes, and you try not to get on anyone's bad side. The seniors posture and make you do things you know you aren't supposed to do, but you do them anyway, because you want to be included. Sometimes you forget your manhood and grovel. You don't stand up for yourself, because you know that what would come of it is pain, more pain than you can conveniently bear. And you see what happens to those who do stand up to it. They are ostracized. Hurt. Made to stay behind.

The worst thing you can be in war is left behind.

I yearn for kinship. I long for the brotherhood I was looking for when I stood in the recruiting office a year ago. But it's elusive. Bonds are formed through shared struggle. How can you form a bond if you're the only one suffering? You can't connect with the senior Lance Corporals, let alone the Sergeants or the Corporals. Sure, everyone's training, but they aren't enduring the extra misery, the additional humiliation shoveled on the boots. You connect with your fellow boots only because they are just as unhappy as you are.

You remind yourself: this is the Marine Corps. You are a member of an elite fighting force. You'll be in combat soon enough, and you'll forge the bonds then. But these thoughts don't help when you're waking at dawn on a Saturday to go on a run with drunk seniors, or having all of your gear stolen because another boot went absent without leave, or being manhandled by someone you can't fight back against.

Questions the recruiters never asked us: do you want to go to war with someone who extinguishes a cigarette butt on your arm? Who pours bleach on the floor of a shower, turns it on to full heat, and makes you do pushups wearing a gas mask and poncho, a boot pressing down on your back? Who does disgusting things to your protein powder and watches you drink it, unaware? Who punches you in the nose for a minor infraction, then watches as you lie to your squad leader about it, too afraid you'll incur more of the same?

Preparing to go to war, I feel no sense of brotherhood. Grimly I realize the forehead-smashing, Code Red-giving relationship between senior and boot that I romanticized prior to enlisting is in practice simply brutal, a brutality that makes young men hate the organization they idolized enough to sign their lives away. I decide then that if I am given the opportunity, I will never lead men like this. When it comes time for me to be in charge, things will be different.

Still I hope, naively, optimistically, that combat will bring us closer together, that the coming war will create the Esprit de Corps that training did not. I have no choice but to hope. The alternative is something I don't want to think about.

A few good leaders, many bad leaders. The good ones you never forget. Even if you don't know they're good at the time. Sometimes, even the good ones make you miserable. But it's a misery you respect, a shared misery that builds you up.

The Marine Corps gives you the criteria for a leader. Can this person run faster? Hump more? Yell louder? Does he know your job better than even you? Does he seem to genuinely care? Do you respect this person? Would you charge a machine gun if he told you to? Would you think twice?

One time, we're up on the north side of Oahu, humping around the Kahuku Training Area in the Koo'lau mountains above the Turtle Bay Golf Resort. You know it. It's where they filmed *Forgetting Sarah Marshall*. When we train there, we watch the golf course with dejected envy.

It's raining. Thick, heavy drops, all day and all night. Somebody loses a compass, so we stop land navigation training to look for it.

Eventually we find it. It's in somebody's tent, or in a pocket, or on the ground. It doesn't matter. We are miserable despite the compass.

So we stand around, waiting for someone to tell us what to do. Boots, seniors, NCO's alike. We start to freeze. It's Hawaii, we think. Why is it so cold? We're soaked to the bone. Why? The explanation lies in The Marine Corps Way.

We've all packed our Goretex rain jackets, but nobody's allowed to wear them. Why? Couldn't say. Who gave the order? Couldn't tell you. But nobody's wearing one, and we're all freezing, the whole platoon, standing in a circle, our hands in our pockets, not speaking. Some brave souls light cigarettes and pass them around.

Is this brotherhood? Is this shared suffering?

An officer jogs up from somewhere.

"What are you all standing around for?" he exclaims. "Are you cold?"

Nobody says anything.

"Well then, let's get warmed up!" he shouts. He runs off. We know what to do. We follow.

We jog to the middle of a clearing, stack our weapons neatly so they don't get dirty. We begin to exercise. Squats, pushups, burpees. We count each repetition, but it's not enthusiastic enough. We count louder. Every repetition we do, the officer does better. When we count ten, he's halfway to twenty.

After ten minutes or so, the officer decides we're done, or remembers some other meeting he needs to be at. We stop exercising. Pick up our rifles, try to wipe the mud off our uniforms.

"Now, I don't want to see you all standing around looking miserable any more, understand?"

Aye sir, we say.

"We're Marines. We're tough. Rain doesn't matter. If it's not raining, we're not training. Oohrah?"

Oohrah, we say.

I go to sleep wet. I wake up wet. I think about wearing my rain jacket the next day, but don't.

Another week in the field, this time at Bellows Training Area, windward side of Oahu. In the night something wakes me. I open my eyes and stare at the ceiling. I hear nothing. Not knowing what disturbed my sleep, I realize I need to pee, but I'm too comfortable to get up. If I get up, I'll have to get all my clothes on, grab my rifle, and walk outside to the port-a-shitter. I suppress the urge. Again I drift away.

Then I hear a scream.

I keep my eyes closed, still not fully awake. It must be part of my dream.

Nobody gets up. They rustle in their sleeping bags. A cough or two. Silence.

Suddenly, another scream. A real one. I sit up, slowly, hesitantly. I see someone far down the line from me shaking his sleeping bag. I notice that I'm the only person who sat up. Did nobody else hear that scream? Am I imagining things? No—the guy shaking his bag is real. He finishes, stops, lies down and goes back to sleep. I do the same.

And then I hear another scream. I sit up once more. It's the guy next to the first guy, one closer to me. Ten guys away. He's shaking his bag, too. Again, I'm the only other person up.

The bag-shaker lies back down. I drift. I wake again. How many times, I don't remember, but each time I wake I think I hear another scream, another rustle, another scramble in a sleeping bag. Each time, getting closer to me. Each time, I'm the only other person who wakes up.

In the morning I'm packing my gear into my rucksack, getting ready for the morning's movement. The events of the previous night are a distant memory. Perhaps they weren't even real. Perhaps I imagined the whole thing. The screams fade into the recesses of my psyche, disappearing like ephemeral clouds behind a mountain range. Then I overhear a Marine say:

"...motherfucker bit me last night," as he pulls up his shirt, showing a pair of holes underneath his ribcage. "Centipede. Biggest I've ever seen. Got me good. Thought I got him good, but I couldn't find him. Swear it was a centipede. Huge fuckin' thing."

Maybe it was real. Maybe it was all a dream. Maybe it's all just one long, shitty dream.

Too young to legally drink so I take my car up into Kaneohe proper every other Saturday to get tattooed. I escape the barracks, avoid my seniors, blow my paycheck, and permanently disfigure my body all in one go. Win-win-win.

Usually I take other boots with me. We are grown adults, but we can't leave the barracks without at least one "battle buddy" accompanying us. Sometimes, when the company leadership feels like our rate of degenerate behavior is too high, they make us sign out in groups of three. I grab a boot or two and drop them off somewhere while I get inked. Sometimes we go out together afterward.

The tattoos I get are banned. Sleeve tattoos, like that on my right arm, were prohibited before I even joined the Marine Corps. Still I let artists cut and color my skin. It's the infantry, I rationalize. First Sergeant doesn't seem to care. He knows we'll all get out after four years. The Marine Corps doesn't need us any longer than that. Four years, two or three deployments, they'll shove us head-first into the GWOT grinder until our bodies and our minds are close to breaking or already broken. We will work tirelessly for little pay until our enlistments are over, and then they can kick us to the curb without a second thought.

Unauthorized sleeve tattoo, the Marine Corps will say when they deny our reenlistments. Lucky we didn't get punished for it earlier.

We go to Waikiki if we want to spend money or look for women. Most of us are underage, so getting into a bar is tough. There are a couple of seedy strip clubs just off Kuhio avenue that don't care how old you are, the kind that hand you a beer as soon as you walk in the door, then sit you down and force you to watch as a geriatric grandmother takes off all her clothes. You pay her handsomely to leave you alone.

Honolulu is like a different country. You stalk the streets, a pack of Haole white kids with high and tight haircuts, Affliction shirts and plaid shorts. You're a target and you don't even know it. A mark for the roving bands of locals, whose ancestors are Hawaiian or Japanese or Pacific Islander, who are much larger and better at fighting and drinking than you are. A target for the working girls, who wear clear plastic heels and force Marines to pull cash from ATM's to pay for services they were too drunk to take advantage of. A target for the plain-clothed military police and shore patrol Marines in their dress uniforms who are looking for fucked-up kids like you to bring back to the base and stand before The Man.

And you don't know it but you're right in the middle of the Great Recession and when you walk by Señor Frog's on your way back to where you're staying you can hear *Pokerface* and *Like a G-6* and *Boom Boom Pow* pulsating out of the club, music of a culture you're largely removed from because all you know is the Field and the Barracks and the Base. You spend months Not Fucking. You can't get laid because you're a copy of a copy of a copy, all of you going to the same clubs, talking to the same women, haunting the same streets. Everyone is lonely. There is nothing to be done about it, unless you look for the girls with the clear plastic heels strutting down Kuhio avenue. They'll do something about it.

You spend your nights in shared hostel rooms, sheets stripped because there's a toga party going on, listening to a song by Ratatat on someone's brand new iPhone. Every time the wildcat roars, you drink Jägermeister and chase it with a shot of Monster Energy. You get nice and toasted and head down to the toga party, where the four of you stand around looking awkward, wondering what to say. A giant Polynesian man named Lou pats you on the back and tells you to come into his office. Strangely, conveniently, this office is located in the hostel, and it is here he offers you a kind of tea called kava and life-coaching services to go along with it. The drink makes you numb. You stumble back to your room and pass out on a bare mattress.

The next day you wake up to the elder boot drinking warm leftover Budweisers. You hang out at the beach, snorkel, have a late lunch at a diner by the Hilton. Maybe you get a tattoo that will mean more to you ten years later than it does today, something like an Eagle, Globe and Anchor on your chest or an *0311* down your triceps. You return to Marine Corps Base Hawaii, sober, and drive through a yellow light as it's turning red. The ultimate buddy fuckers—military police—pull you over. Because of a ticket you got before you entered the Marines, you find out you're driving on a suspended license. You thought you took care of it, but you were wrong.

They take away your driving privileges for the next three years. Your car ends up abandoned because the shitbag you sell it to leaves the island without registering it.

One time the company's staying at Camp Wilson, over by the training areas on Marine Corps Base Twentynine Palms, California. It's right after we finish our big pre-deployment exercise, Mojave Viper. We have a day off, maybe two, before we head home to Hawaii. I spend a night in the base lodge with four other boots, drinking and watching television. It's good to get away. I can finally relax. No seniors, no sleeping bags, no dirt. No huffing and puffing on a live-fire range. No carrying rockets. I sleep on the floor but the floor's better than a squad bay.

I wake up in the middle of the night and one of the other Marines, a guy I don't know very well, is throwing up. He's still asleep and he's lying next to me and some of it starts to pool and come toward me so I get up and throw my covers off. The drunk part of me gives way to the annoyed part. Nobody else is doing anything about this guy, checking on him, so I decide fuck it, I'm going back to sleep. I pick up my covers and go to another corner of the room. Lay down, close my eyes.

I'm dozing when I hear footsteps, shuffling, retching and a thud. I open my eyes and the guy is on the floor by the bathroom, a pool of vomit coming from inside. The smell burns my nostrils. All of a sudden he rises, lurches over to the bed and tries to lie in it. He is kicked off by two other boots. The room is hot. I am no longer sleeping, and my drunken sense of forgiveness has eroded. I decide it's time to go. Better to risk dealing with seniors and sleeping in a cot than to not sleep at all.

I grab my things and leave. The night wind is cool on my hot skin as I exit the door, escaping the puke sauna I was sleeping in. I'm walking through the courtyard toward the front desk when I hear my name.

"Yo, Aaron!" shouts a voice, which I recognize as Lucas, a guy from another platoon. We call him the Old Man of the Marine Corps. He's maybe twenty-seven, ancient, withered, experienced in life but a boot all the same. Always off on his own. Always tan. Always smoking.

"Hey," I say. "I didn't know you were here." I want to leave.

"Yeah, yeah, man, had to get out of the cans, you know?"

"Same."

"Who are you here with?"

"Some guys from another platoon."

"Oh yeah?" Checks his watch. "What are you doing? It's like, one-thirty in the morning."

I nod at the front office. "Heading back."

"Why?"

"Just over it, man."

"No worries, no worries." He drags on a cigarette.

"I'll see you later—" I begin, but he cuts me off.

"Hey listen man, this dude wants me to fuck his wife."

"Oh, wow."

He leans in. "I bet I could get you in there, too."

"Uh, no thanks." I taste bile.

"Are you sure? She's not bad-looking. I mean, not *that* bad-looking."

"Yeah man, I'm good. I'll uh...I'll see you around," I say, inching away.

Lucas shrugs, puts out his cigarette. "Your loss, bro. I think the husband would have gone for it."

"Um. Okay," I say stupidly, and go to the front office. I talk to the desk clerk. Half an hour later a taxi picks me up and takes me to Camp Wilson. I find my quonset hut and lay down on my rack. I notice the guy sleeping next to me, Jensen, isn't actually Jensen but one of our seniors, Marty. He's facing me and even in the low light I can see he's thrown up on the side of the cot as he's been sleeping. There's a still, wet cone of vomit hanging out of his mouth. Puke everywhere: all over Jensen's gear, his pack, his tarp, his sleeping bag, his pillow. I look around for Jensen—he's sleeping on another rack nearby. I pass out. This is tomorrow's problem.

In the morning Marty's gone, sleeping on his own bed a few rows down. Jensen's sitting on his rack, quietly angry.

"What's up, man?" I rotate my feet to the ground. My head hurts.

"Puke everywhere, dude." He points at dry stains. "Someone threw up on my cot. Everywhere. All over my poncho liner, my plate carrier and my Kevlar. My fucking pillow, dude."

"It was Marty," I say. I tell him all about it.

A look flashes over Jensen's face. His anger fades to resignation. "Whatever, man. I'll just clean it." He moves slowly to get up. I put a hand on his shoulder, holding him.

"*No,* man, that's bullshit." I point at Marty. "Ask him to help you clean it up. He fucking puked all over your shit. That's disgusting."

"He's a senior."

Jensen's right, but I feel like making a stand. "I don't care if he's a senior. There's some shit we just shouldn't have to do. Seniors, boots, whatever. Doesn't matter. You shouldn't have to clean someone else's puke off your gear."

Jensen just shakes his head.

"Look, I'll just go ask him," I say, standing up. "He doesn't seem like a bad guy. He probably doesn't even remember it."

"Kirk, don't," he says, but I'm already walking toward the other side of the Quonset hut. Marty's dozing, but another senior Lance Corporal sits nearby. Frank. He's watching a movie on a portable DVD player, dipping tobacco.

"Excuse me, Lance Corporal," I say. Customs and courtesies. Seniors and boots. The Marine Corps Way.

"What?" Frank's a boulder. Tall, wide, completely hairless. Crushes smaller rocks.

"Lance Corporal Kowalski puked on Jensen's rack last night. I just wanted to see if he could help Jensen clean it up."

Marty opens his eyes. He's been listening. "No I didn't, boot," he murmurs.

"Solved that quick," Frank says. "Fuck off."

I point to the vomit on Marty's collar. I explain that the vomit matches the pattern on the cot. I explain the extent of the damage. I ask for consideration.

What I get instead is Frank's fist, clenching my t-shirt, pushing me backward.

"Listen, motherfucker—Marty didn't puke on that rack. I don't care what you *think* you saw. It wasn't him. Go away, before I give you something to complain about."

He lets me go. I don't move. Against my better judgment, I open my mouth.

"Lance Corporal, Marty puked on the rack, and I think it's pretty messed up if he doesn't—" and suddenly there is a great flurry of movement, a powerful pair of hands on my chest and I'm flying backwards, tumbling, soaring into a pile of rucksacks.

I help Jensen clean vomit from his magazine pouches.

It's one thing to be a boot. It's another thing to be an unpopular boot. It's an entirely different thing to be the *most* unpopular boot.

My friend Levi was that guy. He didn't fit in with anyone. He was smart enough to be an assaultman, but at the same time he was airy. Detached, like he was off on some adventure. He certainly wasn't stupid, but he certainly did stupid things. He would forget things, like where he left a piece of expensive serialized gear, or to bring a tarp to the field. Our seniors didn't like the way he talked, or dressed, or looked. He incurred the wrath of just about everyone he came in contact with.

Despite his gift for attracting trouble, nothing the seniors did to him ever seemed to matter. I've never seen someone smile so often when yelled at, belittled, pushed around. It didn't help that he didn't need or want their approval. He was fiscally responsible. He drove a white Toy-ota Yaris. He had local friends. He was into poetry and Rennaissance fairs and technology.

When I found out we were going to be in the same squad together on the upcoming deployment, I felt a selfish, guilt-ridden relief. Levi would definitely get the brunt of our seniors' anger. Maybe, just maybe, they'd leave me alone.

5

War, Take One

Nawa District, Helmand Province, Afghanistan
December 2009

Our squad leader, Sergeant Hernandez, works alongside us. He helps fill sandbags, move boxes, organize water bottles and chow. No task is beneath him. When he works, others notice. If you're a boot, you run to make sure he's not the only one unloading trucks. If you're a senior, you move a little slower, but you get there too.

Sergeant Hernandez's friends call him Dez, for short. We, boot and senior alike, are not his friends, so we call him Sergeant Dez.

Our squad rotates between three locations: two small, squad-size observation posts and the company-size combat outpost. For this deployment, we shed our weapons specialties. We are all riflemen. We live out of rucksacks, packing up our belongings and patrolling between three different bases. We are weighted with the accoutrements of the field: sleeping bags, poncho liners, tarps, books, ammunition, body armor, flashlights, knives, first aid kits, tourniquets, goggles, Oakleys, gloves, white socks we're not really allowed to wear. We walk through knee-high mud, taking two hours to clear two kilometers.

Two of these bases are little more than drab, gray, Hesco-barrier triangles surrounded by wheat and poppy fields. They are situated near intersections which we are told are important. Our job is to watch for activity. To observe. To make sure nobody puts bombs in the road. We do not have enough Marines to patrol and man the base at the same time, so for two weeks we stand post until it is time to move to the next base. We are isolated, but not remote; the main company combat outpost is only a few kilometers down the road. Out of sight, but not out of radio range.

Most of the seniors have changed little, even in Afghanistan. It is clear the boots are not part of the club and never will be. Sometimes, if the seniors don't want to stand post, you stand post for them. You pick up the squad's refuse in the morning and drag it to the burn pit and light it on fire. You police-call the patrol base while they sleep. You drive engineer stakes into the ground and fix concertina wire and fill sandbags and clean machine guns and do all of the jobs of the infantry all at once because you are a boot. After a few weeks of this you begin to stay away from the squad's shared tent so that nobody throws an odd job at you or accuses you of malingering while they malinger.

Within a few days there begins a silent claustrophobia. It settles in slowly, gripping your heart, raising your blood pressure, filling you with anxiety. The sum of it is that you are living in hardship, performing menial tasks, with some men who do not like or respect you and others who are indifferent and others who are in your same situation. And maybe this lack of respect is because you are a boot, and maybe it is because of your own poor attitude, and maybe it is because of your sense of indignation at not being accepted, not fitting in to begin with. Whatever the cause, you are still convinced that one of these days it will end. Someday soon, you are sure, the squad will endure a classic trial by fire and find a brotherhood forged by blood and lead and death and shared danger.

But for now there is no respite. Nobody shoots at us. There are no gunfights, only purgatory and bored senior Lance Corporals. There are no bombs. No green and red tracer rounds flying back and forth. No exchange of fire. No mortar that binds the bricks of friendship together.

We stand post and wait.

For all the times I think I have it bad, Levi has it worse. When you're marked, you're marked. And when their attention is on Levi, it is off me. Though I feel terrible, it is always better for me to slink away when they lay into him.

Our only saving grace is the panther-like presence of our squad leader, working harder than us, sleeping less than us, moving with the grace and lithe muscularity of a predator. Sergeant Dez scares everyone. His mere presence is enough to quiet a room. He walks unchallenged.

An example. Fast forward seven months. We return from this deployment and turn in our guns at the armory. The company is formed around the First Sergeant, a giant of a man with a booming voice. But even that is not enough to quiet a particularly salty senior Lance Corporal. So Sergeant Dez hurtles through the crowd like a Greek trireme cleaving an ancient enemy ship in two. He barrels through a dozen Marines and uses his bodyweight to propel the offending Lance Corporal rearward, chest to chest, until he is nearly to the fence, bellowing, berating him for his transgressions. When he finishes, he walks back, exasperated, then suddenly, in a fit of rage, hurls his notebook toward the company office. It lands on a basketball court.

The First Sergeant pauses briefly for this, then continues his speech. Only one person could do that, could keep balance and order the way he did, effectively and permanently. Sergeant Dez was that man.

Despite his work ethic and his sense of fairness, he seems to know not to disrupt the balance. Senior, boot. Team leader, rifleman. There is a place for everyone. There is a Way. We, the boots, accept our fate with quiet claustrophobic desperation, praying the deployment goes by quickly.

Around Christmas there begins an interesting fashion trend at the company combat outpost.

It involves a Gunny. Gunny is an archetype. Gunny tends to be the loud uncle you wish would shut up at Thanksgiving dinner. The same uncle who comes up to you afterward, slips you a hundred bucks and says "don't tell your mother." In the Marine Corps, Gunny is the most senior infantry guy in the company and he knows it. His job? Supply, maybe. Theft and brigandry, more likely. He is an enforcer of the Marine Corps Way, although he is not the chief enforcer; that job falls to the First Sergeant. He is the darkness of the infantry. He is one-third cigarette smoke and one-third machine gun lubricant and one-third unbridled fury. He is the antithesis of the poster-perfect Marines on the billboards.

The fashion trend is unauthorized beanie hats. Black or coyote are the only approved colors, until Marines start getting hand-knitted beanies in the mail, or beanies that look hand-knitted but were really store-bought. Out of some sense of sentimental family connection, the company authorizes the wear of these hand-knit beanies and their hand-knit-looking counterparts.

My father sends me a beanie. It is not hand-knit. It is a gaudy Tapout brand hat, the mixed-martial-arts apparel company that went mainstream when Chuck Liddell mohawks were popular. The kind that wanna-be tough guys wear. I'm a wanna-be tough guy, so I like this beanie. It is a nice Christmas gift, and it is warmer and more comfortable than our issued kit. And my dad sent it to me. It is a bright spot in an otherwise dreary existence.

My seniors make fun of me for it, as they do for just about anything. They tell me to take it off, but I interpret their instructions as more ribbing. Besides, whose beanie is less authorized? Mine is black, while theirs are bright rainbows of color. I keep wearing it. It drops from discussion. I go about the life of a deployed boot.

After a week, a senior pulls me aside, a genuine-looking smile on his face.

"How you doing, Kirk?" he says.

"Good," I say. "Cold."

"Yeah, me too. How's your dad?"

"Good," I say, taken aback. I'd mentioned my father, still in the Army, was deploying to Afghanistan soon, along with my stepmother. There had been talk about trying to link up in-country later on. He had that kind of pull. I didn't even have enough pull to get a Chili-Mac MRE.

"He's fine," I say. "Just training, getting ready to deploy."

"Good," he says. "Hey, listen, Gunny wants to talk to you. I think it's about that."

"Oh." I'm surprised. "Okay. Really? About my dad?"

"Yeah, definitely. Just talked to him."

"Right now?"

"Yeah, as soon as you can. He's over by the fire pit."

"Okay. Thanks, Lance Corporal."

"No problem," he says, smiling.

I trot away. I'm intrigued that Gunny wants to talk to me, but I'm more enamored that one of my seniors asked a personal question. Showed interest. Cared. A budding victim of Stockholm syndrome, I'm suddenly the happiest I've been the whole deployment.

I grab my rifle and bounce over to where the company leadership sleeps, separated from the rest of us by Hesco-barrier walls. There's a roaring fire in a grated pit. I spot Gunny smoking a cigarette by it and make a beeline for him, a slight smile on my face.

"Oohrah, Gunny, I was told—"

"Who the fuck do you think you are, cheese dick?" he shouts at me. "You think you can just walk around wearing whatever the fuck you want? You think you can ignore your team leaders? Stand at parade rest, motherfucker. You think you can just wear whatever fucking beanie you want, even though you've been told not to? Take that fucking hat off. Right now. Throw it in the fire. Look at it. Watch it burn. Don't you ever fucking disobey orders again. Get the fuck out of my sight."

I run away. In the hooch my seniors look at me with smirks, snickering to themselves as I walk in. They stop laughing when they see the dirt-streaked tears on my face, the way I'm trying to hold back more. I grab my issued beanie and run to an unseen corner of the landing zone, where I sit in quiet claustrophobic desperation, playing the scene back in my head, imagining retribution, knowing it will never come.

Post. You don't truly know yourself until you stand in one place for six hours. Eight hours. Some guys do sixteen hours straight. Usually it's a punishment for falling asleep on the first eight hours. The Marine Corps Way.

Your mission is to guard the base, to observe, to watch for activity in the fields or on the road. But what you're really doing is passing time. Daydreaming. Dissociating. Meditating. Fuming. Wishing the months would pass in a blur. Knowing they won't.

Your companions are a machine gun, a pair of night vision binoculars, a thermal scope, four hundred rounds of ammunition, a pen flare, a red star cluster, a logbook, a radio and the flock of sheep outside your concertina wire. If you're lucky, a camel spider will grace you with its presence during the night.

At first, you count the hours one by one. You celebrate as they pass. The problem, you find, is that in checking your watch, you discover you have misjudged how much time has actually passed. You think: this must have been two hours. But it's only thirty minutes. This is the road to despair, and you must avoid this practice at all costs.

You must release yourself from the concept of time. You must sever your connection to the present, leaving only a small remain-behind element of subconscious to ensure there are no threats approaching the base. You must never allow your thoughts to drift back to the hour or the minute or the second. If you are able to master this phase, you can spend an entire shift in a pleasant daydream and find yourself startled by your relief as he walks up the ladder to send you back to sleep.

You learn to relax. To exist and not exist. Sometimes, on quiet early mornings, as the sun rises, and the roosters crow and the smell of burning trash fades and gives way to dew and haze and mist and wet grass, a revelation comes: this country, viewed at certain times, through a certain lens, in a certain mindset, is actually beautiful. And so these sunrises witnessed from behind a machine gun stick in the recesses of every grunt's brain, a vision that never leaves us, as long as we live.

While on post you learn a form of meditation, ad-hoc, improvised, made up as you go along. The meditation helps you realize that post is nothing, that the war is nothing, that you are nothing and nothing bothers you. You become one with the world. Your seniors, your squad leader, the Marine Corps, Gunny, none of it matters any more. You are the post. You are the post and you are the sheep and you are the burn pit and the Hesco barrier.

Like any meditative state it begins with the corporeal form. You must lose your sense of body.

It begins when you take a couple of steps to the left or right. You lean against the gap between the Hesco barrier and the roof, where you could shoot if you ever needed to shoot anything, although you don't need to shoot anything because you are one with everything and anything.

You rest your thumbs inside of your body armor. Lean your head on the wood boards supporting the roof. Unfocus your eyes, slowly. Be completely still. Let the weight of your body armor remove itself from your shoulders.

Let your thoughts wander. Hundreds of hours of post is a gift. Solitude. Reflection. Internal soliloquies and revelations, passing as soon as they come. A chance to muse on every important and unimportant event that has happened so far in your miserably short life. Every mistake, every embarrassment, every triumph. Your situation and your attitude toward that situation.

Perhaps it is a matter of perspective. These seniors are just men. Men are flawed. They know the Way that they know. Marcus Aurelius said man acts according to his nature—so forgive him. But you don't know if you can forgive them. Not yet.

Fine. But maybe you can begin to understand them. No matter what cruelties you endure, perhaps it is important to realize that these flawed men learned this from their seniors, and they from theirs. There must be a reason.

Perhaps it is this: in this profession, you do what you can to prepare for war, even if there is no war. And if there is war, and it is not quite as much of a war as you expected, then still you act like it is a war. You do the same drills, learn the same knowledge, master the same systems that you would for any war. You train for an underwhelming war the same way you would for a hellish, kinetic war. You train your subordinates most of all, hoping that what you instill in them will keep them alive, keep you alive. You do the best you can with what you know.

With their insistence on training and misery, these seniors have shaped you into someone who knows that though you could give in to sloth, or laziness, or indifference, you must not. You realize they are doing the best they can to teach you the lessons they think you need to learn. And maybe, though you do not forgive them yet, you can at least appreciate what they are trying to impart to you.

Then again, you think during your thirteenth hour of post, maybe not.

Sometimes you stand post alone. Other times you're with another person. My favorite, though I couldn't always tolerate him, was Levi. He had an interesting upbringing, religious family from West Virginia, something like that. He didn't talk about them much. He was always more interested to hear what I thought about current events, or to read the books I'd grab from the company patrol base whenever we'd rotate through. We shared the entire *Twilight* series between the two of us. We talked literature, fantasy, science fiction.

Levi told me about LARP'ing: live action roleplay, where you dress up as a fictional character and fight other people dressed up as fictional characters. He said you could be whatever you wanted: a barbarian, an elf, a wizard. He explained that the weapons were foam but, if you swung them hard enough, could bruise or injure your opponent. It was the closest you could get to real medieval fighting, he would say excitedly. Sometimes, battles would get so brutal that you'd find yourself charging full-speed into the opposing team, knocking people over, tearing through nerds with a blood frenzy. I was interested. I promised to find him later, much later, after we both got out, and LARP with him. I don't think we ever told the seniors about that.

One time, after I had climbed the wooden ladder up to Post Three to relieve Levi, I spotted drops of some milky substance all over the sandbags that held up the machine gun. It took me a couple of seconds before I realized what I was seeing. Immediately I recoiled in disgust.

"Levi! Hey, Levi! What the fuck?" I shouted, holding on to the edge of the door frame as I leaned out from the post. He turned to face me. He had the look of someone who walked through life oblivious to its difficulties.

"What's up?"

"You fucking jerked off all over the sandbags, dude!"

A look of genuine shock. "Oh!" he says. "I'm sorry. Let me clean it up."

So he put dirt where he needed to put dirt, and poured water on it, and promised he would be more careful next time. Water under the bridge. It was just post. It was just Afghanistan.

Things are blurry. Sometimes I do not know what I see. Sometimes it is crystal clear.

One of the blurrier days. I watch Levi come off a post we only man during the night, watch him disappear around a corner. A moment later one of my seniors comes out from where Levi just went, what looks like a black bag for a high-powered night vision optic in his hands. He walks to the post Levi just occupied, enters it, and leaves. The black bag is no longer in his hand. He walks around the corner, to the tent. When he returns, he returns with Levi, who is back in full gear, carrying his rifle. They walk to the post. The senior raises his voice. Levi stares through him. Yes, Lance Corporal, no Lance Corporal. The senior points to an adjacent post, one we man during the day. Levi replaces the Marine on that post.

I do not say anything. I do not stand up for Levi. I do not stand up for anyone, not then, not for the entire deployment. All of a sudden things are crystal clear.

6

Marjah

February 2010

For a grunt, the worst thing you can be is left behind.

Early in the new year Charlie Company prepares to fly over to the outskirts of Marjah, a big Taliban town on the west side of Helmand province. Our mission is to secure Five Points, an intersection where five major roads meet, a few miles east of the city. We'll land there a few days in advance of the main air assault, which is being handled by the Sixth Marine Regiment out of Lejeune. Their First and Third Battalions will clear from west to east, meeting up with us at a patrol base we're supposed to establish.

Until they get there, we're to hold the intersection, at any cost.

We spend weeks preparing for the operation. Tensions are high. Some of us will have to stay behind. The company needs a skeleton crew to man the bases, to stand post, to answer the radio. Though the official message is that competent people are needed so things don't deteriorate, we all hope our squad leaders like us enough to recommend us for the mission. As I drift from foot patrol to post, from trawling MySpace on the computers at the company position to sitting on an MRE box drying my boots, I pray that I'm chosen.

You might only get one chance to fight like this, say Marines with hands in pockets, bullshitting by the burn pit. One chance to do what you trained to do. Infantry shit. Real grunt shit.

It's going to be the Fallujah of Afghanistan, one Marine tells me. They've been dropping leaflets for months, telling the civilians to leave. Just like Fallujah, they say. House-to-house fighting. Taking the city block by block. And we're going to be first in.

All I know is that I can't be left behind, so I grovel extra hard to the seniors. Defer and deflect. I try to befriend them. It doesn't work—it never works—but somehow, one morning, my old section leader finds me at the company outpost.

"You're going," he says. "And you're a gunner."

The day before the operation I'm loading my rucksack. People keep giving me things to put in it, even though it's already the heaviest it's ever been. For this operation I'm a rocketman again. A looming punk-rocker named Corporal Jessup, an older Marine removed from and entirely unfazed by the boot-senior hierarchy, will be my team leader and assistant gunner. He'll help me get on target, spot my rounds, clear my backblast.

My weapon is the Shoulder-Fired, Multi-Purpose Assault Weapon. The SMAW. I carry the launcher (sixteen point nine two pounds) cross-body. I stick three rockets (eighteen pounds each, fifty-four pounds total) through the top of my rucksack, underneath the detachable top pouch. Someone shoves four PRC-117 radio batteries (about four pounds each, sixteen pounds total) into my face, which I find a spot for. I pack three days' worth of food and water, a cold-weather marshmallow suit, rain jacket, rain pants, polypropylene warming layers, neck gaiter, a personal tent, sleeping bag, flashlight, headlamp (altogether thirty pounds, maybe less). Two uniforms, underwear, socks, gloves, eye protection (five pounds). Personal night vision device (eleven ounces).

Body armor: a lightweight (but not too lightweight) plate carrier, ceramic front, back and side bullet-proof plates (seventeen pounds), six magazines of 5.56 rifle ammunition and a smoke grenade (six pounds eleven ounces), a Kevlar helmet (four pounds), and an M4 fully loaded (seven point five pounds) in front of me. A pack of Marlboro reds, though I don't really smoke.

And *Breaking Dawn,* the last novel of the Twilight series.

We wake sometime around midnight and ready ourselves. We move to the landing zone where the helicopters will pick us up, a short distance from the company outpost. Our packs are so heavy we cannot lift them ourselves, so we lie upon the ground and scoot into the pack-straps, our friends deadlifting the weight from the bottom. We move with little tactical grace. We reach the landing zone and wait. When the time arrives, we watch MV-22 Osprey aircraft, the ugly bastard of a plane and a helicopter, approach and land with all the grace of a walrus belly-flopping onto an ice floe. We struggle to load, one at a time, trudging onto the rear ramp of the aircraft. We avoid the whirling rotors that light up green with infrared through our moonlit night vision monocles, an orchestra of movement, more drums than violin. We take off and fly for Five Points, clutching our weapons in the bucking darkness.

I'm riding in the Osprey on my way to Marjah and I'm not afraid. The bird is landing, hitting the ground hard, and I'm not afraid. I'm unloading my ruck from the Osprey, dragging it out into a pile, and running to form a circle around the still-whirring helicopter, guns facing out. Still I am not afraid. As we exit the aircraft I'm thinking about being in the right place, having enough dispersion between me and the next guy, facing outward in a satisfactory Marine Corps high kneeling position, and still I am not afraid.

The birds lift off and leave us with the early morning silence. We wait

one

two

three

moments, and then we're moving, bounding toward an outcropping of buildings a few hundred meters away. The mortars section stays put, guarding our packs, setting up their 60's behind a few deep canals, prepping for a fire mission. I'm running, sprinting, hauling ass, holding my rifle with one hand, steadying the SMAW with my other hand, two rockets on my back. I am in prime fighting shape, ready to kill, but still the lactic acid builds in my legs and my lungs burn like paper. I leap deep irrigation canals carrying the SMAW and the rifle and propelling myself to the crumbling far bank of each canal. It's a long way down but my feet never touch the bottom. Others do. They are helped up. We keep moving.

We reach the intersection. The engineers run up carrying charges they spent the whole week making, big cardboard cutouts with explosives attached, two, three times more C-4 than they need, and they run up to the nearest compound wall, a marvelous huge thick thing made of nothing but mud, and they stick the wall charge to the side, duct-taped on, so we stand fifty yards down, shielded by another wall, and they give us the three-count:

Fire in the hole!

Fire in the hole!

Fire in the hole!

and there is the most marvelous explosion, a beautiful blanket of blast wave, concussion in my unprotected ears and I'm running again, sprinting, following the other Marines through the gap, and it's as my foot is about to fall over the new hole in the wall that, for the first time, I feel it

fear

and I stop, something about stepping through a threshold that catches me like trout in a net, but then someone pushes me through

move it Kirk, they say

and I'm through the wall, blinking at a family of four or five or six, an old man and a young man and a woman and some girls, fully covered in blue and black and grey, the man standing with his hands up, talking to the Afghan soldiers

and I forgot the Afghan soldiers are here, too, they're supposed to be in the lead but they don't even have night vision

and big skeleton Corporal Jessup pushes me and says hey Kirk, let's go, we're following this platoon

and we rush out the front door of the compound, following a line of men as they bound and walk and start breaking open corrugated-iron doors and

this place is called Five Points and it is a bazaar and a marketplace, I suddenly remember

and before I know it I'm front and center, pointing my rifle into shops, helping clear houses, all the while carrying a rocket launcher and fear.

It's early in the afternoon. We've consolidated inside the first compound, which becomes the company headquarters. There are two or three other compounds that have been taken over by the company, their occupants told to move down the road and avoid the fighting. I'm standing around, drinking water, smoking cigarettes even though I don't smoke, when I hear it for the first time

crack

above everyone's head, way over the wall, just one, then

crack crack crack crack

and it begins, the firing toward us, and then the Marine response

the response

is this percussive and deadly symphony, a lethal orchestra conducted by the company commander, his platoon leaders, his squad leaders, the weapons platoon section leaders. I climb a wall, take a knee on a low roof, take cover behind a section of thick hardened mud, and before I know what or why I'm staring down a four-times-magnification riflescope, firing, blasting away, all of my fear dissipating as dozens of

Marines shoot in the same direction, toward the same brown blobs in the distance, and there it is,

symphony, as the machine gunners let loose on the eastern rooftops, their 240B's singing, answering, calling to each other, the bursts lasting as long as it takes to say

diemotherfuckerdiemotherfuckerdie,

harmony, each gun picking up as the last stops firing, talking guns, three or four or five of them on line, the whole section, beautiful, the most magnificent performance I've ever seen, the truest, most authentic expression of the grunt's purpose, tracer rounds dancing in the afternoon haze, and you could never plan it like this, never imagine you might do this, never in a million years, even when you're at the School of Infantry, and yet here you are, witness to something extraordinary and irreplaceable and unique and inimitable.

This is what your seniors have been waiting for, what they have been preparing for, and now they are doing it with aggression and violence and precision born of years of intense practice, and as you watch you think maybe some of what they taught you makes sense after all.

A massive wire-guided TOW missile, fired from a truck, *shooooops* out of its tube, sails and sails for what feels like forever and finally lands, and there are thunderous roars and applause from the Marines of Charlie Company. A direct hit on someone's abandoned home, now a Taliban firing position.

A Javelin missile, shoulder-fired, and the shooting stops again, everyone waiting, waiting, waiting, and suddenly it falls from the heavens, drops onto a compound, another grand slam, and the crowd roars for the away team.

I blast away two magazines and stop, just watching. I don't see any targets. I don't hear any incoming fire. Eventually we all stop shooting. Make our way down off the walls. One of my seniors falls from a rickety ladder and lands on my head. Four Corpsmen berate me for moving my sore neck.

Come up with a post rotation. Strip off our gear. Eat some First Strike rations. Read a little bit about werewolves. Go to sleep in the shit-filled animal shelter around the back of the house, inside the wall with the new entrance. Slumber, deeply.

More Marines from the battalion show up with heavy weapons, riding on trucks. They dig fighting holes, set a perimeter around the compounds we're occupying. Emplace huge fifty-caliber machine guns, with bullets the size of your thumb that'll tear a man in half with a solid burst. The next day is more of the same, shooting starting in the morning and continuing intermittently all day long. We move out to another compound, Corporal Skeletor and I, taking our rockets with us. More Marines arrive, engineers with bulldozers and backhoes, and they start building a patrol base for us, a rudimentary thing just outside the Five Points buildings, starting with a perimeter Hesco wall they build with dirt.

We're tasked to protect them, so the backhoe digs us a fighting hole and we sit in it for a day, smoking cigarettes and taking pictures on a digital camera. I haven't shot a rocket yet. We sleep all together under someone else's blankets, in someone else's bed, next to someone else's chickens, in a house that was, until two days ago, someone else's home.

The company starts doing patrols, whole platoons going out at once, flanking the road as the engineers' specially-built trucks clear IED after IED. I find myself out wide on the flanks, two rockets and a SMAW, hopping canals and walking in a diamond formation with four other guys from a line platoon.

A screaming sound followed by a boom up ahead, a rocket-propelled grenade and the start of an ambush. Immediately we run to the nearest embankment, a perfect source of cover from the machine gun and AK fire that starts from our left flank. Again I find myself shooting into the distance, my ACOG reticle hovering over distant houses and trees and other likely targets.

"They're calling in artillery," Corporal Jessup says, looking at his radio.

"Where?" I'm not shouting; the firing has come to a comfortable lull, only the repetition of evenly timed suppressing fire coming from our side. We're waiting. Adrenaline recedes. The gunshots are suddenly very loud.

"That compound over there," he says, pointing, "I think."

It's a massive one, four hundred or so yards distant. I've never seen artillery before. I'm excited.

The platoon, fanned out along the crumbling earthwork remnant of a deep irrigation canal, talks and waits for the artillery to strike. Nearby, a long convoy of Mine-Resistant, Ambush-Protected vehicles halts. Lumbering vehicles, tailor-made for this war, some equipped with minerollers, devices hooked to the front of the truck with wheels to trip any pressure-plate IED's in the ground, in the interest of having them explode in front of, rather than under, the truck. The turret gunners in their sand-colored goggles and neck gaiters lean against the back of their protective turrets, each alternating direction, ready to shoot over our heads. There's a platoon on the other side of the convoy, too.

They must wish they were over on our side, I'm thinking, when suddenly I hear the screeching approach of a crashing jumbo jet aircraft, except it's not a jet, it's the artillery, and I have half a second to think

this seems awfully close

and then a friendly 155mm artillery round strikes the mine roller of the lead vehicle in the convoy and explodes with tremendous force, mangling the truck, so close it shakes my teeth. I watch the turret gunner's head recoil far too fast for a human neck to absorb, his head slamming into the steel armor plate in the back of his turret. He falls into the MRAP's innards.

Immediately I'm up and running, grabbing the nearest Afghan Army soldier, sprinting back the way we came as four more 155 shells land nearby, a slow, rhythmic cadence of incoming jet-engines aimed at us, and we bear the shockwaves and rocks and dirt they kick up as they land, impossibly close, and I keep running away, the Afghan soldier at my side.

"Cease fire! Cease fire! Cease fucking fire!" screams the platoon leader and Corporal Jessup and the squad leader and everyone else who has a radio while the rest of us run, sprint for our lives as fast as we can.

We regroup a couple of hundred yards back, a mess of men and gear, no order or discipline, all of us crouching behind the same mound of dirt, delirious and wondering what went wrong. Impossibly, unbelievably, nobody from the patrol seems to be hurt.

Later, back at the company patrol base, I share a cigarette with a stunned Major while Corpsmen check us for wounds. Nobody speaks.

Nobody tells us what happened to the turret gunner.

One day Bradley, another assaultman, shoots a rocket from seventy yards away into a machine gun murder hole, blowing away whoever's on the other side and earning the title "Mad Brad." I'm behind on rocket-shots. On that day, or maybe another, an element hits a massive IED, which wounds several Marines, some badly, some of whom are flown out. Nobody dies, and even though I don't believe in miracles I think that it must be.

During one firefight Corporal Jessup and I get the green light for a rocket shot. It's a rough one. Someone in charge wants to blast a hole in a distant wall. He wants us to breach it so we don't have to go in a potentially booby-trapped front door. Except the compound he wants us to shoot is three or four hundred meters away, pushing the accurate range of the weapon system. I have no idea how thick this mud wall is, or whether my rockets will do anything to it. Regardless, I'm filled with an eagerness and adrenaline that I've never felt before.

This is my moment. My time to shine.

We find the best spot we can, just in front of a canal. There are at least thirty other Marines on line with us, waiting for a show.

I think to myself: you could not be more prepared. You've waited a year for this, ever since you shot your first rockets at the School of Infantry. Ever since you heard about the Rocketman of Fallujah, who they say shot fifty rockets there, clean shots into windows, at trucks and technicals and fighting positions. Ever since you found out about the Novel Explosive round, which can take down a whole building with one shot. Ever since your instructors first told you stories about putting projectiles on textiles in Iraq, evicting terrorist tenants from their apartment window firing points with smoothbore high explosives.

I sight in and pop off some spotting rounds, but for the life of me I can't see where they land. This troubles me, but I try not to show it. I can't lose face. I can't back out now. This is maybe my only chance to ever shoot a rocket in combat, to earn the single most important assaultman combat credential. Dozens of Marines are watching me, waiting for the grand finale, the climax of the afternoon's festivities. Like the platoon and company assault ranges we run, the rocket shot becomes the focus of all eyes. I am the main event.

Corporal Jessup says we're on target. I don't know if I believe him but I don't have much of a choice. I have to trust him. With my a-gunner reassuring me that the spotting rounds hit the wall, I flip the safety off.

"On target," I say. Out of the corner of my eye, I notice a Marine recording with a digital camera.

Corporal Jessup waves his hands and cranes his neck, making a big show of clearing our backblast. This is his moment, too.

"Backblast area all clear!" he screams to the platoon, the enemy and God above.

"Rocket!" I yell and cut off quickly, exhaling completely to steady my chest and the scope's reticle. I depress the trigger and the firing lever and

whoomp

goes the familiar explosion next to my head.

The projectile sails and sails, building an infinite moment of combat hangtime, sailing and hanging and then finally the rocket impacts and explodes with a dull thud just below the wall, where the foundation meets the dirt.

A miss.

My stomach drops. I feel the disappointed eyes of every grunt on the patrol. We load and shoot another rocket, scoring a direct low hit this time. The rocket does not penetrate the wall. A pointless shot. Nevertheless I imagine I already know what everyone thinks of me. My reputation as a rocketman diminishes that day. So passes my moment of glory.

After three weeks our time in Marjah comes to an end. We hand over the patrol base we built to the Marines who cleared the city from west to east. They keep the base's name: Combat Outpost Reilly, after Charlie Company's fallen Marine from the last Iraq deployment.

We go back to the day-to-day drudgery of Nawa. I rejoin Levi on post at the company outpost, where he's been wallowing since losing the popularity contest a few weeks earlier and staying behind. The status quo resumes, and we endure the rest of the deployment together.

Part Two

*We were
chasing ghosts in killing
fields, where adolescence
ended and the war began*

7

Degrees

Everything is measured in degrees. Degrees of temperature: it broke a hundred-ten today. Degrees of discomfort. Degrees of convenience and inconvenience. Degrees of suffering.

It's a contest to see who has it the worst while they're deployed. A race to the bottom. How do you determine who got fucked hardest? Ask questions. You live in containerized housing units? You have Wi-Fi? You get lattes at the coffee shop? You have a gym, with treadmills and barbells? Bed, with sheets? Air conditioning—adjustable? Privacy? Can you jerk off without anyone watching?

Do you shit on a toilet? Porta-john? Plywood seat? Hole in the ground? What do you eat? How often? Is your water cold? Hot? Do you wear cammies, or FROG blouses, the kind that are only authorized in real combat?

It's all covered in dust. Manas Air Base in Kyrgyzstan, the last stop before you get in country, they have it the best. Nawa is not that bad. Marjah was the worst that you'd been through. The guys who invaded Iraq lived in chemical suits for weeks. Korengal was worse. Baghdad was easy. Ramadi was bad. Fallujah was the worst, really the worst—what year? Only lost two guys in 2007. Degrees.

Degrees of combat. You draw hostile fire pay at a big base like Leatherneck, but you don't get shot at. That is, unless some Taliban decide to dress up as U.S. soldiers, sneak past the sleepy, non-infantry types guarding the perimeter, and blow up your planes.

You take indirect fire? Mortars? Rockets? You—you? Or your buddies? Or some other part of the base? Or do the sirens just wake you up? Are you so used to it you don't wake up at all?

Do you leave the wire? Do you leave your rifle in Condition One? Bolt forward, round in chamber, magazine inserted, safety on? Or are you always Condition Four—magazine removed, bolt forward, chamber empty, safety on? Do you ever rack a round?

Do you ever get shot at? Blown up? Find IED's? Find caches? Enter houses? Kick doors? Dismount? Leave the protection of your vehicles? Did you earn a Combat Action Ribbon? How many gunfights were you in? Did you shoot back? Did you see who you were shooting at?

Would you give all your ribbons away to get back the friends you lost?

Degrees of war. The further you are from the real war the more you endure.

These bases, this war, Afghanistan. All of these Marines, we all walk around with our version of who's got it worse, who does more, who suffers the most. It's ingrained in us, burned into our collective psyches through hazing and tradition and our Senior Lance Corporals. Redemption through combat. A fervent admiration for true warriors. A love of killing, though most of us have never killed, will never kill.

The Cobra gunship pilots, the grunts, the motor transport truck drivers, the weather guys, the artillery unit that "does mostly grunt stuff," they all know about it. And they perpetuate it and they live it and they need it. Everyone has something. Some degree of war-related suffering that you can lord over somebody else around a smokepit or outside a chow hall or back home in front of your old high school buddies or ten years from now when you meet another veteran at a construction site.

When you're heading into the worst parts of war, the most-far flung reaches of the empire, you imagine you're more important than you really are. You're a god at Dwyer. A legend at Manas. A warrior in Hawaii. You imagine that at every intermediate stop on your way to Helmand there are guys wishing they were you, wishing they'd go out and get a deployment. A real deployment.

But maybe it's the other way around. Maybe those guys are glad they're living in a heated room, eating hot chow, showering, not worrying much about death.

Even in Helmand you might not be anything special. Sangin. At least you're not in Sangin. And especially not *that* part of Sangin. Nawa? Ain't shit in 2010, but in 2009 it was something. Marjah stood out. Sangin took a quarter of a battalion out of action. Let's be honest—Afghanistan has nothing on Peleliu or Iwo Jima or Belleau Wood or the Chosin Reservoir. Talk about dick-measuring. Tarawa Marines need a yardstick.

Everyone wants a bad deployment. Until you get a bad deployment. Then you just want to go home.

Degrees.

The gap between one round of war and the next is ten months.

Ten months from leaving Afghanistan as a boot Lance Corporal and going back to Afghanistan as senior Lance Corporal.

Ten months of seniors departing, commanders changing, platoons re-organizing. Re-orienting yourself to a newer position of increased responsibility. Learning to lead. Field operations on Oahu, on the big island, at 29 Palms. Rockets and grenades. Squad and platoon and company assault ranges. Re-learning the basic infantry skills. Drinking in the barracks and playing FIFA and watching one of your friends throw all the laundry in all the barracks washing machines off the catwalk. Wrestling him to the ground. Ripping your Disneyland shirt. Making nice with him. Drinking more.

Skipping out on mountain warfare training when the battalion heads to California and spending three weeks learning Pashto instead. Hitting pristine Pyramid Rock beach on the north side of the base by three o'clock every day. Falling in love, having your heart broken and doing it all over again. Joining your father and stepmother on their vacation trip to Hawaii. Willing them not to ask the questions they're holding just behind their smiles.

Attaching out to a new platoon. Spending nights in the field with them, grasping for stars. Firewatch and foxholes. Slowly, bonds begin to form. Friends gravitate toward each other. A certain kind of absurdist humor binds you to the man next to you, who is doing what you do, which is filling in the fighting hole he dug yesterday, the hole he found half-dug, in just the right spot. The hole that will be dug again in the same spot by the next platoon that comes through this part of the field. There, you think. There is the thing you've been searching for. We are peers, friends, and mostly we do not treat boots like our seniors did. It is good to make conversation without worrying what the man you are talking to will do to you if he doesn't like what you say. There is no tension in our words, in the tone of our voices. We huddle around the same coffee dispensers, mugs steaming in the rain. We wear our Gore-tex jackets. Only one or two of our minute number of new noncommissioned officers seem to take themselves too seriously, but they are noncoms. They are in it for the long haul. They have bought in and succumbed to the Way. There is little measuring of dicks, but when we do measure a little, they are little measurements we can laugh about.

Months of training and field days and the garrison Marine Corps bore. Endless Wing Nights at the base enlisted club, dunking port-a-potties by the softball fields into Shit Creek for the nth time. One last field problem and one last night out, and you're finally ready to leave again for the war. You pack all of your belongings into a series of cardboard boxes and send them off to a warehouse on the base, where some private in supply will inevitably damage them or steal from them. The rest of your gear you stuff carefully into two seabags, a rucksack and a daypack. A series of briefings in the base theater, powers of attorney and living wills, routing numbers and extra socks and flashlight batteries and then boom, you're headed off to Afghanistan again.

The only difference is that this time, you're a squad leader instead of a squad member.

How do you get to a war?

Buses. Parking lots. Goodbyes. Kisses. Sitting. More goodbyes. Energy drinks. Cigarettes. Loading seabags. Unloading seabags. Loading again. Goodbyes. Finally you get on a bus. You put your headphones in, turn on *Grow Up and Blow Away* by Metric and stare blankly at jungle-covered mountains as you drive across Oahu. Your heart rate rises.

You arrive at Hickam Air Base on the other side of the island. You get off the buses, sit around. You ask yourself questions: are you ready? Are you really ready?

What do you do if someone gets shot in the neck? Plug it. When someone loses a leg? Tourniquet, high on the thigh, into the crook of the leg. When an Afghan soldier gets angry? Calm him down, or maybe he'll waste you when you're not looking.

You visualize catastrophe after catastrophe. You think of the consequences of inaction. Any decision is better than no decision.

Again and again you imagine explosions and flying limbs and one of your friends lying in some field looking up at you. You failed. You didn't do enough. You weren't prepared enough. All you want is to be prepared enough.

You know the nine-line casualty evacuation request back to front. How to clear a house. How to fire and maneuver. Speed, surprise, violence of action.

A deployment is a seven-month long boxing match. These are the weigh-ins. You feel like you've made weight, but barely. Second deployment. Second round. Second chance to lose your legs or keep them.

Something different about this one. You no longer feel untouchable. No heroic illusions. You could easily die, and others could die because of you. You are charged with keeping three fireteams worth of Marines alive. Maybe that's the wrong attitude—worrying about keeping the men alive instead of completing the mission. As you wait for a chartered plane in the passenger terminal of Hickam all you can think of is taking casualties. Watching one of the friends you've made in Second Platoon torn asunder. You vow to put their safety first, even if it means the mission takes a backseat. Everyone comes home alive. Whatever the consequences.

In the terminal a few civilians sit on white plastic benches waiting for space-available flights to the mainland. There are Ritz crackers and bottles of water and vending machines and televisions. We read fantasy novels about a dark elf named Drizzt Do'Urden. We call our mothers while we still have cell phone service. We check and re-check to make sure we aren't missing gear. The staff NCO's give a few ass-chewings, light things, routine things.

We carry hundreds of devices to help kill and maim the enemy, our own equipment and spares. Extra night-vision devices, thermals for crew-served weapons, extra M16's, M249's, M4's, daypacks filled with rain gear, poncho liners and toothpaste. Machine guns and magazine pouches and GPS wristwatches. One poor soul hauls around a gigantic locked bag full of bayonets that nobody will use.

Huddle into a jumbo jet. Machine guns under our feet. Takeoff and blue water. The flights are snapshots and fragments, moments of lucidity dropped into a Nyquil-induced dream. Later on you think you remember loading seabags and rucksacks into the belly of the plane. You are pretty sure you recall trudging across the airstrip and up tall portable stairs onto a massive Boeing 747. The look of the cheery, red-clad Omni Air flight attendants who give you Sprite and 7 Up and coffee. You remember the vast azure ocean as you take off.

You remember stopping in different places, but for how long? Where? What airport? Maybe you fly to Alaska, or Minnesota. Then Ireland, where there's a bar but you can't drink. Or maybe it's somewhere in Germany, where you buy a t-shirt with a red and yellow and black flag on it and you don't even know why. Each flight is timeless and interminable as you doze and wake back up and doze again. You lay your head on your buddy's shoulder, and he on the next guy, and so on. You snore and move your head and dream and in a day or so you're in Kyrgyzstan.

In 2011 Manas Air Base is the gateway to Afghanistan. The base is situated on the outskirts of Bishkek, the capital of Kyrgyzstan. You get off the plane and the first thing you see are these massive mountains in the distance and you think: has anyone climbed that? Like a series of sharp white knuckles they punch the sky and seem to tower over the world. The base gives off an air of semi-permanence. Between the Hesco-barriers, off-white steel structures and grayness there is an undercurrent of nervous energy, as if everyone on the base were walking to fight the war right then, right there. It is wholly deconstructable. In the blink of an eye, Air Force engineers could take it down and pack the whole thing up. A base-in-a-box. Manas feels alive and urgent, even at night, as soldiers from a half-dozen countries power-walk to and from Pete's Place, the MWR center, the phone banks. As you walk around you pass formations of soldiers, sailors, airmen, foreign soldiers, other Marines, all talking hurriedly among themselves, all preparing to fight Their Personal War.

We are a tight-knit group, bulky seasoned lower enlisted grunts. We spot a group of Army officers and as we near them they stop talking and eye us uneasily, as if unsure what to expect. We don't salute. We don't care. These fat-faced Army officers, who wear clear eye protection as they meander from exchange to chow hall, are beneath us. We are young and arrogant and we believe we are on our way to experience a higher degree of combat. So we fail to salute and we walk away and the Army officers say nothing.

In the chow hall a Kyrgyzstani woman serves lasagna and green beans and spongy garlic bread. I drink dehydrated milk and stare at a female Air Force member's hair. Blonde, tied in a bun. I wonder what she looks like when she's not wearing tiger stripes. The exchange here sells lingerie. I push it from my mind; there is a war waiting for me.

We spend a few days here. We kick hip-pocket classes. We go to the gym. We talk. We walk over to Pete's Place, where you can watch movies and shoot pool and get on a computer. We arrive to an unexpected sight: a group of Mongolian soldiers arrayed at the counter, checking out all of the laptops.

In minutes every available computer is on a table, surrounded by two or three Mongolian soldiers, typing away, and over their shoulders I see they are checking Mongolian Myspace or Facebook and I am bewildered because I did not know Mongolia had a military, nor why it would choose to send soldiers to Afghanistan, and even more disorienting is my realization that these websites exist outside of America and have made it as far as Mongolia. But somehow they have, and so the Mongolian detachment uses the computers while we move over to the televisions, where we watch *The Bourne Identity* with a group of overweight U.S. Army soldiers, waiting for our turn.

We leave Pete's place, head to the gym or the chow hall or for various working parties. We lock up our weapons and spend the next several nights in massive Quonset huts on gravel lots, waiting for a flight.

Something I'll never forget.

The hooches next to ours are full of Marines, but I rarely see them outside. When I walk by their doors, I catch glimpses of men, endless rows of men, just sleeping on their racks. I learn later it's Darkhorse, the men of Third Battalion, Fifth Marines.

They look like ghosts.

Thin from stress and too many foot patrols. Gaunt-eyed from too little sleep. They venture out of their lodgings sparingly, only to take showers or smoke cigarettes under metal awnings as the rain beats staccato rhythms on the roof. When I see them they look at the ground or their pillows. No trash talking. No football throwing. No roughhousing. None of the hallmarks of a unit returning from combat, happy to be headed home. They are surrounded by each other but each man looks very much alone. These are my impressions. They are strong impressions.

We ask them to brief us on Helmand, on how they fought the war in Sangin District. How they took back the district, despite losing twenty-five men dead and two hundred wounded.

We assemble by the picnic tables, our green notebooks out and ready. Our lecturer is a mustachioed Corporal in sun-bleached utilities. His long hair, low-bloused boots and manner of speaking silently scream combat. He speaks to us with his hands in his pockets, sunglasses on, spitting dip in the ground. He addresses none of us by rank.

We are wearing clean uniforms. Our rifles are unfired. Our boots are bloused high.

He talks about what Darkhorse learned over seven months of death and mayhem and heroism and hard-earned victories. For a while I take notes. Then I just listen.

Walk single file, he says. Walk in each other's footsteps. Always have multiple pointmen carrying metal detectors, because they are the ones who get blown up most often. If this happens, the second pointman clears a path to the wounded Marine, and then to the medevac landing zone.

Keep hundreds of bottlecaps in your dump pouches, he insists. The second man lays them down so you know exactly where to step. The last man collects the caps so the Taliban won't know where you walked. Mark every few feet, or every footprint. Spray paint where you turn. Sweep everything with a metal detector.

Patrol in two elements. When one element strikes an improvised explosive device (and they will) or is fired upon (and they will be, right after the IED explodes), the other element maneuvers on Taliban positions. Don't drag the wounded on uncleared paths. Clear the landing zones: you might also find two, three, four or five more booby traps while clearing for the medevac bird.

To get a bird spinning, you only need the location, injury, and zap-card identification number. This information alone will get the bird off the ground. Send it quickly.

Use polar instead of grid fire missions for mortars. If shot at, simply lay down, even if you are in the middle of an open field. Do not run to cover. There are IED's in every embankment.

The Taliban is two steps ahead of you. Shoot rockets into trees to rain shrapnel on hidden machine gun positions.

Tourniquets on every man. Not one or two — five, six. As many as you can carry. Create your own openings with explosives because doorways are booby-trapped. Don't run to collect casualties. Clear to them with a metal detector. Don't, and you will die.

Ensure every man knows how to fasten a tourniquet on his own leg. His own arm. Two-handed. One-handed. Blind.

The Darkhorse Corporal speaks automatically. He is mechanical, emotionless in his description of mangled limbs and groin wounds and triple amputees. It is distant to him. He seems detached, as if he were giving us this brief in a patrol base in Sangin. Addressing the realities, the horrors of combat as though he were still in the midst of fighting. It is chilling to watch.

When he leaves us, the Corporal does not say goodbye or good luck. He does not salute the Lieutenant. He spits his dip on the ground and nods at us. Then he walks back into his hooch. We are in Manas three more days. I don't see him again.

Comfort in Kyrgyzstan is fleeting. Soon we're getting a flight out. We're loading our rucksacks and seabags and coyote deployment bags onto pallets while airmen in tiger stripes secured the piles with ratchet straps. This is their part of the war.

We grab our body armor and helmets for the combat flight. Until now we've been on civilian planes, but because of the danger inherent in flying into a combat zone, it's an Air Force C-17 with a military crew in tight-fitting jumpsuits.

We fly over the jagged mountains, the grasslands and the greenery and the peaks of Tajikistan and Uzbekistan and finally northern Afghanistan. The plane rocks and bumps. I don't sleep.

I imagine what's happening below.

I think of Army infantry in their ugly grey uniforms slugging up and down the mountains of the Korengal. I picture them climbing, exhausted, one hand on each knee, looking out over valleys filled with baboons and red-haired Pashtuns and houses built into cliffsides. I imagine a whole city of Hazaras in Mazar-e-Sharif, probably working with Army Special Forces, building wells and sneaking around. How many firefights are raging right now? How many bombs are about to explode? Now, right now, as we fly over, are Americans dying? Afghans? Brits? Whoever else found themselves unlucky enough to be here? Shit, nobody *finds* themselves here. Volunteers, all of us. Except the Afghans. They don't have a choice.

My eyes stay open, my mind racing as I think about what lies ahead.

Land, taxi, file out onto the tarmac. There it is, as if it never left. The smell.

Afghanistan.

Anywhere else in the world, I might smell it for a few fleeting seconds, moments that bring back clear memories of this place, and then the smell is gone and the memories are gone as fast as they came. Here, it's all around us. Inside us. Soon I'll become accustomed to it, forget it's even there, but for now, I smell it perfectly. Bizarrely, I feel I've missed it, as if I've come home to it.

The smell of Afghanistan is machinery and diesel fuel and gunfire and shit. It is burn pits and moon dust and sandbags and Hesco barriers and grey water inside of trailer-bathrooms. It is early morning dampness, humid fields and poppy stalks and marijuana plants taller than the top of your helmet. When we get to Garmsir, the scent will change subtly, enough that it will show up again in our noses and be gone again just as quickly. A few minutes from now I'll acclimate and the smell will disappear. But if I make it—if we make it—out of here alive, I'm sure that I will remember the scent again. I'll remember the first whiff of it I got, standing on the tarmac, just a few miles from the war.

8

War, Take Two

I don't know for sure who's going to be in my squad until a conversation with my platoon commander. The squads have been kind of fluid lately, says the Actual. He tells me a few guys got pulled to different positions, and we got a couple of new guys to the platoon. He tells me he's sitting down with all the squad leaders, hearing our thoughts about how to allocate the new guys and the experienced guys. He doesn't guarantee it'll happen the way we want it to, but he's open to my thoughts.

"First," he says, "who do you want to be your first team leader?"

No hesitation. "Jason, sir."

The Lieutenant's skeptical. Jason was caught with hard liquor in the barracks right after we got back from our first deployment. He and a friend both got a cut in pay and restriction to the barracks. The event killed his morale. He felt he had behaved well; he hadn't even left his room while he was drinking. Were it not for an overzealous senior pounding on his door, nobody would have known.

After that, Jason seemed to lose interest in being a Marine. He slacked, skated and pissed away his talents in favor of staying drunk every night after work. But then, almost reluctantly, he turned it all around. During the last two training events he'd reverted back to being a squared-away, competent grunt. When we were out in the field, he couldn't help but fix things and take charge. I'd seen it firsthand. It was as if he had no choice but to lead; his brain told him to take it easy but his heart made him mentor, coach and work.

A field Marine if there ever was one. The first into town on liberty and the last to return, but without the distractions of Hawaii life I judge he'll be the exact team leader I need.

I make this case. The Lieutenant comes around without much fuss. Jason as first fireteam leader, in charge of three guys. He'll also be my assistant patrol leader, my number two.

I choose Terrance as my second team leader. Another assaultman, turned mortarman, turned assaultman again. There's a picture of Terrance's helmet in Marjah that became famous. In the photograph, he's facing away, and he's written "GOD" in capital letters with a sharpie on his goggle-strap. Years later, this picture still circulates on social media, collecting likes without context.

Terrance also happens to be the guy I saw get screamed at, way back when I first got to the fleet, for having an out-of-regs haircut. At the time it seemed to me he was being singled out like so many other black Marines, men whose tightly-cropped hair doesn't ever look the way white hair looks, even when it's shorter and still in regs. Terrance is a little older, more mature than the rest of us. A principled and disciplined bulldog who takes shit from nobody. I need him to watch our collective backs, and he needs to be in charge of a team, whether he knows it or not.

Another concurrence from the Lieutenant.

We go back and forth about the rest of the squad. We are creating a band of misfits. The guys with hiccups in their pasts, like Jason. Perceived attitude problems. Recent arrivals to the company. Former Weapons guys who always kept to themselves during training. Most of them I know; we're friends, or at least friendly. Some are new to me. I welcome these odd men out. I identify with them. They seem by and large to be competent grunts. I just hope I'm up to the task of leading them.

I grab two machine gunners, one a Yankee from the Northeast, one from somewhere south of the Mason-Dixon line. Tony and Russell. One's loud, and one's quiet. One's a little older and outgoing, and one's young and subdued. I've worked with both. Tony's got a Jersey-shore kind of tough guy thing going, but he's confident behind a machine gun. I know Russell from his time tasked out to Assault, where he adapted to being an assaultman, running a SMAW with the best of us. He stays quiet most of the time, observing, but moves to the sound of the guns quickly and violently. They'll be fine.

A mortarman, Cody. The weapons platoon comedian. Midwest bred. Hard working, smart, and fit. Everything's a joke for him, even war. Except you can't always tell when he's joking, which makes it even funnier. He is fearless and confident.

I get a grunt-turned-dog-handler, Ivan, and his working dog, Willie. Ivan strikes me as mildly neurotic, foul-mouthed, an overgrown skateboarder, but his integrity and work ethic are beyond reproach. He's the best dog handler in the battalion, and he's the only one of us who can program a radio. He's also friends with Jason and has instant rapport with the rest of us. I'm glad to have him.

Willie is a black lab who can smell an IED from a football field away. He's partial to his red Kong toy. He's a good boy.

Ruben. The funniest, most irreverent and talented grunt I've ever met. My impression is that he is quietly competent at everything from weapons employment to patching up casualties. He is undaunted, hilarious, and fiercely loyal, but the one thing he's missing is ambition. Ruben never shows a desire to be anything but an outstanding grunt and a peer leader. I will rely on him heavily.

Mario and Nate. Nate is one of the skinniest Marines I've ever met, a hairy, chain-smoking font of sardonic wisdom who broke his leg falling off a rope in our sister battalion and came to us just before deployment. He's also the smartest person I'll ever meet in the military. We become instant friends. He's strong for his size, and tough. His catchphrase: "I shouldn't even fucking be here right now."

Mario is an interesting case. Though I haven't worked with him directly, I've heard about him from others. He's a little rough around the edges, a little indifferent, a little sloppy with his gear. He's been in trouble, but who hasn't? Where others see a Marine on the wrong side of the Way, I see hope for redemption. I take him on expecting to mentor, coach, teach. I welcome the challenge. My hope is he will go home a different man.

Little do I know how different he'll be. How different we'll all be.

Finally, our Navy Hospital Corpsman. The Marine Corps version of a medic. The only noncommissioned officer in the group, and as an E-4, he technically outranks me.

Three months prior to arriving in Hawaii, Doc was a blueside Corpsman in a hospital who wore scrubs to work. Now he's a greenside medic in a frontline unit, wearing unfamiliar body armor, expected to live and breathe the grunt life, to experience discomfort and hump and to shoot back when shot at. I'm not sure this is what he signed up for.

My impression of him in the short time I've known him is that of a true medical professional, a knowledgeable and adept Corpsman who can treat any wound, fix any infantry-induced disorder, triage any casualty.

The truth is, I don't need another shooter. I need someone to put us back together when we're not whole. I need someone to save lives, not take them. Doc strikes me as an expert at his profession. The rest is just learning to endure misery. He'll be fine, and we're better off for having him.

The platoon does its first training at Camp Dwyer, a few days away from flying deeper into the rich Helmand river valley. My squad learns that we are to occupy an isolated position west of the platoon's slightly-larger patrol base, which is called Durzay. Durzay has a refrigerator, a couple of computers, a generator, a small gym, a place to park vehicles, and hooches with air conditioners.

Our position will have none of that. We are headed to the most austere, furthest south position in the battalion's area of operations. The edge of the edge of the empire. I am a Lance Corporal, leading a brand-new squad of Lance Corporals, and we will occupy a position in an area that, until a few months ago, was overrun with Taliban. I couldn't be more excited.

We jump into the training: zeroing our weapons. Walking IED lanes. Getting briefed by civilians and officers, old men with titles that mean nothing to us, whose briefings don't seem to coincide with what we've been hearing. But we listen for anything of value we can take with us.

Guidance. More guidance. Every officer and SNCO in our innumerable chains of command feels a dire need to give guidance. It's a requirement. If you're not giving guidance, are you even in charge?

The regimental combat team's "Flat-ass rules": every mission has a task and purpose. Clean your weapons, equipment and position every day. Keep accountability of your gear. Improve your position. Know your fire support plan. Uphold the basic standards. Lead by example. You're a Marine first.

The law of war. Military necessity. Distinction and discernment of enemy forces. Proportional response. Limiting unnecessary suffering.

Rules of engagement. Make sure you discern a hostile act and a hostile intent before you engage. Just because a guy has a weapon doesn't mean he's going to shoot you with it. Just because a guy is trying to punch you doesn't mean you should shoot him.

Inherent right to self defense. Escalation, de-escalation of force. Positive identification. Legitimate military targets. Don't shoot if they're demonstrating a willingness to leave the fight. Above all, remember: firefights happen. The subtext: if you do get in a firefight, and we think you did it wrong, we'll fry you.

I come away from that briefing thinking that firefights are to be avoided.

More briefings. The general orders for everyone: no drugs. No dumping of uniforms. No sex. No weapons in condition one on Dwyer. No alcohol. No fun.

Somebody, maybe a surgeon, talks briefly over medical issues. Go see a doc if you're within fifty meters of a blast. If you're in a rollover. If you're shot in the head. If you're not breathing. But first, change your socks.

Other briefers talk about how to get intelligence after a raid, how to work with the Afghan soldiers and incorporate them into our operations. After a few hours I tune out and think about the Mongolian stir fry I'm going to eat in the chow hall later. They serve it every day. I had it yesterday, and I'll have it today, and I'll have it tomorrow if we don't get a flight out.

I spend a little free time in the MWR center, looking around. Inside on a white picnic table there's a pack of playing cards. Peppermill, made in Reno, Nevada. I pick up the pack and spread the cards around my hands, shuffling them just a little bit.

On a whim I pick out a two of spades and a three of clubs. Second Platoon, Third Squad. I check to make sure nobody's looking, then I stuff them in my shoulder pocket. They stay there for the next seven months.

Eventually, the briefings are over and we leave Camp Dwyer on helicopters, headed south.

As I'm buckled in, catching glimpses of the Helmand River, the bird pitching back and forth, flying low and fast over Garmsir district, it occurs to me that all of the platoon's black members are in my squad.

I don't know what to do with this information.

9

The Hill

Garmsir District, Helmand Province, Afghanistan
April 2011

Someone shakes me and whispers the time. Zero-four-thirty. I'm already awake, lying on the pebble rocks of Patrol Base Durzay in my sleeping bag. I thank my human alarm clock. He leaves.

The silence that precedes the sunrise makes my ears buzz. In combat, silence is comforting. If you can take the silence without considering the isolation, danger and anxiety of your day-to-day life, it can be quite peaceful. If you can't, then silence is your enemy. Harmful and counterproductive thoughts begin to drift around your head. The plunge of a pressure plate. The snap of a bullet. The sickening thud of a limb hitting the ground.

I spot constellations I know. I pretend I see constellations where I don't know any. I look for Orion's belt. I savor the peace.

The squad slept outside last night. Correction: *my* squad slept outside last night. On our foam isomats, in front of our rucksacks, neatly arranged in accord with unwritten annexes to the Marine Corps Way.

The spring dew condensed overnight on the tri-color waterproof bivvy sack which covered my sleeping bag. I'd covered my boots, too.

Leave your boots out in the dew and the insides would be soaked like you'd stepped in a puddle. In the field or on deployment, you take precautions. No matter how tired you were, you always covered your boots with something. A blouse, a tarp, a waterproof bag, a new pair of socks. Anything to keep the moisture out and your feet dry when you put your boots on at reveille.

These are the things you need to convey to the Marines you are in charge of, I remind myself.

You. Squad leader. Two fireteams: nine Marines, one Corpsman, one dog. And soon, one isolated, remote, primitive patrol base in the middle of southern Helmand.

I take a few deep breaths.

This is it. It's real now.

Afghanistan.

Again.

Every couple of days you wonder how you got here. Why would anyone trust you with a squad?

First, your seniors had to leave. That's critical. They leave, and their impressions of you go with them. Even if they were good impressions. You, now, this new you, needs to make new impressions. You've been on a deployment, but you still need to prove yourself. Your seniors will never see you as a leader. They'll only see you the way they did when they first met you: naive, without expertise, boot. Take what they taught you, and wish them well as they become civilians or move on to other billets. Their time ends. A new cycle begins.

Then, you need new leadership. A new commander. New First Sergeant. New platoon leaders. New platoon sergeant. Someone to give you a chance.

With the change comes a clean slate. A chance to start over with a brand-new set of men who come to the job with no preconceptions about your abilities or potential. Their opinion of you is entirely guided by your own actions. And you can control your actions, so you can influence their opinions. You finally get a vote in your own fate as a Marine.

Finally, you need boots. New Marines to guide and teach and discipline and mentor. It doesn't matter how many. Even one will do. One direct report makes for one example of your leadership style. He is a reflection of you, for better or for worse. His actions are your actions. If he leaves his rifle at a water buffalo during a movement, and someone brings it to you, you're expected to discipline him. To give correction. In giving this correction you reject the belittling approach taught by your seniors in favor of empathy and teaching. But there are some things you learned from your seniors that have a place. For grievous infractions, like falling asleep on firewatch or leaving a weapon behind, you know what to do.

You smoke him. You run gun drills with intent. You run until he's learned two lessons: how to properly operate a SMAW, and how to keep his rifle from leaning on water buffaloes, so he doesn't have to run gun drills when he could be relaxing, eating, drinking. You smoke him, and you smoke yourself right alongside him. You smoke him until he's learned, once again, to keep his rifle in arm's reach at all times. And he knows you've gotta smoke him, and he's grateful to you because after you're done smoking him, it's over. You explain the lesson. The message is received. He's a person. A boot, but a man nonetheless. Though you may have learned how to punish from your seniors, you do not go further, and you fulfill the promise you made to yourself a year ago.

To be considered for squad leader, you need to show initiative. In the field and in garrison, you're the first to move when a task comes down. You solve problems for your new platoon leader and platoon sergeant before they know they have them. You watch as several Corporals from Security Forces, who get promoted too early, crash and burn as team leaders. Rank doesn't mean a thing if you don't know anything. When everyone's tired from the hump to the range, and you're tired, and you just want to sit and take a nap with everyone else, instead you get up as the ammo trucks come in and start unloading. And then men follow you and start unloading right next to you. Teach classes, mentor, fill in when needed. Initiative. Endurance. Perseverance.

The new leadership takes notice of your performance. Nobody's there to tell them about all of your failures, about how you missed the SMAW shot in Marjah or fell out of your first hike in the fleet or got your driver's license revoked on base. The old senior Lance Corporals, Corporals and Sergeants are gone. You have one chance at a fresh start. You take advantage of it.

The new Actual, a mountain of a Lieutenant with a moral compass as straight as a Roman road, notices your peer leadership. The new Bravo, a veteran of multiple kinetic deployments, a wiry, intellectual Marine with an affinity for precisely allocated gear, whose opinion as the platoon's senior enlisted member makes all the difference, has some reservations about your rank. He knows how challenging it will be to lead a group of peers. But even he, too, sees your potential.

And because of them, one day the company commander calls you into his office and says

Well, Lance Corporal Kirk, are you ready to be a squad leader?
And you say
I think so, sir
And he says
I hope you can do better than 'I think so'
And you say
I'm ready, sir.

Rank. I'm a Lance Corporal. An E-3. The third enlisted rank. The third lowest in the entire military. There are literally twenty-eight higher ranks, from Corporal to Chief Warrant Officer to General. I'm so low-ranking the Marines who serve veal parmesan at the K-Bay chow hall outrank me. Yet going into Afghanistan this time, I'll be in charge of ten men, five Afghan soldiers, an interpreter and a dog. The head honcho for daily operations on a solitary hill in the middle of nowhere. Isolated from higher-level commands. Completely independent of day-to-day supervision. Outside of the orders I get from the platoon leader and platoon sergeant on the radio, there will be nobody to tell me no, or yes, or anything at all.

When I get on the Hill I'll be able to call in a Blackhawk helicopter (flight cost $30,000 per hour) to drop off food or to pick up a wounded man. I'll be in charge of making sure serialized equipment worth hundreds of thousands, even millions of dollars remains accounted for. I can call in F-16's to drop bombs on compounds. If I wanted to, I could shoot mortars into the Helmand River and say we were attacked by a horde of Taliban dressed up in Navy uniforms, riding camels. I might not get away with it, but you never know.

I'll need to tell my friends what to do. To lead other men of the same rank is something that can only be done by being the example. I'll need to sleep less and work more. I'll need to negotiate a series of complex relationships between groups of men with vastly different backgrounds and two things in common: the title of Marine (or Navy Corpsman), and their placement on a faraway hill in a dangerous section of a deadly country.

Sixteen souls on my Hill, all in my hands. The lives of every Afghan in every surrounding village. The security of roughly twenty square kilometers of Garmsir district. The shared success or failure of the Afghanistan counterinsurgency campaign.

As a Lance Corporal, I will be trusted to occupy the furthest, most isolated, most austere, most dangerous position in the entire battalion.

I am David Kilcullen's strategic (Lance) Corporal.

I am twenty-one years old. I make $1838.70 per month.

By the book, I have absolutely no business being a squad leader. That position should go to a Sergeant, an E-5. In the Army it's even higher, an E-6's job. Doctrinally, the E-5 squad leader should be in charge of two or three E-4 Corporal team leaders. Those Corporals should each be in charge of two or three Lance Corporals and Privates who can run guns and kick doors.

A squad leader should have attended Corporal's course, and Sergeant's course, and the infantry squad leader's course, or the assault leader's course, or the machine gun leader or mortar leader's course.

Any course at all. He should have proven himself for more than four years. He should be experienced and wise and a little older. He is the moral authority, the ultimate arbiter of a grunt squad. He must be above reproach, professionally, physically, mentally, and simultaneously brutal with firepower, a multi-tasking coordinator of systems, quick to make decisions, swift to kill the enemies of the United States with unmatched speed and precise violence.

But there just aren't enough of those guys. And men are imperfect. In the convoluted and counterintuitive Marine Corps system, the infantry is a beaten dog chained out in the yard. You don't let him in from the cold, or else he'll get used to it and lose his edge. The entire Corps is built around the infantry, and it needs its grunts interchangeable and angry.

Grunts don't get promoted; the cutting scores are too high, and the main factor is how long you've been in. If the cutting score for your job is 1600, and you've only got a 1430, it'll be a while until you make up the difference. With only a couple of meritorious promotions each quarter in the whole battalion, you're looking at a long time as a Lance Corporal.

Other jobs, like admin clerk or recon, have low cutting scores. You graduate basic reconnaissance course or admin school and immediately you're a Corporal. You don't know a goddamn thing, but you rate a greeting of the day from Lances who've been downrange and could run intellectual circles around you with their professional expertise.

So you're in the infantry, and you're a lowly Lance Corporal, but so is almost everyone else. Except the security forces guys, who got a big bonus for their time fast-roping and pretending to be Delta Force somewhere in Virginia. Very special operators.

So what sets you apart? Why would a Lance Corporal be a squad leader?

Combat time—that's the key. You don't get a boost on your cutting score for being deployed, but if you've been downrange and you're going again, it matters a lot. Of course you can lead in combat without ever having been in combat; the country would not win wars if it did not throw untested men into the fire. But at the squad-leader level, for a long-running war whose nature changes slowly, if at all, it helps.

Take a battalion that's been deployed to Iraq or Afghanistan every six months for six years and you've got a deep bench of combat-hardened Lance Corporals still eating up time on their four-year enlistment. Guys with months of direct experience doing exactly what is required in Helmand. Spread them around and you're bound to end up with lots of E-3 fireteam leaders and a few E-3 squad leaders.

When I tell my dad, a 25-year Army veteran, that I'm going to lead a squad as an E-3, he flips shit.

"You can't even grow a fucking beard!" he shouts through the phone.

I do my best to follow the examples of good leaders, and try to discard things I learned from the bad leaders. I follow the golden rule: never, ever make a man do anything you wouldn't do.

Other good maxims: Always set the example. Don't be a hypocrite. Leaders eat last. Keep it in-house. Don't throw your men under the bus. Allegiance to the Corps, loyalty to your men. Do the right thing, even when nobody is watching.

You don't need to run faster than everyone, or shoot better, or know more. You just need to run fast enough, know enough, and shoot well enough. On the bloody field of bad leadership lie the bodies of fast men. You need to set the example, then you need to show, and tell, others how to do what you just did.

Leadership is simple—except when it isn't. What happens when all the people you lead are the same rank as you? When you become a Lance Corporal in charge of Lance Corporals?

What if you don't know what the right thing is? What if you're just making things up as you go along, following your instincts, hoping it turns out okay?

What if you think you're doing the right thing, but it's the wrong thing? What if the leadership lessons you learned aren't the lessons you needed to learn?

Mission first, they always say.

What if the mission isn't worth dying for?

Patrol Base Durzay's command operations center is a muggy nook between two Hesco walls, underneath a plywood roof reinforced with sandbags. I am standing next to the bored-looking guy who woke me up, fifteen minutes early to my patrol briefing, in accordance with the Marine Corps Way.

I'm checking out the maps and charts tacked onto the side of the wall. Friendly positions marked with dry-erase markers. Radio watch and patrol schedules. Rules and regulations in capital block-letters. Furniture hand-made from excess Hesco, high-backed chairs and a plywood table with a toughbook laptop and long-distance radios that could reach all the way to the regimental combat team dozens of miles away in Leatherneck. Black Mr. Coffee machine, stacks of magazines, a few books and a Game Boy Advance. A white, military-issue air conditioning unit.

War comforts.

The guy who woke me up is drinking a green Monster Energy, and unless he got that drink in a care package (unlikely) it means only one thing.

"How often does the PX truck come out here?" I ask. A convoy to sell cigarettes, protein powder and junk food to isolated bases.

"Like once a month."

"Does it go out to KT-4?"

He shakes his head. "Can't make it on the roads."

This intrigues me. "How does KT-4 get resupplied?"

"They come here, pick stuff up, load it onto the John Deere Gator, and drive it out through the fields. Gotta unload everything at the bottom of the Hill and carry it up. Sometimes they hire a tractor. Or they get resupplied by helo."

I mull this over. A short, tired-looking Marine walks into the COC. He nods at me.

"I'm Corporal Kim," he says. "Where's your squad leader?"

"That's me."

"No shit? You're a Lance Corporal?"

"Yeah."

He raises his eyebrows a little, a small reaction to a small abnormality. He moves on.

"Okay, so we're here," he says, pointing to the map. "And we're going here. It's called KT-4. Sergeant Dorsey's squad is up there right now. When we get there, my guys are gonna wait at the bottom of the Hill while you guys walk up."

"Is it a tough climb?" I ask.

"Yeah, it's a pain in the ass. So excuse us for not joining you." He grins wryly. "Some of Sergeant Dorsey's guys are coming back with us to Durzay. A couple are staying behind to do handover with you."

"Okay."

"For the patrol itself, just fall into the middle. We'll take front and back. Single file. Try to get good dispersion. It should take us about forty-five minutes to get there."

"Roger, got it."

A few more details. Radio frequencies. What to do if we find an IED. Medevac procedures.

It's his show. I ask a few questions and we part ways. Walk back to find the guys moving around, packing up their stuff, Jason and Terrance taking charge of their teams. For some of my guys, this will be their first time outside the wire. Their first time on a combat patrol, and we're carrying heavy rucksacks, which will make it difficult to be vigilant. But it doesn't matter. I have faith in each of them, perhaps more faith than I have in myself. We will get there. We are grunts. This is what we signed up for.

Grab bottles of water, check and re-check magazines. Get on line and conduct pre-combat checks and inspections. These PCC's and PCI's are where the tactical leader makes his money. It's about insuring against disaster: enough water, enough ammo, working night vision. "Kill" cards in your shoulder pocket with your name, rank, social, blood type. Both shoulder pockets and your leg pockets in case any of those limbs get blown off. Check for anything that could keep you from fighting, like wearing a warming layer when you don't need one. Pack straps that are too loose. A dirty rifle. A radio that doesn't work. Someday, the new guys will inspect the veterans, learning their craft in the process. But today is not that day.

The guy who gave me the brief earlier walks up with his three men. "Ready?" he says.

"Ready."

"Okay, let's go. Condition one."

As we walk out of the patrol base, single file, we pull the bolts of our M4's and M16's to the rear, chambering a round. We are ready to fight.

Our anticipation rises. The sun begins to peak over the horizon behind us as we walk toward a looming landmark in the gray morning fog.

They say that Alexander the Great built it as a watchtower for his armies. A giant mound of earth, rising as if from nothing, overseeing the fields and the villages and the countryside. It is encircled by twenty-foot high walls, weathered and decaying but still standing, thousands of years after they were built.

Perhaps once a garrison for Macedonian warriors, now an inconvenience for emaciated goats and their child shepherds. Its denizens are camel spiders and short, thick, triangle-headed pit vipers who haunt its caves and tunnels. Its southern and western faces are sheer and cliff-like, while its northern slope joins the ground only a bit more gently. The sole path to the top is from the east.

Standing on the Hill, on a clear day, you can see other, similar hills stretching in a long line from north to south. Perhaps in antiquity these watchtowers would have been used to signal distress with fires lit in sequence, a system stretching for dozens of miles along the Helmand River. During the height of this most recent war, these hills were largely occupied as observation posts by the Americans. Lost to history were how many battles had been fought for this key piece of high ground. How many men had died defending it, taking it, re-taking it.

And how many had died in the surrounding farmland, the Hill the last thing they ever saw.

On hazy mornings, when the dew evaporates from corn and poppy and watermelons, the other hills and villages and roads are all but invisible, the Hill's walls the only landmark visible in the fog.

The middle of the twentieth century saw the construction of hundreds of canals, built by American optimists, which divided farms and created artificial treelines. Farming allotments the size of football fields were tilled by the villagers, who worked for local landowners.

When the fields flooded, the dirt would turn to mud, the mud to muck, and the men would come forth from their single-story walled compounds. They would stroll unhurriedly over their stick bridges, to shovel and plow all day by hand. They would work until the fields were crisscrossed with knee-high furrows, ready for seeding. Men and boys would roll up the legs of their *dishdashas*, tilt their sparkling caps to a jaunty angle and work the land. They survived on the proceeds of their poppy harvest, one of very few ways to make a living in Garmsir.

The men of the villages around the Hill would smoke cigarettes and hashish in the early morning, eat *naan* mid-day and lounge under metal awnings in the evening. Women in blue *burqas* would travel between compounds, fully covered, in groups of three or more. Older women had the privilege to dress in black, their faces uncovered, and travel alone. Perhaps their husbands had fallen victim to one of the country's endless wars.

The Hill bore witness to countless sunrises and sunsets. It heard roosters herald the morning light, saw villages come to life, villages with names like Hajji Zulmai Kalay. It saw young girls in bright colors fetch water with yellow buckets from the foliage-covered canals. It watched the moon wane and wax in a clear night sky. It heard the call to prayer from bamboo-and-metal speakers sung by the *mullahs* of a half-dozen mosques, a competition of pious crooners.

It saw the things that the Pashtun people of Helmand kept hidden: the *chai* boys, enslaved and raped by older men; night letters left by the

Taliban; beatings by Afghan police; heroin-addicted migrant workers, eyes glassed over, leaning against a tree. The torture rack an affluent man had rigged up to punish his wife when she displeased him.

The Hill watched men grow from naked filthy children to orange-nailed teenagers to bearded adults. It kept an eye on the *Hilmand* and *Ghazni* motorcycles rolling by on dusty roads. It scrutinized the tired old village leaders, men who had made the *Hajj*, who drank *chai* with red and green candies in them when the Soviets came. It watched the Macedonians and the British and the Russians fight and die and retreat. It regarded the Americans dispassionately when we showed up. And when we left, the Hill saw that, too.

Our patrol reaches a bend in the road. When we turn the corner, we catch a close-up view of Patrol Base KT-4 and its walls. We're only a few hundred meters away now and we can easily see the camouflage netting and sandbags on top. I'm struck by how much taller it is than anything else in the surrounding countryside, how there's an Afghan flag on top, but no American flag.

We pass through a gap in the wall and approach from the east. We walk through a double strand of concertina wire which guards the base of the Hill from stray intruders. There is a well dug just outside the entrance. I take a knee and count the men as they come in.

The Corporal who took us out here stays behind, waiting for the men up top to join him and head back to Durzay. He shakes my hand and wishes me luck.

I count the last man and trudge behind my squad as we begin climbing. It is exhausting work. The incline is steep, so steep that in some places we scramble, placing our palms on the ground, stepping on our tip-toes, trying not to stand lest our heavy rucksacks tilt us backward. It occurs to me that we'll be making this climb every day, at the end of every patrol.

We huff and puff until we reach a sandbag wall just over the crest of the hill, where we're greeted by a lanky, mustachioed Sergeant with out-of-regs hair and Oakley M-Frames, whose men pass us on their way down the Hill.

We drop our packs.

"You the squad leader?" says the Sergeant.

"I am." I immediately feel inadequate.

"I'm Sergeant Dorsey. This is Polo, and Fernandez is up on post one. They're my team leaders."

I introduce Jason and Terrance. We shake hands.

"How long are you staying?" I ask the Sergeant.

"You're taking us back day after tomorrow. We have until then to get you spun up."

"Sounds good."

"Let's do the tour, then."

The men scout out cots to sit on and water to drink while Jason and Terrance and I walk the perimeter with Sergeant Dorsey. As we move around the Hill I notice how deeply he and Polo contrast with us. We're wearing pristine new combat uniforms; their FROG tops are near-black from sweat and grime. Our hair is freshly shorn; theirs is oily and long beyond regulations. They wear bandanas and baseball caps. They are serious and resigned, like Sisyphus might have been. The grime on their faces, their indifference to it, reminds me of documentaries I've seen where flies buzz and land on children in distant countries, who pay the bugs no mind. It is as if the entire war had been thrown at and stuck to them, and their defense was to ignore it.

Is it that bad up here?

The hilltop is dug out in places and flat in others. On the other side of the sandbag wall is a shallow bowl and a sleeping area covered by double-strand camouflage netting and tan sunshades. We walk on hard-packed dirt, tan as everything, with green, military issue, collapsible cots scattered around. A square plywood table with MRE boxes for legs. Gear, Hesco baskets, water bottles.

"This is where most guys sleep. The team leaders and I sleep down there." He indicates two partially dug-out sandbag bunkers, their roofs incomplete.

"This is where the terp sleeps," he says, pointing to another bunker, this one with a roof. It is very dark inside.

We follow him up to the highest point of the Hill, about fifty feet from the berthing area. We roll into a wide, dug-out sandbag position, with sheer cliffs, two machine guns and a radio.

"This is where we stand post," he says. "Comms. Mark nineteen, sighted in on Hajji Zulmai. Pig, sighted in on the road. TOW launcher. We use the sight for looking around."

The grenade launcher and the machine gun both looked dirty and unused.

"Don't worry," he says, noticing that I'm looking at it, "We keep the insides lubed. The outsides never stay clean with all the sandstorms up here."

I examine the TOW launcher. This is the first time I've ever seen the missile system on a tripod. The whole contraption is as tall as I am. There's a high-tech thermal sight that can zoom in on targets miles away, day or night. Even with no missiles, the optics give a strong advantage here on the high ground.

He shows me the gear that comes with the base. Thermals, binoculars, radio batteries. Maps, flares, pen flares, extra grenades, extra ammo. A radio that can reach Durzay and the company outpost, Rankel, far to the north.

He says they keep most of the important stuff in this post, under constant watch, in case the Afghan National Army soldiers decide to steal it. On the east side of the Hill he points to a patchwork of blankets and tarps where the ANA sleep. "They steal all sorts of shit. Food, water, especially. But other stuff too. Random shit. Leave your iPod lying around and it'll be gone, along with your belt, or your flashlight, or whatever."

"How many ANA are there?"

"Five right now. Should be six. One guy went on leave and never came back."

He shows us where they store food, on the south side of the Hill behind our hooches, under a triple layer of camouflage netting. Meals, ready-to-eat; a few Halal meal boxes, for the Afghans; bulky First Strike Rations, meant to last three days. Stacks of water bottles, the only way we can drink safely.

"Resupply is by helo every two to three weeks. You have to request it through the company. They come out a few days later." He gives me the resupply frequency, and the frequency they use for medevacs, and the frequencies for the company and the platoon. I write it all down in a tan spiral rite-in-the-rain notebook.

"Piss tubes," he points. Engineer stakes, taped together and funneling urine off the south face of the Hill. When you go, you go in full view of the world. Exposed. The entire Hill is like that.

He shows me the Afghan Army post, little more than a pile of sandbags around a camp chair. He tells me they almost never occupy it, so his men have to stand up two posts at night.

We walk back toward the hooches. He kicks a broken generator. "They're supposed to come out and fix this." He shows me a set of tiny solar panels. "You can use this to charge your iPod, if you have one."

He shows us the burn pit, little more than a deepish hole on the north side of the Hill, its depths nursing a smoldering fire. We see the shitter, which is just Hesco barrier over plywood with a hole in the middle. Next to it, a box of wag bags, portable plastic containers you shit in and seal up, sit just outside for easy access.

Sergeant Dorsey puts his hands on his hips.

"Well. That's about it," he says. "It's your Hill now. Welcome to KT-4."

In two days I learn more about being a squad leader than I did in the last two years. Sergeant Dorsey is patient and answers all of my questions without irritation. Many things are unique to the base, to the area of operations, to the war. Some things are unique to his unit. Others are gaps in my knowledge, the result of being selected for the position as a motivated Lance Corporal who never attended Infantry Squad Leader's Course.

He shows me how to send up patrol intentions. To detail when, where and how we're going to walk around. How much water and food to order from the company. How to send up fuel requests if someone ever gets the generator working. He shows me the post schedule he uses. How to incorporate the Afghan soldiers into the patrol and meet the eight-man minimum. Things to look out for in the fields, in the villages. How to tell if the ANA have been using hashish before a patrol. What the Pashtuns in the surrounding villages can and can't carry around with them.

I tell him I've never done a real patrol order, so he helps me translate the doctrine that I've copied into a notebook into something I can brief to officers if I ever need to.

He tells me about the Hill. His men had lived there only a few months, enduring the cold winter out of their rucksacks. His company had pushed all the way down to the Durzay bazaar, further south than any line infantry unit in Afghanistan. Noting the importance of the terrain, his platoon registered the Hill as "Known Target Four," or KT-4, for on-call mortar fire. After being shot at from it a few times, they decided to take the high ground.

As they climbed up with sandbags, entrenching tools and shovels, the Hill turned from Known Target Four to Patrol Base KT-4. They spent a week digging out fighting holes before leaving on their first patrol.

Taking the Hill changed the strategic calculus for the Taliban in the area. Marine snipers and designated marksmen picked off targets at ease. The Taliban, who had previously fought running gunfights with the Marines, were now far outmatched. So they switched up their tactics. They observed the Marines as they walked. Instead of engaging in direct firefights, they would watch Sergeant Dorsey's platoon and emplace bombs wherever they walked. These IED's were cheap and easy to make, so the enemy put in scores of small ones that would take a leg or two. After a while, Sergeant Dorsey's men learned to predict and find these bombs using simple tools and techniques honed by instinct. They looked at their own movements and patterns the way their enemy would, and in doing so they figured out how to avoid setting patterns, how to find IED's before the IED's found them.

By the time we show up, the bombs come slower. During our two days with Sergeant Dorsey we find none.

We are taught how to patrol the way they patrol. To walk single file. To scrape—not like we were taught during the train-up, but better, with a shorter stick. To use the metal detector quicker and more efficiently than we've trained. To march through the muck and stay off the easy routes.

We need eight men per patrol, and we're to do two patrols each day, so Jason and Terrance's fireteams will be on separate outings unless we need more men. We can go out with or without a dog: Jason, Ruben, Cody, Nate and Ivan; Terrance, Tony, Mario and Doc. Two or three Afghans per patrol. Cody and Tony are the designated sweepers. Mario and Nate, carriers of the Thor. Everyone is scheduled for post, except Doc and me; we'll jump on as needed.

I'm eager to get familiar with our area of operations, so I ask Sergeant Dorsey to take me to each of the villages. We do a couple of long patrols, walking from one identical set of compounds to another. I meet the village elders, old Pashtuns who gave their namesake to a cluster of compounds they call home. Influential men, some of whom are called *Hajji*, although that doesn't necessarily mean they've been to Mecca. It's used more as a sign of respect. A local would never know if someone actually went to Mecca or not.

Sergeant Dorsey takes us to the Durzay bazaar, a conglomeration of twelve or fifteen shops with blue corrugated-iron doors, selling everything from drugs to radio parts to motorcycles to sodas and cigarettes. Five dollars for a carton is the going price, so we grab some: Pine Lights and 88 Milds and Seven Stars. The perfect garnish for any patrol. I keep a pack of Pines in my shoulder pocket so they don't get wet when I jump in a canal. Different year, different district, same old war.

At the Hill, while Sergeant Dorsey's men relax, my men work on position improvement. We learn what it takes to keep a patrol base going.

I have in-country experience with this, the result of endless boot working parties, and so do my team leaders, but this is the first time we've been on our own, so it takes some time to get it right. Terrance and Jason mentor the boots in how to report their post. To talk on the radio when summoned by Durzay. To load and unload the machine guns. To replace the batteries as needed. To keep track of the shifts, and the battery counts, and things that go missing.

Polo, in an act of benevolence, gives Cody a baseball cap that says *Kentucky* on the front. Totally out of regs, and the Marine Corps Way looks unkindly on uniform irregularities. Even so, I tell Cody he can wear it around the base, but only when the squad's here alone. He shoots me a sly grin and plops it backward on his head. Polo offers to send us booze when he gets back to the world. I halfheartedly decline, but when I turn away I notice Jason and Ruben talking to him in whispers, smiling from ear to ear.

I make Tony and Russell responsible for keeping the machine guns properly lubed and cleaned. They yank back bolts and brush dust from ammunition and lube the pig's insides until it slides like a luge on an icy run. They are in their element and happy.

Doc stashes his medical supplies in a divot and sets about constructing a makeshift medical aid station. He commandeers a cot, lines it with a poncho liner, and sets up an expedient IV-bag holder above it. In a slew of cardboard boxes he finds bandages, tourniquets, chest seals, ace wraps and eight-hundred-milligram ibuprofen tablets. He asks me to request certain items for the squad aid station, things like IV bags, seasickness medications, anti-diarrheals, foot powder. I make a note to send these requests to Durzay.

On the second day Polo holds a hip-pocket class by the green PRC-117 radio and teaches us to roll crypto: to change the encryption on the radio frequency in order to keep the enemy from listening in. It is a process I, as a worldy and strategic Lance Corporal, find unnecessary. In what world could the Taliban possibly decrypt our radios once, let alone every week?

Nevertheless, Polo tells us, at three in the morning every Saturday a call will come over the radio to switch it out. We'll need to patrol to Durzay once every couple of weeks to get the new sets of encryption. I put Ivan in charge of making sure this happens, since he's the only person who pays enough attention to figure it out.

"Jack. Jack, you up?"

A voice echoes from the darkness.

"Yes, Sergeant. Yes, I am up. Yes."

Scuffling feet. The sound of sandals being pulled on. A handsome, weather-worn Afghan face appears in the entrance of the dark hooch I passed earlier.

"Jack, the new guys are here. I want to introduce them to Sergeant Mike and the ANA."

Jack shakes my hand.

"Hello, Sergeant. Very nice to meet you." He puts his hand over his heart, in the way Afghans do to symbolize honesty. I take him to be the interpreter. He wears a strange sort of off-brand combat blouse and sandals, and his face is very angular, his brow thick. He shuffles out, squinting against the sun, and we walk toward the Afghan Army tent. On the way, I ask Sergeant Dorsey why Jack called me by a different rank.

"If I were you," Sergeant Dorsey says, "I would just let everyone call you Sergeant. To Afghans, it doesn't make sense for a low-ranking guy to be in charge. It doesn't really make sense to me either, honestly. But the only rank they know is Sergeant. So just be a Sergeant." I nod, absorbing the sage wisdom. I smile inwardly at my secret promotion.

The Afghan area smells of fresh-cooked rice and rich spices and body odor and feet and marijuana. Soldiers lounge on a wide rug surrounded by blankets. The scene is little different from what I remember of the average Pashtun's house, except here there are AK-47's and rocket-propelled grenades and a PKM machine gun, Soviet weapons fighting an American-led war. The Afghans wear a blend of old-school tri-color camouflage and new, green-and-black-and-brown digital patterns made specifically for the Afghan Army. They complete the look with sandals and soccer shirts and tank tops. A large bowl of steaming rice and *naan* lies in the middle of the group, having been cooked somewhere outside the tent.

A scrawny, mustachioed Afghan pops to his feet and greets us with gusto.

"Sergeant! Good morning! How are you!" His words are choppy, heavily accented.

"What's up Sergeant Mike? I'm good. How are you?" says Sergeant Dorsey. Hands over hearts.

Sergeant Mike speaks to a portly soldier, who stands up from his pillow nest and retrieves for us a kettle full of tea. I dump an absurd amount of sugar into my cup. Fantastic.

Jack interprets for us as we speak.

"Mike, this is the new guy we talked about. The one taking over the Hill from me. His name is Sergeant Kirk."

As Jack and Mike speak, I search for words I can understand. The Marine Corps had seen fit to send me to Pashto class instead of Mountain Warfare School with the rest of the battalion. I'd spent three grueling weeks not hiking up and down mountains, instead learning the basics of a language spoken only in Afghanistan and Pakistan. By three o'clock every day I was forced to stop training and soak up the sun on Pyramid Rock beach. I embraced this burden with resigned determination.

After several minutes of paying close attention, trying to decipher fast sentences, I realize they're speaking Dari, the other language of Afghanistan. I don't understand anything.

Sergeant Mike and the cook-soldier have strong Asian features. They're of the Hazara ethnic group, which hails from Northern Afghanistan and has long been friendly to the United States. Jack, I later find out, is from a place called Khost, and barely even speaks Pashto. Of the others, one is Pashtun and the rest are of various ethnicities, calling Kabul their home.

I have a long conversation with Sergeant Mike. His name is not really Mike, of course, the same way Jack is not really Jack. They do this because as Americans, we are often both too stupid and too lazy to learn the names of the men we may fight and die alongside. In time I come to know Jack very well. I never learn Sergeant Mike's real name.

Sergeant Mike is a quirky and animated caricature of a soldier, in dire need of protein, obviously stir-crazy. He makes sure we know he is Afghan Army, and proud of his record of working with the Americans. He tells us about the differences between Afghan Police and the Afghan National Army. There are no police around here, he says. He says they are not to be trusted. He tells me the ANA is comprised of recruits from all over Afghanistan, who are normally stationed outside their ethnic home areas. This makes them better soldiers. You can be assured of their loyalty, he informs me.

I ask him how long he's been in the Army.

"Seven years," he says. He shows me little pea-sized shrapnel wounds all across his legs. For him and the other men, the Hill and these blankets and pillows and sandstorms comprise the experience of being in the military. Garmsir is not a deployment for them. This fighting is not irregular. It is their normal occupation. Home leave is the abnormality. They are stuck here until reassigned, when they will go to another part of the country to continue fighting the war.

I have a time limit on this combat tour. They do not. Their war does not end unless they die, retire, or the Taliban stop fighting. Only one of these outcomes seems likely.

My job is to ensure the security of six villages. Four of these exhibit positive atmospherics. Friendly, by Sergeant Dorsey's account. One he rates as negative, while one displays a kind of indifference that he views as neutrality. The village that doesn't like Americans, Hajji Zulmai Kalay, happens to be the closest.

I am tasked to routinely talk to the elders and find out what they want from us. To meet and collect useful human intelligence. To show presence. To win hearts and minds, whatever that means. To conduct two patrols a day, and to come up with a mission for both.

I am armed with the authority of one of the lowest ranks in the military. The men I am charged with leading are my peers. I represent the United States Marine Corps. I am the face of America.

I am barely old enough to drink a beer.

The day I drop him off at Durzay, Sergeant Dorsey takes a pair of metal Sergeant's chevrons out of his shoulder pocket and hands them to me.

"Wear these when you're around the Afghans. All of them, the locals, the terp, the soldiers. They'll think you're important."

I take the chevrons and thank him. He points back at the Hill.

"You're up there for a reason," he says slowly. "Don't forget that."

"I won't," I tell him.

And then he's gone, and the Hill is mine, and though I am surrounded by my men I suddenly feel very much alone.

10

Bomb Squad

How do you run a patrol base? What does it need?

First, Marines. A patrol base is just so much mud without men.

So what do men need? Men *think* they need things they don't really need. Internet. Hot water. Hot food. Blankets. Dry clothes.

What they really need is merely the bottom rung of Maslow's hierarchy: air, water, food, shelter. But even that is too much.

All a grunt needs is food to keep him moving and water to keep from passing out and weapons to fight and kill the enemy. Chow, water, guns. Everything else is a luxury.

So you capture this, and everything else, in a daily report on logistics statistics. Logstats. A condensed list of needs. A short blurb of wants. I decide to track this for myself, and delegate when I'm comfortable. So I learn quickly.

What do nine Marines, a Corpsman, a dog and an interpreter use every day? What do they need? First—what do they have?

United Group Rations-Express, six-seven cases. Water, six-two-zero cases. Meals, Ready-to-Eat, one-six boxes. First Strike Rations, one-zero-eight boxes. Toilet paper, seven packages. Wag Bags, five-three. Fuel-zero. Oil-zero. Radio batteries—One-five two batteries, one-zero. One-five-three batteries, one-one. Twenty-five-ninety batteries, six. Fifty-five-ninety batteries, thirteen. C-Batteries, six-four. Three-Volt batteries, two-one. Double-A batteries, two-five. Triple-A batteries, two-five.

Requests: request one generator mechanic. Request fuel. Request oil. Request better solar panels. Request a shovel and a pickaxe. Request machine gun lubricant and brushes. Request sandbags.

You don't need to request bullets if you don't shoot bullets. Keep yours clean. Keep the stores clean. Preventative maintenance.

What else does a grunt need to fight? He needs water, yes, and food, yes, although he needs less than the average man once he becomes conditioned to it, once he patrols and lives in the dirt and sheds his excess pounds. But he needs bullets and he needs uniforms and he needs his equipment and he needs his machine guns lubricated and he needs his feet to be free of blisters and he needs the men around him to be able to carry him if he falls. He needs to make sure his gear does not fall apart and that he has a uniform to wear. These are the things that a Marine needs to fight in any war.

To fight in this war, Afghanistan, this country-wide minefield, this booby-trapped hellhole, this bomb-laden landscape, is different than fighting in France, or Vietnam, or Liberia. And to fight here, in Garmsir, is different than to fight in Korengal or Ghozni or Kabul. To fight here, Marines need batteries for their metal detectors and their Thor packs. They need duplicates for the times they fall and break metal detectors. They need night-vision devices that work and they need litters to carry wounded men and they need tourniquets to stop arterial bloodspurts. They need ultra-high-frequency antennae to communicate with helicopters as they fly into landing zones and jets as they drop five-hundred-pound bombs on mud huts. They need two methods of marking a landing zone for night and two for daytime. Purple smoke grenades and orange air panels and red lasers and infrared strobe-lights and infrared buzzsaws, which are just infrared chemlights attached to 550 cord and swung in a circle. And they need killcards with blood types and identification numbers and they need maps to know where they're going and global positioning systems on their wrists to know where they've been.

If you're out in the countryside, away from the big bases, away from the medium-sized bases and even most of the small bases, if you're out there—way out there—you need stuff you can only get at an Afghan bazaar. Cold Fanta and charcoal-filtered Seven Stars, weak Pine Lights and true-to-their-name 88 Mild's. Five dollars a carton. Even that's too much.

What do we need in war?

Cigarettes. If nothing else, cigarettes.

You don't know how much you crave cold water until you don't have any.

No matter how many nets you throw over it, the sun will always heat your water until it feels like it came out of a hot kettle. There are, however, ways around this. With some preparation you can get your water cool in the morning. Cold, even, if the night cooperates. And it can stay that way the whole day, if you're careful.

First, dig a hole in the ground. A narrow hole, like a cylinder. As deep as your extended arm. Line it with a frame of Hesco with the fabric still attached. Put your water bottles in there and cover the hole with more Hesco fabric. Walk down to the bottom of the Hill, fill up some buckets from the well, and pour the well water over the blankets. Fill it up in the evening, pour it over, and keep pouring over the hole all day. If you put in the effort, you'll have cool, crisp water ready for your morning patrol. If you don't, you'll have to drink water hot enough to burn your mouth. But you'll still be hydrated. Always be hydrated.

And change your socks often. The Marine Corps Way does not permit white socks in uniform. Green, brown, black or tan only. But in Garmsir, in the furthest reaches of the empire—in the grunts—it is sometimes permitted. Problem is, you can't wash your socks. Not effectively. Two buckets, one for detergent and one to rinse, is not enough to keep your socks from getting uncomfortably stiff and itchy.

So you do what you do in a modern war. You grab a satellite phone. You call your dad, or your mom, your Uncle Joe in Montana, both sets of grandparents, your cousins, and you ask them for white socks. Normal white cotton crew socks. The socks will arrive quickly. Regular delivery of care packages is an integral part of the modern war experience. It takes two or three weeks for a package to get into country. Another week to get to you. Sometimes things get lost, but even all the way out here on the Hill, we can still walk to Durzay and get our mail reliably.

I start asking my family to send white socks before the deployment begins, so two weeks into it I've got a stash of socks that'll last me the whole deployment. I distribute these to the men. I make them change their socks whenever theirs become soiled. We have that luxury now, in this modern war. If you jump in canal and your boots get wet enough times, those socks are done for. But if you walk around for a couple of hours and don't get too sweaty, you can probably re-use them. It's a long slog of a deployment. You'll need your feet.

We hit the ground sprinting. Two patrols a day, minimum. Our operational tempo is fierce. Combat does away with your sense of invincibility. I am thoroughly vincible. I am tired. Even without firefights, even in the beginning, the war exhausts. The Lieutenant wants us to patrol at different times each day, so sometimes I'll take the guys out at six in the morning and six at night. Other times we'll go at noon and midnight. If I'm feeling really masochistic, I'll do a late afternoon patrol, say, six o'clock, and follow it up by heading out at two in the morning.

At night, you're picking your way through the same terrain you do during the day, but you're walking slower, and you're tripping over everything, and you're making noise despite your best efforts. Everything you carry jingles and smacks together no matter how you tie it down. Huge, snarling, invisible dogs bark at the last guy in the ranger file, who tries to walk backwards so they won't sneak up on him. He trips a lot, but eventually he gets it right. He learns how to lift his legs so his toes clear obstacles as he walks backward, because if he doesn't, that dog gets way too goddamn close. And then you have to choose. Do you shoot the dog, and incur the wrath of the Bravo, and the First Sergeant, and maybe even the Sergeant Major? Or do you throw a rock, and hope it doesn't bite you?

The Marine Corps Way says you throw a rock. Because in a head-quarters somewhere, someone decided that these dogs Mean Something to the Pashtuns of Helmand province. That killing one is a Big Deal. We're not so sure. But we don't shoot the dogs, because that's The Guidance. To violate The Guidance is also a Big Deal.

At night you can't see any indicators that might mark an IED. Not that you could during the day, but at night, your lack of awareness is especially frightening. Every step terrifies you with its uncertainty. The Thor helps you to not get blown up by radio-controlled IED's, clicking when it blocks a signal, but even so it gives no comfort because you never know what it is actually blocking. You sweep and the metal detector beeps and your two-man comes up with the sickle, and he can't really see what he's scraping up in the ground. He's wearing a night-vision monocle, a PVS-14, which is terrible at just about everything, but it's especially bad at discerning details. I spend long nights with a PVS-14 over my eye, wondering if an object fifty yards away is a person or a goat, only to find out that it's a tree. It's always a tree.

So you stay off the paths, and you sit more than a daytime patrol. You move a hundred meters, and you sit down again, and you call up your position. And you tell the Lieutenant you're doing an "ambush," and it's true: you are in position, hoping some armed insurgent types will come along so you can politely blow their fucking heads off. But what you're really doing is smoking cigarettes in a cupped hand, talking about girls and music and home.

On a cool, overcast morning a sound like an oversized firecracker *snaps* through the air as I'm leading a patrol back to the Hill. We stop as one. Some of us take a knee. Some of us stand stock-still.

"Everyone okay?" I shout to the column. The guys roger up. The Afghans flash me a thumbs-up.

"Nobody move," I say. "Who stepped on it?"

I'm certain one of us has triggered a pressure plate, and that what exploded was the blasting cap, and that this blasting cap failed to det-onate the main charge of an IED. Now we're standing on at least one bomb, and I'm worried about a second or third charge we haven't triggered yet.

"Who stepped on it? What was the noise?" Nobody answers. Everyone's frozen in place, ice-sculptures, only their eyes moving.

"Did anyone step on anything? What happened?" I'm quickly becoming confused. What was that sound, if not a blasting cap?

Slowly, sheepishly, one of my guys raises his hand. He tells me he unintentionally shot his rifle into the dirt. We all breathe a collective sigh of relief as we shake it off and continue the hump. I tell him we'll table this and talk about it back at the Hill.

We finish the long march to the base, strip our armor off and grab water. I pull the guy aside. We sit face to face on opposite sandbag berms and have a conversation. Negligent discharges are one of the cardinal sins of the Marine Corps. In the rear, a man who shoots his rifle without intending to, or in the wrong place, or at the wrong time, gets official paperwork at a minimum. He might get busted down a rank. If he's junior enough, he'll probably receive an informal, physical "counseling" from his seniors.

But this is not the rear. This is not Hawaii. This is not even Earth; this is the planet Mars. This is an alternate reality, where we're fighting a war and there are more important things to worry about.

So I talk to the guy. I reiterate rifle safety. I acknowledge that we're walking around with loaded guns for hours at a time. That we're sliding down embankments, leaping gaps in creeks, tripping over furrows and plows and going in and out of the prone. I tell him that to keep things like this from happening I always keep my right thumb pressing up on the safety, no matter what, and how my index finger never goes near the trigger unless it's time to kill. I let him know that by having the rifle pointed in a safe direction, he at least prevented one of us from catching a bullet, and even though he screwed up on one thing, he did another thing right. He knows all of this, of course. And he knows he screwed up. Sometimes you screw up, but screwing up doesn't mean you're a screw-up. It just means you're human.

I handle this incident, and others like it, by following a principle re-iterated by Drill Instructors, NCO's and even senior Lance Corporals alike: keep it in-house. Handle things at the lowest possible level. Don't throw guys under the bus. Don't be a buddy fucker. Punish by training. Counsel, train and re-train. Your squad's baggage is your baggage. No need to run to mother unless it's absolutely necessary, unless you've tried and tried and can't fix it, or someone's going to get hurt or die. Fireteam, squad, platoon first. Remember loyalty goes both ways. For grunts, this rule may as well be written in blood.

Blind loyalty to your fellow Marines has its downsides. Its toxic side-effect is that junior Marines never tell their commander about hazing even when they're asked. Keeping things in-house is why "request mast," every Marine's right to talk to his Commanding Officer about anything, becomes a punchline to a sad joke, an act guaranteed to ostracize. In some respects, this loyalty is a hindrance to the Corps. But for small units, it is more critical for lethality than even a clean weapon system or rations. Trust is everything in the grunts. A squad can fight without food. It can't fight without trust.

We're at war. If we strike an IED, I need this man to listen to my instructions without question. To trust my every directive. Will he do that, knowing I tanked his career instead of cutting him slack? I need him behind a gun on the Hill if we're attacked. The squad needs his heart, and he deserves my loyalty until proven otherwise. The choice is clear. What happens on the Hill stays on the Hill.

Early on, I realize I can't sleep at all during the day, only at night, no matter how tired I am from the previous evening's patrol. I begin to count every hour of darkness. When the hours and minutes pass, I subtract these from the total night-time hours and end up with the difference. This difference is the maximum potential sleep I can get in a twenty-four hour period. I begin an obsessive, running tally that I keep for the rest of our time on the Hill. I keep a mental running esti-mate for the squad as well. I track whose team had which patrol, who stood post during the coolest hours of the very early morning, sacrificing the best sleep of the day. As the mornings and evenings get longer and the nights shorter and the temperatures grow hotter we lose more and more sleep.

I begin to let Jason take out patrols every once in a while so I can rest. Terrance follows. Letting them take responsibility is difficult; I was never taught how to delegate, only how to lead by example. I feel it is my duty, since I don't stand post, to go along every time we leave the wire. But there are many excursions, and few hours to rest. So I begin to let Jason and Terrance take patrols, and I sleep some, but not enough. You never get enough sleep when you're at war. We adapt to a schedule of chronic involuntary insomnia.

One day we're walking around, visiting villages, jumping canals. The furthest friendly village is Hajji Ismail Kalay. We head out there for what officers call a "key leader engagement." My job is to bullshit with an old guy for twenty minutes and tell him we're working on projects or providing security or conducting an operation nearby. In return I receive assurances he'll cooperate with us. He gives me gifts of chai, bread and candy. I pass out hand-crank radios.

We roll up into town from the south. Men smoking, talking. Children playing. Old women filling yellow buckets with brackish water.

Terrance's team takes up positions watching the roads. Entrances and exits. A relaxed kind of awareness. We're not there to cordon and search people. We're there to say hello.

Jack and I knock on the door of the elder, the town's namesake, Hajji Ismail. He goes by just the one name. Jack tells me that "kalay" means village in Pashto, so the "Village of Hajji Ismail Kalay" is redundant. We are Marines, so we call it the wrong name anyway. You can only ask so much of us.

Hajji Ismail isn't home. There's no *chai* for us today. I spend my time in the village walking around with Sergeant Mike's boys, Wali and Abdullah. We shake hands with smiling men. I give pens to children. A lot of hand-to-heart action. I round up the guys and we start to leave the village, heading eastward. We're in a jolly mood. It's nice to feel welcomed and safe in a village.

Tony leads us out, his metal detector up in the air as we cross a bridge out of town.

Suddenly he stops. He backs up, quickly, avoiding something only he can see. Terrance, one step behind him, asks him what it is. I can't hear, so I start to move closer. Terrance's already walking up, passing Tony, tentatively crossing the bridge, and then he's backing up, sprinting, yelling

"It's an IED! It's a fucking IED! Run, motherfucker!"

We run backwards, a mildly disorganized bundle, limbs and guns and jingling dump-pouches. When we're a safe distance away I right our posture. I have my guys take up positions of security, ensuring nobody else has access to the bridge from this side.

"What did you see?" I ask them.

"Like a tube. Some sort of cylinder. Pointed right at us," says Terrance, breathlessly, seriously.

"You sure it was an IED?"

"Hell fucking yeah I'm sure, dude. It was right *there*, that far away," he says, pointing to where my knee touches the ground. That's close.

"Okay," I say. "What kind was it?"

"I don't know. I couldn't tell."

"Probably wasn't a pressure plate," I think aloud. "Maybe an RC?"

Terrance points to Nate and the Thor. "I don't know, man."

The Thor is humming. I assume that means it's working, which means a radio-controlled bomb wouldn't be able to detonate within its radius.

I see an Afghan carrying a bundle of poppy stalks begin to walk across the bridge from the other side. I try to wave him off, but it's too late. He keeps moving toward us, confused. Jack yells at him that it isn't safe. He crosses anyway. We stop him. Through Jack, I ask him if he saw a bomb on the other side of the bridge.

"*Nishta,*" he says. Nothing.

I make a decision.

"We have to get closer and confirm this is what we think it is. These guys are just walking across like it's nothing." Terrance begins to protest. I put up a hand. "I believe you. I one-hundred percent believe it's an IED. But they told us EOD needs two methods of confirmation, and you only saw it for a split second. They might not even come out here if we can't tell them for sure."

Even Terrance has to admit this is true. If we call it up, it's likely they'll just ask us to do what we're doing now. "Let's just go around the other side, look at it through our RCO's, and see what kind it is. Then we'll call the EOD guys out here. We need to get security on both sides of the bridge, anyway. Prevent people from walking up to it and getting blown the fuck up, like this moron." I motion to the Afghan who crossed. He smiles, teeth blackened by Persian chewing tobacco.

Terrance sees my point. We split up. I take Nate and Tony, leaving Terrance with Doc and the Afghans, and walk a couple of hundred yards down the canal, jumping down into waist-high water and clambering up the other side, rifles first. We sweep a wide arc, cautious for any secondary bombs. I spot the corner of the bridge where Terrance saw the cylinder, but even with my rifle scope I can't get a good view. It's obscured by nearby corn, chest-high. I decide I've got to get closer, so I lead Nate and Tony to the edge of the field and take the metal detector and the Thor myself. I tell them to wait for me at the edge of the field. I feel for the two playing cards I placed in my left shoulder pocket before the deployment. Two of spades and a three of clubs. I touch them without knowing exactly why. I start moving forward.

In the corn field, sweeping with a metal detector is difficult and pointless. I inch forward, my heart pulsating in my chest, my hands and underarms wet with perspiration. I've never heard my heartbeat in my ears before. Beads of sweat slide along my lips and I taste salt.

I crest the edge of the corn field, some twenty yards from the bridge. I can see something where Terrance described it but I can't tell what it is. I put the metal detector down and bring up my rifle. I look through the scope and

holy fucking shit

and I about face and I'm sprinting as fast as my legs will take me, holding the Thor and the metal detector, gear sliding back and forth, until I'm all the way back with Nate and Tony. They ask me what I saw.

"You guys were right. It's a fucking IED," I say.

I call up the nine-line.

"Bitch, I told you!" Terrance says on the radio when I tell him.

It turns out to be a kite-string IED, the type of bomb you have to pull to detonate, where you have to see your target or have someone relaying directions to you. It was only partially covered, as if we'd stumbled on it right when they were setting it up. Had it exploded, Tony and Terrance would have been wounded seriously by shrapnel, maybe killed. When I looked through the scope, I saw a metal cylinder propped up on wooden sticks, pointing upwards toward the bridge. Two green kite-strings were attached to it. They blended in perfectly with the heavy vegetation on either side of the canal. Easy to miss. Later, when the EOD techs come, we follow the kite-strings two or three hundred meters down the canals. The emplacers, the spotters, whoever was responsible for our near-death experience, are long gone. Chasing ghosts.

The squad that brings the EOD techs out is full of our friends from Second Platoon. It is the first time I've seen them in weeks, and at first I am happy for their company. We greet each other with handshakes and hugs. But after a few minutes pass there is a conspicuous silence. An underlying tension I've never felt with them. It's as if they are scrutinizing us. Too-close looks at our rolled sleeves. Our gear. Our cordon surrounding the bomb. Assessing our tactics. Monitoring us. It feels as if my peers, the men I've known since squad bay times, are judging me as a leader.

Then, an illuminating exchange.

"So," one of them says to me. "Just out here looking for bombs, huh?"

"No," I say, irritated. "We weren't looking for anything. It was just...there."

"Sure," he says. "Sure it was."

"What are you trying to say?"

"Nothing," he shrugs.

Perhaps it makes sense. For some of them, I am what they wanted to be. There is no doubt many of my peers believe they deserved to be a squad leader instead of me. To add insult to injury, I have now found the first IED of the deployment, a milestone that rates some sort of absurd status among us, Lance Corporals with a deployment under our belts. Perhaps they are right. Perhaps they would be better leaders than me. And if our positions were reversed, I would probably feel the same way they do.

Nevertheless, their obvious frustration fosters a bristling, defensive reaction in me. I'm not ready for a deployment filled with friction. But this seems to be the path things are destined to take.

By the time EOD blows the bomb in place, I'm exhausted and confused and disappointed. I was told Sergeant Dorsey did a lot for this village, and I'm angry that Hajji Ismail allowed this to happen. In the early evening hours Jack and I talk to the elder, who seems as bewildered as we are. He tells us he will organize a *shura* of all the village men tomorrow morning. He says he will try to help us get to the bottom of this. We accept him at his word and return to the Hill. I report my findings to the Actual on the radio that night.

Terrance's team tells Jason's team about the interaction with the other squad. We are incensed at the idea that we went looking for a bomb. We take umbrage at the insinuation that we are out here looking for trouble. It was chance and circumstance. But really, we reason, if we find IED's and blow them up, what's wrong with that? How else do you mark progress here? There is nobody to shoot at. We already own the territory. A bomb found is a life saved.

We embrace the day's find as a marker of success. We decide that, no matter what our friends might say or think, we will not shirk or deflect from what we did. What we do. Who we are. Over fire and Fanta we are re-christened. Ruben gives us our name.

"Bomb Squad, baby," he says suddenly. "We're the fucking Bomb Squad!" We are in jubilant agreement. Two-Three. Bomb Squad. KT-4.

He paints this phrase, along with our callsign, on a piece of plywood, posting it at the entrance of the Hill for all to see. We drink celebratory coffee in the absence of beer. I change my socks. I ready myself for the next day, the next patrol, the next bomb.

I am eager for the morning *shura*. Sergeant Mike insists on coming with this time. I welcome his help, the Afghan face on the meeting. We get to the village around nine to find a large gathering of men in the village center. A hush comes over them as we roll into town. I shrug my shoulders back, hold my gun in a cool-guy way, try to look important, to convey some sort of gravitas. When Hajji Ismail comes over to greet me, I take off my gloves and sunglasses to shake his hand.

Jason's team spreads out to provide security. I'm excited and nervous. The squad searches villagers for suicide vests and weapons. A crowd of men pack themselves into a sort of outdoor meeting house.

Sergeant Mike and I sit against a wall, facing Hajji Ismail, who is clothed in white. His turban and salt-and-pepper beard convey more authority than the skullcap and brown *dishdasha* worn by most of the others. He's relaxed but hard to read. He turns a set of prayer beads over in his hands, a ritualistic tic, his thumb rubbing each wooden bead as it passes through his palm.

"*Assalamu-ailakum,*" I say to the group, hand over my heart. "*Zeh Sergeant Aaron yum.*"

I meet the eyes of each man in the room. They are uniformly older and thinner than me, but I do not sense distrust or hatred in their eyes. Rather, I see expressions that I interpret as genuine concern. I hope this is the case.

Hajji Ismail speaks to me. Through Jack, I ask questions.

Who saw the bomb? I ask.

Nobody knows, is the reply.

Where did it come from?

We did not see anyone put the bomb in.

But it was right outside your village. I saw people walking there.

It was well-disguised. Nobody noticed it.

What am I supposed to do?

We will make sure it does not happen again.

Is that a promise?

A promise.

How can I be sure? When we've done so much for you? The well? Security? And still this happens?

We are very grateful for all that you have done. The Taliban are not good. The Americans are good.

And the Afghan Army, I say.

Yes, the Afghan Army, too.

So no more bombs?

No more.

And will you help us find the people responsible?

We will watch out.

Will you help us?

Yes. We will help. We will ask and try to find out who it was.

I come away from the meeting with a glowing feeling, like I've accomplished something. My naivety leads me to believe that these people will help us find the person who emplaced this IED, and that yes, they really do want us here, and that yes, they think the government of the Islamic Republic of Afghanistan is worthwhile and will ultimately help them. I am satisfied. I am content in the outcome of my mission. I have provided security to this village. I have conducted a key leader engagement. I have come away thinking Hajji Ismail is my friend, and I am his. And friends don't let friends get blown up.

There is an anecdote in the Marine Corps. It goes something like this:

You can be a master bridge builder. You can build the most beautiful, largest, most structurally sound bridges in the world. People come from all around to marvel at the ingenuity of your bridges, to stare in wonder and ask: how did you achieve this? Hundreds, thousands, millions of people cross your bridges. You can receive awards for your bridges. You can be the most renowned bridge builder of all the bridge builders in the world. Your bridges never collapse. Your bridges are beautiful, durable, architecturally ingenious. You spend your whole life reveling in your bridge-builder fame.

But, the anecdote goes, if you fuck one goat, you'll be known to history not as a bridge-builder, but as a goat-fucker.

I come back to the Hill and send my *shura* notes up to the Lieutenant. Good atmospherics, I tell him. Excellent meeting. We're really building a relationship, this elderly opium farmer and me. The Actual says good job. Says to put a couple of observation posts out in that area the next few nights, see if there's any more activity. I tell him okay, sounds good sir, roger. Get off the radio, drop gear, walk over to my rack, drink water. Take my shirt off, walk out onto the hard-pack over by the shitter and take a look around. Life's good.

I'm getting ready to duck into the shitter, when all of a sudden—

"Kirk," comes a voice from post one.

"What's up?" I yell back.

"Durzay. They can see you on the tower cameras. They want you to put your shirt back on. And they want Cody to take off that Kentucky hat."

11

Trash, Goats, Bugs

How do you get rid of trash on a remote base in Afghanistan? Easy. First, you dig a hole. As deep and as big as you can. Dig it right outside your perimeter. Maybe surround it with extra c-wire, make sure the dogs can't get in. Make sure you can see it from one of the posts, in case a bad guy tries to sneak into the hole and surprise you.

Then you collect your trash. Plastic spoons, MRE containers, leftover sugar packets, socks, magazines, plastic wrappers, water bottles, batteries. You stuff all this inside trash bags; if you're short, you can open one of those small-group tray rations, UGRE's, that are used to feed several guys at once. There's a bunch of trash bags in each of those. You grab all the refuse and you put it all in the trash bags and then you take the bags right outside of the concertina wire on the north side of the Hill, out to the hole you just dug. You grab a jug of diesel fuel, dump it all around the center and the edges of the trash pile. Then you stand back and pinch a match between your thumb and the lighting strip on the matchbook and you *pop!* it quickly. There's an art to it; if you aim right the sulfur catches on fire just when it lands in the middle of the diesel fuel. JP-8 diesel fuel doesn't explode, per se, but it makes a decent fireball. You watch it all go up in flames.

Congratulations, you have yourself a burn pit.

For the rest of your time on the Hill you toss in anything you want to get rid of: broken flip flops, letters, bags full of human shit, dead animal parts. You stand ten feet away and smoke cigarettes while you watch it all burn. You hack up yellow or orange or green phlegm every couple of days. Years later you sign up for the VA's burn pit registry.

Everyone wants to eat a goat, so we get one. It's a process. Bartering with the goatherd—he sells you the runt, the smallest goat he can find. The whole squad goes in, gets it for sixty bucks. We all know it's too much but we're ravenous for fresh meat. You lead it back to the patrol base, two or three klicks. Guide it up the Hill, tie it to some Hesco. Now what?

If you're smart, you let the Afghan Army guys slaughter it. They'll do it Halal, nice and easy, bleed it out, and then they can share the meal with you. That's the best way. Why is that the best way? I'll tell you.

My first deployment. We buy a goat, same process, same haggling. We're staying at a squad-sized outpost. Americans only, no Afghan Army. We have to slaughter it and cook it ourselves. What's the best way? We mull the problem. You can't shoot it. This isn't Vietnam; if another base hears a gunshot they'll probably call it in to higher. I mean, maybe you can explain it away. Say a car backfired. Say you didn't hear anything at all. Problem is, each bullet is accounted for. Sure, you can say you lost a round, it fell out of your magazine, your dump pouch, whatever. But how many times can you do that before someone catches on? This isn't fucking Vietnam. It's Afghanistan. Different war, different rules.

Back to the goat. My first deployment. We figure out how we're going to kill it. Ideally, we want it to be quick and painless, and since we've spent our entire lives watching movies where people die instantly after having their necks twisted, we figure we'll do the same. Our biggest, strongest guy puts the animal between his legs. He pinches it so it doesn't move, which isn't easy, but he's a wrestler and knows how to pin. He grabs the goat by the chin and the horns and he twists as hard and as fast as he can. He's looking to break the neck, like in all those action movies. Except instead of breaking the neck he just turns the head one hundred and eighty degrees. Things crack but do not break. The goat's bleating in agony. The squad's shouting, frantic, taken aback. Why didn't it die? The goat's trying to get free. The Marine keeps turning the head. The goat's head cracks and twists. It bleats and cries. My hands reach unconsciously to my mouth. How is this goat so flexible? He keeps twisting, twisting, twisting, and it gets harder and harder to gain each degree of rotation, and the squad's shouting, screaming, oh my god, what the fuck, how the hell, and finally the goat stops bleating and the burly Marine throws it away from him, lets out a cry of frustration. We all watch the twitching goat die.

Except it doesn't die. The goat jumps to its feet and runs straight toward me and before I can think I've jumped up the ladder to post one and I'm watching a goat, its head rotated five hundred and forty degrees, slam into stacks of water bottles. Someone grabs it and shoots it in the head, twice, because it's hard to hit a tiny brain even at close range. We grill and eat it.

Levi makes a terrible soup. I'm the only one who will eat it with him. I pour it out when he isn't looking.

Back to the Hill. My Afghan Army soldiers offer to prepare the goat and invite us to dinner. It's an event. We all go.

The ANA soldiers slaughter it in accordance with Islamic custom. Things go smoothly this time. For a skinny little animal, it produces a lot of meat, way more than we can eat in one night. Everyone chows down. Sergeant Mike doles out big portions of rice and *naan* bread and a deliciously spicy chutney sauce. The goat meat, cooked in a pot with spices, turns out beautifully. It's stringy but fresh, so fresh. It's worlds away from MRE meat. Degrees.

We savor the juice and the texture and the heat. The amazing heat, the warmth of fresh meat, something we haven't had in weeks, a gift, hot goat, newly slaughtered. We laugh and jest and smoke cigarettes. Sergeant Mike tells a joke in bad English. I tell him he can take patrol off tomorrow. I relieve the guy at post one so he can eat. It's a good night.

The next day the Afghans tell us we will have more goat meat that evening. This intrigues me. It's over a hundred degrees outside. I go and talk to Wali. Wali is the cook because he is loud and fat. He explains this to me without me even asking.

I ask Wali how they store the excess meat without refrigeration. A simple process, he tells me. A yellow bucket contains the meat. Salt thoroughly to preserve it. Cover it well and keep it in shade. Wali tells me it will be good for three days. I'm a little skeptical. I tell the guys. They are more than a little skeptical. Later that night I go over to eat, but only about half the squad comes with me. The Afghans don't seem to care. We have another good night. The meat is still very good. Not quite as fresh, but still delicious.

The next day Wali tells me they have enough meat for one more night. No way, I say. It's been a hundred and ten degrees for two days, I say. There are flies around the bucket, I say. He tells me he keeps the flies away. How? I ask. Like this, he says. He uses his hand to flick them. It is not very effective.

I tell the boys. Everyone except Jason decides to abstain. Jason gives his signature wide-mouth grin. He gives this grin when he's excited or happy, but also when he's nervous, and sometimes when he's scared. Jason smiles and tells me Terrance will have to take the squad when we both die of food poisoning. Sure, I say, and Willie the Bomb Dog will be first team leader.

We head over, just the two of us, and have one more meal of un-refrigerated goat meat. This time, Wali has added some beans from a Halal MRE we found among our last helicopter resupply. The beans are a good touch. The meat's fine. I thank them for their hospitality. What a great three days, I think. Goat.

The next morning I'm geared up, talking on the radio. I'm telling Durzay about the patrol that's about to leave the Hill when I feel a warm gurgle in my colon. I let out gas only to realize too late that it's not gas at all, but hot liquid diarrhea. Shit rolls down my leg. I grab the radio from my flak jacket as I take my gear off. I key the handset, clenching, waddling, shuffling toward the head.

"Durzay, Two-Three Actual."

"Send it Two-Three."

"Roger, patrol is going to be delayed about ten mics, how copy."

"Solid copy, Two-Three. Two-Bravo wants to know why, over."

"Roger, I shit myself, over."

A long pause. "Roger, Two-Bravo copies."

"Roger, out."

I throw my pants in the burn pit.

"The rules are simple," says Ruben. "Everybody lets their bug go at the same time. The last one standing wins."

Five men, five containers, five bugs. One miniature arena, a foot-high wall of cardboard and Hesco barrier dug into the ground. A bug-fighting coliseum. The gladiatorial games begin tonight.

Over the course of the week, since coming up with the idea, Jason and Ruben and Cody had constructed the arena and encouraged the squad to collect and capture bugs. The nastier the better.

There was no shortage of potential gladiators around the Hill. You'd toss your rack up and dislodge enterprising camel spiders who found warmth under your sleeping bag. At night they scurried about, stalking prey in the moonlight, finding their way into boots or Crocs, which we'd shake out in the morning. They were part of the Hill's ecosystem, eaten by the pit vipers that dwelled in the base's nooks and crannies. Cody captured a bug we didn't know the name of, so we called it a dildozer. It was a powerful-looking type of camel spider, all black, with short, stubby legs, a massive torso and gruesomely sharp fangs. Ruben, unafraid as ever, pulled up two scorpions by their stingers and plopped them into separate water bottles, which he cut off and capped ingeniously with duct tape and carboard. One was milky-white and thumb-sized, the other a beastly black creature the size of a cell phone. They say that the lighter-colored scorpions carry more venom in their stingers. It's probably bullshit, but we believe it.

Rounding out the roster tonight are Ivan's lanky, ghoulish camel spider, Russell's ordinary-looking spider, and Nate's dung beetle, Samson. I let Nate know his beetle's chances are slim.

"Samson's fucked," I say.

"Have faith," he replies.

We gather around the coliseum after dark. The boys are playing Waka Flocka Flame, *Hard in the Paint*, the lyrics slapping the air through a blown-out aux speaker. We're excited, electric, animalistic. Bets are placed, hands rubbed, wild promises made.

On the count of three we loose the traps. Bugs scuttle and scurry their way across the dirt floor. Some dart for the sides of the arena and attempt to escape while others head straight for their prey. We're mad with bloodlust, spitting and howling at our bugs, urging them to victory.

Inside the arena, chaos. Black scorpion darts toward normal spider, who stands no chance. The scorpion's stinger thrusts one, two, three times into the spider's body as his claws tear it limb from limb. On the other side of the arena the dildozer and the camel spider find each other. They exchange vicious bites, striking quickly and without mercy. The white scorpion tries and fails to climb the arena walls to safety. He scurries away from the melee, then back toward it. Samson the dung beetle does little but sprint along the outside of the arena, avoiding the other gladiators.

As their creatures fight and kill and die, the men laugh and scream and curse.

We make these bugs fight each other because of boredom. Because of impotence. Because of indoctrination. Because we are Marines. Because we want to kill, and we cannot.

The Marine Corps Way: to kill one's enemies is good. The Marine's primary function is to close with and destroy the enemy.

Left foot, kill foot. You scream it in bootcamp: "kill, kill, kill." You sing cadences about killing. You kill paper targets on the range. Kill green Ivans. Kill time. Kill bodies, slay bodies. Kill, kill, kill 'em all. *Get over here, killer.*

The language, the mannerisms, the entirety of Marine Corps culture directed us toward *this*, this overwhelming desire to *kill*, to simply *take a life* and yet none of us, not one of us, could say that we had done so. Instead we are on top of an old ruin in the middle of nowhere, hunted by men we can't see, ghosts who follow our every move and try to kill us instead.

Instead of wolves we are bison. Not snakes, but mice. Trained to be apex predators, we are instead whack-a-mole dummies in an absurd life-or-death game, all of us young and full of testosterone and stupid with rage.

The bugs die and as they die spittle rains from our faces. In another life we might be genial and thankful and sweet but in this one we are mean and hungry and overwhelmed. We let loose our rage as we condemn the fallen insects to an eternity in hellfire, as we praise the warrior instinct of the fat-bodied dildozer.

Kill him! Tear him apart! Fuck him up!

we shout and we mean it, truly we do. Lack of killing makes us feel useless. We are governed by restraint and rules of engagement and dashed hopes and ruined expectations. Perhaps these macabre theatrical deathmatches are but a symptom of the frustration of never really being able to hold accountable the people who place the bombs in the fields, of never being able to *actually fucking kill the enemy*.

So we watch.

Dildozer hunts for black scorpion and black scorpion meets him with no hesitation and stings dildozer once, twice, over and over, the brutality of each sting evident to the men gathered round, gasps and oh's and grimaces and yet dildozer, seemingly oblivious to the pain and the poison, clasps his jaws around black scorpion's head and sucks his face off. Black scorpion twitches but stings no more. Dildozer walks slowly over the carcasses of his enemies to the last remaining threat, the white scorpion. White scorpion, sensing the danger, tries to run away but finds himself backed into a corner, forced to stand and trade with dildozer. He is a weakened dildozer but still an imposing dangerous killer dildozer. Meanwhile Samson the beetle races his circles around the inner edge of the arena. He is the unnoticed third survivor, He has outlasted the normal spider and the camel spider and the black scorpion. Dildozer and white scorpion are going at it now and the gathering takes on a hushed tone as white scorpion's stinger pierces dildozer's thorax again and again and again—*nobody can take that much venom!*—screams someone but dildozer can and he does and as he does he eats white scorpion's eyes and white scorpion dies bit by bit and you can see dildozer is fucked up from the venom and the fights and as dildozer moves away he moves so slowly that you think he might collapse at any moment and every time he moves it seems to take a tremendous amount of effort and you wonder if bugs can feel pain but even as you think this thought *there he is* Samson the dung beetle creeping up from behind and we stare at each other slack-jawed as Samson crawls atop the dildozer and sucks his brains out, leaving an empty cavity that looks like a sinkhole in the dildozer's head.

12

Battle Rhythm

Our relationship with the rest of the platoon at Durzay grows more tense. They watch us with cameras attached to a hundred-foot tall tower called the GBOSS. The GBOSS was designed to look for fighters placing bombs in roads and insurgents running away from firefights. Instead, some of the Durzay Marines use its precise thermal cameras to watch the Hill for signs of uniform violations. Instead of monitoring patterns of life, they monitor the sleeves of our uniform blouses for improper rolling. Stuck with the platoon sergeant and platoon commander, they are subject to a higher level of self-discipline and scrutiny that comes with the semi-functional air conditioning, the dumbbells and internet access. Rather than follow suspicious cars, they follow us, watching as we fill Hesco barrier by hand with our shirts off, as Cody wears his Kentucky hat around the base. Fellow Lance Corporals in Durzay's muggy operations center turn the cameras toward us, monitoring for some minor infraction of the Marine Corps Way so they can tell the platoon sergeant, who is honor-bound to correct us. He doesn't always do so. I can tell he empathizes with us. But he's a lifer, a guardian of the Marine Corps Way. He has little choice.

So the Eye of Sauron watches us. We stay under the camouflage netting. The war goes on.

Life on KT-4 follows a rhythm. There is a never-ending list of things to do. Reports to higher. Mission cards and patrol intentions and logstats and serialized gear lists and broken equipment lists and requests and PCC's and PCI's and trash burning. Two patrols, one night and one day. You leave the Hill at different times so as to not set a pattern. But you set a pattern anyway.

Daily tasks. No bulldozers, so every afternoon for a few hours you get the squad together and use your entrenching tools to shovel dirt into the Hesco barriers, shielding us from northward fire. The barriers only ever seem to fill halfway.

Hygiene. You shave every day, or every couple of days, or whenever you know someone's coming to the Hill, or when you're patrolling to Durzay. Grab a water bottle, flip it upside down, puncture the top and spray your face. The dirt streaks and when it's gone you're a different person. You do your best to shave with a dirty, half-broken electric razor or a Gillette from a care package. Your chin and cheeks stay clean for a day, then the dust reclaims them.

If there's a sandstorm, you endure it. If things are blown away, you pick them up. If supplies are delivered, you go out and get them, then carry them up the Hill. We take our flak jackets off, post an overwatch, and spend days stooped over, carrying boxes. Sometimes it takes a week to finish. We leave the supplies overnight, in the field just beyond the concertina wire. Nobody steals from us. Our fields of fire are wide and deep.

The first time we're resupplied by helicopter I'm on the radio, talking to the bird, a big Marine Corps CH-53E with a cable underneath, carrying along a giant pallet filled to the brim. I'm talking to the pilot, telling him to circle around to the south and come up on the east side of the Hill. It's an amazing feeling: communicating with an aircraft, telling the pilot the best way to drop our supplies off, watching him do it. I've only got a little bit of training in this. I'm stoked.

Until he drops the load off and then flies right over us, his rotor-wash blasting our fragile camouflage netting setup to pieces and throwing chunks of burning refuse all over the hill and the surrounding area.

We spend the rest of the day picking up trash.

Once in a while, you decide to get clean. Doc does it almost every day. The rest of us do it when we can.

The key to a successful combat shower is having a real towel. Lots of guys bring those micro-fleece things, the coyote brown ones that roll up nice and small. Problem is, they get dirty after a while. They become greasy and transfer the grime back onto you. No, you need a normal towel. Grab your hygiene kit and a dry pair of silkies. Put your sandals on, walk out by the Hesco. Get naked. The good people in the nearby villages can only see you from the shoulders up, but it's enough to feel like an exhibitionist.

The water bottles in the Hesco-crate nearby have been in the sun all day and hold a nice, warm temperature, so you flip one upside down, pop it on the sharp Hesco grid-metal to puncture it, and raise it over your head to soak your hair. Days of muck separate from the thick, oiled strands of hair grown way out of regs. You can taste the salt and carbon as little rivers stream over your lip and into your mouth. Dry off with your real towel, hang your clothes up on a line and put on a new skivvy shirt.

Try to do this every couple of weeks.

Most evenings, patrol schedule permitting, I eat with the Afghan Army soldiers. The food is hot and cooked, rather than just reheated in trays. Like making friends with a school shooter, dinner is my strategy to keep them from killing us out of insult or irritation.

We recline on the ANA's cots or sit against pillows on the floor. The ANA serve us good rice and chicken they steal from our First Strike Rations. When we're done, we go back to our berthing and they to theirs, and I hope against hope that the next day Sergeant Mike will make his men carry the Thor.

I try to keep the Afghans informed of my patrol intentions, but I rarely tell them exactly where we're going, or for how long. I'd been told that sometimes the ANA feed information to the Taliban for money. I don't think the ANA on the Hill are doing that, but you can never be too careful.

The end result is that in this war, a war that Afghans are supposed to be fighting, I keep them in the dark about how we're fighting it. This does not sit well with me.

Sergeant Mike is friendly most of the time, unless he doesn't feel like working, or he thinks we're taking advantage of him, or he gets into an argument with Jack, our interpreter. He oozes the cross-cultural sliminess of a used-car salesmen or a multi-level marketer. He smokes constantly. He prefers American cigarettes, but has nowhere to buy them, and couldn't afford them if he did. So he bums them from us.

He's only got a few lines of English. Always the same shtick.

"Patrol no good," he says, to our endless amusement.

"Patrol double no good," we say back.

"Patrol triple one-hundred no good," he exclaims. And he does this every time before we go on patrol, and it never seems to get old to the guys, even though to Sergeant Mike I'm sure it's very old, because he's probably been saying it for half a decade now, saying it to many different units of Americans, in different provinces of Afghanistan, making his living while fighting his county's endless internal war.

But he says it, and we laugh, and he bums cigarettes from us, and somehow he keeps skirting danger and dodging bullets and avoiding whatever Good Idea the Americans come up with now.

His faults aside, Sergeant Mike tries to be useful in dealing with the local Afghans. He has no cultural ties to the region, being a Hazara in a Pashtun province. He tells us, in simple English, if a local is telling the truth or not.

"Good," he'll say.

"No good," he'll sometimes remark.

"Double good. No Taliban," he'll explain.

"Double no good. Taliban! Fucking Taliban!" he'll exclaim.

On his advice we detain a couple of guys, bring them back to Durzay. They're released for lack of evidence. In time I come to realize that Sergeant Mike's instincts are not very good. I learn to look at Jack for a fact check when Sergeant Mike tells me anything.

To pass the time we play Spades with grimy cards on the plywood table. We blast music from a battery-powered aux-cord speaker. We debate about rap and country. I am exposed to music I've never heard. Our days and nights become opportunities for intra-squad cultural exchange, like an excursion during a study abroad. A cross-cultural experience inside of a cross-cultural experience. When you have nearly all of the platoon's minority Marines concentrated in one squad, stuck on top of a tiny Hill in the middle of nowhere, you have no choice but to come away influenced. Terrance and Mario and Doc play Waka Flocka Flame and Plies on the speaker, singing *No Hands* and *Racks on Racks on Racks*. They stack imaginary money, dance on top of boxes. It is an education. They try to explain the trap to me. I can never really understand.

Nate and I play chess or *Magic: The Gathering*. We use cards my dad sends me. We bullshit. We put water in the cooling-holes. We shake out our boots and pull new socks from our care packages. Jason and I gravitate toward a particular song, which we play often, on repeat, just sitting and listening and thinking. It's a fast-paced remix of a Metric song called *Monster Hospital*. One aching refrain haunts us now and later:

I fought the war
I fought the war, I fought the war but the war won't-
Stop, for the love of god
I fought the war
But the war won

It sticks with me, and with Jason, long after we are gone from this place.

Sometimes, when I'm not too tired, I lift weights by the piss tubes. We craft two sets of dumbbells, just bamboo sticks connecting vegetable cans, filled with concrete. A bench from plywood and MRE boxes, a kettlebell from a sandbag, a hammer and a tire. Somehow I expect that my workouts will yield results, even though I'm wearing body armor and jumping canals and walking for ten hours a day. I lose pound after pound, unable to replace the calories I'm expending. In a month on the Hill, I've lost a pant size and untold muscle mass. My body has re-engineered itself to the ideal shape and size of a counterinsurgency grunt. I am lean and agile. I can march all day, fueled by hot Rip It energy drinks and chocolate MRE pound cake. I am a panther who stalks the surrounding villages and roads, looking for a prey that never appears. I am young and wild.

We walk to Durzay to fetch the Gator and load it up with supplies. We take advantage of the amenities there. Durzay is austere by anyone's standards but our own. Big generator. Four computers, two sun showers with rudimentary plumbing systems. Three fully enclosed plywood shitters. A gym with a barbell, one-hundred-eighty-five pounds in weights and a set of dumbbells. Couple of tires and chains and makeshift dip bars and pullup bars. A seventy-pound kettlebell. An abmat. Perfect pushup. Jump ropes. Air conditioning units in the hooches mean you might actually sleep when the sun's up, if they're working. The guys at Durzay are a little bigger and a little more muscular than us. Outside the wire, we all do the same things, but inside, it's a different story.

The trade-off for even moderate creature comforts is proximity to leadership. Constant tasking by the platoon leadership. Visitors coming by in MAT-V convoys. Haircuts and higher-ups. A stricter uniform code, more in accordance with the Marine Corps Way.

Degrees. I decide I wouldn't trade the Hill for Durzay no matter what I was offered. Every single day up there is a struggle, but Bomb

Squad takes a kind of sick pride in it. Some days we resent the men of Durzay. Others we pity them. Most of the time we just miss our friends.

Until they start snitching on my guys for having their shirts off. Then I lose all sympathy. I decide I'll stay on the Hill forever. I'm never coming down.

At Durzay you can check Facebook, respond to Skype messages, tell people you love them. Talk to your woman, trying not to let the other guys see.

Did you get the packages?

Yes, and thank you, you say to your uncle, whose company supplied an enormous number of white socks and cigarettes to the squad.

I make sure that everyone logs on the computer at least once every time we come here. It's our weekly escape, at least for the guys on that patrol. You almost forget you're in a war zone when you're seeing status updates from people you knew in high school.

Eventually the computers shut off. You bid farewell to the platoonmates you like, ignore the stares of the ones you don't. With ferocity you meet the glares of the ones you know are behind the new round of bullshit with the Eye of Sauron. You head back to the Hill. Except this time, you're bringing the farm car with you.

The vehicle is a John Deere Gator, a six-wheel powerhouse, made for the farm and adapted for the field. I wonder where it came from, whose idea it was to send it down to us, whose idea it was to use it to resupply the Hill.

The problem with driving back is obvious. We'll have to stick to paths. We don't walk paths. But when we have the Gator, we have no choice.

We spend an hour or two at Durzay tying up a generator, mail, fuel, Rip Its. Two members of the sniper platoon decide they're coming with us, so we throw their fifty-caliber Barrett rifle in there. It can tear a man in half from a mile away, I hear. There's a Corporal with us, a generator mechanic, whose job it is to get power to us up on the Hill.

With power, we can charge radio batteries, Thor batteries, TOW batteries, something we can't do currently. Right now our solution is to hump a rucksack full of batteries and swap them out every time we're at Durzay. With a generator, we'll be more self-reliant. In time, we might even be able to get air conditioners. If we finish the hooches. If we ever get a break from patrolling. If I can get the men to do it.

The last thing that goes on the Gator is a fifty-gallon drum of fuel. If the generator works, we'll need fuel for it. It's heavy, but we manage to cram it in. We ratchet the gear down with thick straps.

The problem with patrolling back to the Hill in a vehicle is that there are only two routes. Both are roads. One is through the fields to the west. Lots of blind spots where the GBOSS can't see, where the Hill can't see. Terrain over that way is often flooded. Roads are busted-up, broken and crumbling and narrow. The other route is straight to the bazaar on the main road. There's only a couple of blind spots, but you might have to fight some small crowds and steep inclines where the bazaar meets the road. We decide on the bazaar route. We don't have much choice. We'll do our best to sweep and sickle, but the thought of sticking to one pre-planned route makes my skin crawl.

The men walk on the side of the road. If anything is getting blown up, it's the Gator. I take the wheel. If this has to happen to someone, it should be me. I'm uncomfortable and deeply anxious with the prospect of driving this thing across IED-ridden fields, but this is the mission. *Do it for the Rip Its*, I tell myself.

We don't walk paths. But sometimes, because it's the only thing to do, we drive them.

Before we leave, I notice the snipers have unfastened the groin-protecting kevlar flaps from their body armor.

I ask why. Don't they care about their nuts?

It's lighter that way, they say.

Yeah, but shrapnel will shred your dick, I say.

They shrug. I shrug. My guys all wear dick pro. Snipers aren't my guys. They can stay that way.

We leave through Durzay's winding serpentine barriers. We head north on a small road toward the bazaar. Easy going. We cruise through, my guys out sweeping ahead. Two metal detectors, one on each side of the road, plus the dog, plus the sickle-man, plus the Thor. I'm not too worried about the hard-pack, or the bazaar. It's one thing to kill a bunch of guys with a suicide bomber, to do it intentionally, to send a signal. It's another thing to have civilians trip a bomb in the bazaar. The Marines, the Taliban, the Government of Afghanistan are all fighting for the people. It doesn't help to kill them. The bazaar's safe when it's crowded. When it's deserted, that's where you have to be careful.

The real trouble comes after the bazaar. Blind spots, soft dirt. I push my dexterity to the limit getting this vehicle over inclines and bumps. I manipulate brake and gas, watching the tires, thankful to my father for teaching me to drive rear-wheel-drive cars in the Colorado snow. The men are spread out, looking for wires. None of them walk on the road. We do our best—a flawed, imperfect solution to the central problem of the deployment. Logistics.

Walking on paths is like fornicating. You can increase your level of safety, but there's always a chance you'll catch something. In sex it's a disease. In combat it's a bomb. Walking through the fields is abstinence. The surest way to stay safe. Even so, what happens when the enemy figures out which fields you always walk through? Like poking holes in a prophylactic.

And I'm not safe, not in this stupid, lumbering, unarmored farm-car, going down one of *only two possible paths* to the Hill. A perfect target. Any sizable IED would flip the vic, kill me and very likely catch the fifty-gallon fuel drum on fire. My skin would crisp to black. There is a lump in my throat when I begin to drive, though this is replaced by a burning resigned anger as I accept the mission is an essential one. I wish there were a different way to get supplies that the helicopters can't carry. I wish someone in a headquarters somewhere would figure out a way to get us a generator without driving on the booby-trapped paths I refuse to let my squad walk on. And though I try not to show it, I am anxious about being blown up. I hope the guys at Durzay are watching when it happens.

We drive and roll and lumber and miraculously we make it to the bottom of the Hill unscathed. We unload the gear. The generator and the barrel of fuel give us hell. It takes engineer stakes and straps to get the generator up, and three of us to roll the fuel all the way to the top. We take our body armor off and sweat until the sun goes down. We place the small generator next to the older, broken one.

"Well," I say to the gen-mech in his pristine uniform and eight-point garrison cover. "Start the fucking thing."

He works furiously, turning dials and moving switches. He presses the choke and pulls the cord, trying to start. Once. Twice. Three times. Sputtering smoke, white and black. A fourth time. Fifth time. Fifteen times. Twenty pulls and the generator does not start.

"Figures," I say. There it is.

13

Osama Bin Laden

In early May I find out from higher that some Navy SEALS killed Osama bin Laden. After I break the news to the squad we have a little party with chicken and rice and soda. We bump Gucci Mane on the portable speaker. We smoke cigarettes in lieu of cigars.

The next morning we set off into the countryside to tell the Afghans about it. Get the message out. Gotta let everyone know we're doing something tangible. One step closer to winning the war. So I take the squad on a grand tour. We go to all our villages, talk to the elders, the townsfolk. Hump to the bazaar, speak with the shopkeepers.

Everyone we talk to already knows about the raid. They know bin Laden's dead. They don't seem to care.

The shopkeepers ask when we're leaving. Never, we tell them. We buy knock-off brand sodas and head back.

14

25 May

"Durzay, Two-Three, over."

"Send it, Two-Three."

"Roger, what is aircon, over?"

"We are in aircon yellow. Hovering between yellow and red, over."

"Roger. Are we good to return to base, or do we have to stay static and wait it out? Over."

"Two-Three wait one, I'm gonna grab Two-Bravo."

"Roger, standing by."

I wait a second. Ten. Thirty. A minute.

"Two-Three, this is Two-Bravo, over."

"Send it, Two-Bravo."

"Roger, how are you on water?"

"We're near-black on water, over."

"Roger, listen Two-Three, it's up to your discretion whether you stay static or head back. Looks like it's gonna be a pretty big storm, over."

It takes me a split second to decide.

"Roger. We're going to head back then. Thanks Two-Bravo. Two-Three out."

I stuff the radio back in its pouch.

Overcast skies. Winds picking up. Black clouds on the horizon. The tail end of a patrol that left mid-morning and took all day. An exhausting expedition, picking our way through thorny trees and brush all the way to the Helmand River and back, visiting the furthest village in our area of responsibility. Though the sun has disappeared, its heat lingers. We are trapped in a sauna between storm-clouds and the earth, almost out of water, a mile or more of fields and gulleys and embankments to cover before we're back at the Hill. Out here, a mile is a marathon.

We push brush aside, jump straight down into chest-deep canals, bypass bridges. I'm moving us along, urgently, but letting Cody and Jason pick a safe path. Over the course of dozens of patrols I've learned to trust their judgment.

During air condition red, helicopters can't fly. Medevacs can't get to us. We'll have to stay static and sit tight with no water until the weather clears. There is so much risk in merely walking around in aircon red that battalion keeps all patrols inside the wire. But before the weather worsens, in aircon yellow, patrols can return—something we're going to do now, if I can manage it.

I key my black gear. "Jason, we need to get back before the weather goes red. Haul ass, but be careful."

"Roger, moving," comes the reply, three men ahead of me.

We force our way through muddy fields and stacks of poppy stalks. Faster than usual, but still cautious. Call it controlled risk. I'm not comfortable, but the alternative is to stay out here with no water, for what could be an entire night, or even into the next day. There would be no resupply. The very rules that are designed to keep us safe would prevent the rescue of heat casualties. And right now, men passing out from dehydration seems a likely scenario.

As I walk, fifth in the column, a hint of fear-induced adrenaline pumps through me, forcing me into an uncomfortable mind game with myself. I watch as Cody mechanically sweeps the path ahead, Jason just behind him with the sickle.

It's fear. Fear of the storm. Fear that we are moving too fast. Fear of a bomb, lurking somewhere ahead. Fear of the Taliban's data, the information they've gathered on our movements.

This game, this back-and-forth, minesweeper, metal detector, Thor, sickle game. They put one in here. Put one there. Hide it in the poppy stalks. In the bazaar. In the goat-path. You find it, you win. You don't, you die. It's cat and mouse. No—wolf and bison. And you have the uncomfortable certainty that you are the bison. Large, heavy, slow, and vulnerable.

My anti-mind game, my mental armor, is to practice the nine-line medevac in my head, over and over and over, like a metronome. Whenever I feel fear coming on during patrol, I recite the lines. I recite the zap numbers of the men I have memorized, which identify who they are and what their blood type is.

Line one, grid location. The most important line.

Another field. We've nearly reached the road that comes before the walls on the north side of the Hill. The wind wails harder. Cody does a good job picking paths. Nothing too obvious. I send a position report to Durzay and touch the two playing cards in my left shoulder pocket.

I scan. My eyes dart like cats from one object to another, interpreting, pushing down fear. Actively searching. I am lightning in a bottle.

Line two, frequency. Second Platoon tac, callsign Two-Three.

Left foot forward, right foot forward, spin and check on Jack and Ruben and the ANA and Doc. Turn back, cross the road, head down.

Time to cross the big canal. Hill's fortress walls on the other side. Down into the ditch. Waist-deep water, no big deal, been wet the whole patrol anyway. Scramble up the other side, get up on top of the road, head west. Hard-packed. I can see the Hill from here, which means if I were Taliban, the Hill could see me, so no bombs here. Hard pack means you can't stick a pressure plate in the road without seeing it, and there's no disturbed earth. So far so good.

You're only ever one rationalization away from death.

Four hundred meters to go. Just a giant wall and a blind spot. The sky, brown and noisy moments ago, now a black tempest, sand and plants and fear. I hear lightning, distant in the south as the windstorm nears. There will be no rain in this storm, only malice.

We're coming up on the blind spot, the one that always makes me anxious. The one we always stop to sickle. We are in a natural funnel. There are only three or four ways through the walls, and we must cross one of them. There's nothing we can do but to be cautious, and sweep, and sickle.

I key my black gear again. "Jason, be careful down there."

"Roger, will do."

Line three, number of patients by precedent. One alpha, one bravo...

I watch Jason tell Cody, watch Cody acknowledge Jason. We keep walking. My heart batters my ears. Down the incline on the south side of the double-road, then toward the gap.

You only need three lines to get a bird spinning.

Down the incline. Fifth. Jack's behind me. He asks me a question, but all I hear is the wind. I realize I can't see Cody any more. We must be coming up to the wall area. Clearing. Jason and Cody, they'll be fine. I think about a landing zone. Right here, to the left. I continue reciting lines in my head. My hands are sweating.

Line one. Location. Line two. Frequency, callsign. Line three. Number of patients by precedent. Line four. Special equipment. Line five, number of patients by type. Line six. Security at pickup site. Line sev—

Up ahead, the earth erupts.

Whump

it hits me, the hardest shockwave I've ever felt, like belly-flopping into a pool, and oddly I can still hear, as if I had clasped my hands over my ears just before the explosion, and then they're ringing and I watch Russell flop down into a puddle, knocked out, and I can't see Jason or Cody in the dust cloud, and before I realize what I'm doing I shout

Corpsman!

and take a knee and my green radio flies out of my pouch and I'm sending up the nine-line just like I've practiced, and from the size of the explosion I already know that at least one of my guys is dead or seriously wounded—

"Durzay, Two-Three, we just hit an IED, standby for medevac nine-line, over—"

and the rocks that were kicked up into the air fall upon my helmet like raindrops on an umbrella

"Roger, send it Two-Three—"

and the dust cloud grows ever larger

"Line one: forty-one romeo poppa zero zero two three three nine zero seven three two—"

and two figures fly past me, the first Ruben, the second Doc, coming from the rear

"Line two: Second Platoon tac, callsign Two-Three—"

and there Russell begins to stir, rolling onto his side

"Line three: at least one urgent, how copy?"

"Roger, solid copy on lines one through three, standing by for lines four through ten, send when ready—" they say, and I tell them to wait one, because now I need to get up and figure out what happened, and Russell's sitting on the ground, dazed, staring at the front of the patrol, where Doc and Ruben are crouched over a figure on the ground.

I run to Russ, pull him to his feet by the strap on the back of his flak jacket.

"Russell! You alright? You good? You hit?"

He shakes his head. "I don't think so," he says. I check him over for wounds. Nothing I can see. Definitely knocked out by the blast, but okay for now. Need to get him doing something.

"Russell. Listen. I need you to drop this Thor right here and post security up there with the ANA. Stay on the cleared path! Do you understand me? Stop any vehicles that come by. Got it?"

"Roger. Okay."

"Good, go. Go now." He runs, stumbling a bit as he goes, obviously off-kilter from the blast.

The wind howls and I am already exhausted but it is time to get things done, and so I move, improvising as I work the problem at hand, trying to pull myself back for moments of clarity in the chaos so I can make rational decisions. I struggle between wanting to do something for Cody, who seems hurt very badly, and working the helicopter and the nineline and the radio. I'm also worried about Jason, since he was at the front of the line, one behind Cody. I whirl around, seeing the Afghan soldiers at the rear of the column, and then back to the front, where a flood of relief washes over me as I spot Jason next to Doc and Ruben.

Jason's standing up, Russ's okay, so they can be evacuated as routine or priority casualties. The urgent issue is Cody, who I haven't had the guts to look at yet. I call up Durzay, update them, and send them the rest of the report.

"Durzay, Two-Three, standby for lines four through ten of the casevac nineline."

"Roger, send it Two-Three."

"Roger, line four: request a stretcher," I say, remembering bitterly that I'd requested a portable stretcher for the squad for the last two months no avail, "Line five: one litter, one ambulatory. Line six: no enemy presence. Line seven, smoke. Line eight, US, Charlie Foxtrot four seven seven three, line nine, tall walls to the south, road to the north, come in west to east. How copy, over?"

Silence from the radio. Moans from the ground. Tentatively, afraid of what I might see, I look over Doc and Ruben's shoulders.

Cody's laying there, head lolling, propped against a knee-high structure where Afghan farmers store poppy stalks. His armor's been removed. The area around him is strewn with bandage wrappers and gloves and sunglasses and rifles. Doc's cut off his bloody combat shirt and pants. To my immense relief I notice his limbs are intact, but he looks bloodied and blasted, wounded all down the front side of his body, from his head to his neck, except where his body armor had been. His flesh looks sand-blasted, like someone took a powerful machine to the exposed skin, etching away the top layer. Holes in his neck. His cheeks. His thighs. Little bb-shaped puncture wounds on a backdrop of flayed flesh. Everything is red and gray and brown.

"Two-Three, say again lines...lines five through nine, you came in broken and unreadable, over," squawks the radio, so I repeat.

"What's the ETA on that bird, over?" I ask.

"Don't know yet. Main says they're spinning it up now. Weather's pretty bad, over."

"Roger, solid."

"Roger, Two-Three, can you send line ten and the MIST report, over?"

I give the numbers. The MIST report I hesitate on. I can give the mechanism of injury, but the injury sustained, symptoms and signs and treatment given all need to come from Doc, and Doc's busy stopping Cody's bleeding. It can wait.

I walk up and examine the blast site. There's a five-foot crater in the embankment where the path turns right. Looks like the explosive itself was in the wall, hit him directly in the front. He must have triggered a pressure plate...here. I spot the device, uncovered by the blast. No way Cody could have picked it up with the metal detector. No metal to find. Just carbon rods and wood. Battery pack would have been separate. Damn.

Back to where Cody's lying. I tap Doc on the shoulder. "How's he doing?"

Doc's hands are covered by black surgical gloves, his forearms bloody to the elbow. "Stable, in and out of consciousness. He's gonna go into shock if we don't get him out of here. Lots of shrapnel, all over his body."

"How's his..." I point to his groin. He was wearing the groin protector.

"He's good." I stop holding my breath. "We need to get him out of here," says Doc.

"I'm working on it."

I call back up to Durzay. "Mechanism of injury is an IED blast. Injuries sustained are lacerations, wounds to his arms and legs, large piece of shrapnel in the knee. Signs and symptoms stable. Treatment is tourniquet on one leg, pressure dressings, morphine and treatment for shock. How copy?"

"Roger. Two-Three, you said the casualty had shrapnel wounds across his body, break. Are you sure he's an urgent casualty?"

Immediately I bristle, even though it's a valid question. From Durzay's perspective, I'd called up a medevac for a casualty that wasn't missing any limbs, in poor air condition, and hadn't detailed the injuries. There was risk involved in the allocation of resources to get Cody out. On the other hand, without an amputation, the injuries are difficult for me to convey. How do I communicate overpressure and unconsciousness and head to toe bleeding in short, perfunctory language, when my senses are on overdrive? In any case, I hadn't gotten the point across, and the question makes me second-guess myself. Is Cody an urgent casualty? I take another look at him and as I do my doubts are assuaged and I am angry and overwhelmed and frightened that he might die, and Cody is covered in a metallic emergency blanket, his head lolls from side to side, low gurgling sounds emanate from his mouth and so I answer the radio:

"Roger, Durzay, with all due respect, he is a fucking urgent casualty."

"Roger, Two-Three. Standby for Two-Bravo."

Out of the corner of my eye I notice Jason try to hold his rifle with his right hand. He nearly drops it. I tell him to turn around.

"Are you hurt?" I ask.

"Yeah, I don't know. I can't really feel my arm."

"Take your flak off." He struggles with it. When it's off I notice several puncture wounds around his collarbone, and blood around his shoulder. I call for Ruben, who immediately works on patching Jason up.

It's your job to control, I remind myself. And Ruben can do the medical work far better than you can. I let Ruben work on Jason, then run down the line of men. I make sure the Afghans are posted, conducting security, Russell in their midst, looking dazed from being knocked out. As Doc and Ruben treat the casualties, and there's no word on the medevac bird, I start to feel helpless. Where's that bird? What can I do, right now? Suddenly I remember the field I chose for a landing zone hasn't been cleared for bombs.

I grab a metal detector and the sickle and strike out into the field behind the patrol, sweeping and clearing for a landing zone, doing a piss-poor job, but how can you clear a landing zone in a storm like this? Cody is clinging to life, Jason and Russell are wounded and I'm out here trying to listen for beeps in a sandstorm. Almost pointless, but better to try than not to do it at all. And if I don't do it, I can't say that I've done it in case the worst happens and a Blackhawk sets down on a bomb.

I'm a terrible sweeper, jumpy as hell. I beep on a soda can and nearly have a heart attack. How does Cody do this every day?

The radio sputters with Two-Bravo's voice. I switch the metal detector from one hand to the other and bring the radio to my ear.

"Two-Three, Main just called down. A bird tried to lift off from Dwyer three times, almost crashed. They're not going to be able to get one out to you, break—"

My heart skips a beat. Unconsciously, numbly, I lower the radio to my side. For a moment I am the only person in the squad who knows this information. I am speechless.

The platoon sergeant continues. "We have an alternative for you. Engineers who were working here on Durzay are headed to the bazaaar, break." My mind immediately starts working on the logistics of evacuating Cody, carrying him, getting him to the bazaar. "They have vics, but they can't get past the shops. Roads too narrow. No room to turn around."

"How do they know, over?" I ask.

"They've tried before. Learned the hard way."

"Roger, we'll meet them," I say quickly. Automatically, I move from planning to execution, springing into movement after an injection of adrenaline and hope.

We need to move, and so I open my mouth to tell the squad about the new plan. Then a thought occurs to me. I key the handset.

"Durzay, where's our urgent going when he gets on the truck, over?"

"Two-Three, the battalion medical officer is headed down here in a convoy. He'll take the casualty, go to COP Payne after you drop him off. They have a trauma center."

Good enough for me. "Roger, solid copy on all. We're moving now." I holster the green gear, take a quick assessment of the situation. Gloves, weapons, helmets, discarded bandage wrappers, used needle from the morphine, backpacks. Jack and two Afghan soldiers and Russ up top on the road. Doc and Ruben, stabilizing Cody. Jason, clearing the area with a metal detector, even after being wounded and knocked out.

Time to go.

It takes us a few minutes to gather everything, then only about thirty seconds to move out. We are one team, united in our mission to save Cody's life.

I tell Jack to work with Russell and take charge of the ANA. I need them to carry gear. To take up the rear of the patrol. To keep cars away. Jack doesn't hesitate. He grabs Cody's flak and rifle and shouts in Dari to the Afghans. They take their positions. I am grateful for Jack. This is not in an interpreter's job description. The Afghan soldiers do not hesitate to pick up extra gear, to take up security positions. They, too, begin to earn my respect.

I ask Jason if he's all right. Not really, he tells me. He can't hold anything heavy in his right hand. And it's too painful to wear his body armor, so someone will have to carry it. One of the Afghans takes it.

"Give me your weapon," I say. It is dented and bent in several places, the optic shattered. I sling it. I hand Jason my green radio.

He nods. I don't need to say anything. He knows what to do. We all know what to do.

So it's me and Doc and Ruben to carry Cody. No stretcher, no sling, no frame. We struggle with the dead weight, finally hoisting him onto our shoulders in a textbook three-man carry. Real infantry shit that you learn in SOI and forget about. You think: when am I going to need this?

Now, apparently.

Except it's exhausting, and awkward. We trip over our feet, a machine with its gears out of order. We're all wearing our helmets and our flak jackets and we get up onto the road and begin to walk, and we don't make it far because we have exhausted the smaller muscles in our triceps and shoulders and we are forced to put Cody down. The infantry textbooks don't account for three different shoulder-heights. Or fatigue, or dehydration. Or a moaning, half-conscious Marine, one hundred and seventy-five pounds of muscle and sinew and bone and dead weight. Or the demoralizing shame of your own failure.

Standing there on the bazaar road, a half-mile or more from our escape, we decide we will need to conduct a fireman's carry. And since this is my fault, and because I know I can manage for at least a short amount of time, I decide to go first.

There is no choice. Today, I am the leader who let his squad run into a bomb. I am also the one who spent the better part of his young life hiding from others in the gym, doing heavy squats and deadlifts and flipping tires, and because of this I know I can carry Cody on my back. I do not know how far, but I know that I can start, and I know that if there is any time to be a leader, it is now. The squad walked right into a bomb because I let us walk there. We were so close to the Hill, and all any of us wanted was to be back, all I wanted was to be back, and now Cody is lying on the ground, bleeding, fading, rasping, because of me. There is no choice.

Ruben and Doc help me load Cody's near-limp form onto my shoulders. I grasp his leg and hand with my right hand, freeing my left arm to swing as I walk. I begin to move.

He is heavy, heavier than my guilt. Slick. Gritty. I feel blood and gravel and bandages falling off, the slick-slime warmth of his blood on my shoulders, sliding, shifting as I try to keep my shoulders from sagging. I bend my knees and try to glide. Lactic acid and mud as I skim along the hard-pack. One leg in front of another, one knee locked in front of another, head forced to look down as Cody's limp form presses on my helmet. The wind buffets from all sides, pitch-black except for the lights on our rifles we use to illuminate the way. Moaning in my ears. Sand in my mouth. Blood on my shoulders.

This is it, I think. All there is.

I am vaguely aware that Jason is walking in front of me, communicating furiously on the radio, his collarbone bleeding, sweeping with his other arm, ensuring we never lose touch with higher, clearing a path. Despite the fact that he was blown up. Despite the fact that he was knocked out. Despite the shrapnel in his neck and face.

Behind me and to my sides Doc engages Cody to keep him from going into shock while Ruben directs the Afghan soldiers. Everyone, Doc included, is carrying extra gear, extra rifles, and Russell's carrying the Thor, and Jack is translating and carrying weapons, and the squad is moving as one unit, and our shared sense of purpose drives us onward.

Meanwhile I am becoming depleted. Sapped. Debilitated. The pain in my legs and chest pushes beyond even the most strenuous of slay sessions I've endured. I want to stop. To cry. To ask for help. To crawl into a ditch and hide from it all.

One, two, three, four, one, two, three, four, one, two, three, four are the sound of my steps.

Keep going.

I can't.

Don't stop.

I must.

You can do this.

Make it stop.

Don't put him down.

Put him down. Take a break.

It is this voice I listen to as I drop him on the ground. He makes a flopping sound that plasters itself inside my brain, never to be dislodged. A sound effect for my failure.

I stand tall, gasping for air. I decide to rip off my flak and helmet. Five, ten, fifteen, thirty seconds, a minute, an eternity. This is cowardice, this is failure, this is not what a leader does, this is enough, no more, pick him up. I tell myself that's enough, no more waiting.

Pick him up, I say to myself, and if you don't it's all for nothing, everything, how Doc kneeled there, blood on his hands, keeping a man from going to the other side, saving Cody's life, and how Jason and Russell got back up and kept being Marines and kept moving and how Ruben ran into the unknown, into the brownout, and how Jack and the ANA and everyone is here, moving, and none of it will mean anything unless you

pick him up.

Pick him up.

Pick him up.

Now.

Right now. Move.

Fucking move.

And I do, and with Doc and Ruben's help again I'm putting Cody back on my shoulders, and I'm walking down a road in a combat zone with a dying man on my back, no body armor and I feel naked and tired but now there is no choice, I decide now that I will die before I put Cody down, and each step is an effort, each yard an achievement, but there is no solace in my pain, no comfortable coasting, just intense lactic breakdown, the single most difficult physical thing I've ever done, and it's all about me now, but it's about Cody, but then I wish for it to stop, to cease, to let me die, let me lie down in the middle of this road, but I can do it and I must do it and even when I think I can't do it I step, one foot in front of the other, so easy to just step, so painful when my knees lock, one after the other and my left arm swings harder, and my right foot plants and my left foot plants, and I'm not thinking about the hard-pack and walking paths and the bombs on the road or the Gator or the storm or the village or the Hill, I'm not thinking about anything, I'm thinking about my breath, and the *schick schick schick* of the bloody dirty sandy scraping stomach on my shoulders, and Cody's semi-conscious and gurgling and then he's unconscious again and my forearm on his hamstring, my hand on his wrist, grabbing and walking and swinging and moving, distance interminable, a yard, a hundred yards, eight hundred yards, my eyes close because I do not need to see, my ears shutter because I do not need to hear, my mouth dry because I do not need to drink, and we are thin and underfed and overpatrolled and dehydrated and I walk so long the adrenaline fades, I accept things as they are, pain, there is only pain, only now, only here, only the slow, debilitating march toward—

headlights

and two figures standing in the brilliant glow, and as I see them adrenaline jump-starts my heart, I am revived. The silhouetted men do not move, they stand stock-still, slack-jawed, as if watching a passing train. Their surprise kindles anger in me but I am far too exhausted to be indignant about these men and I have no time for them because a man is dying on my shoulders.

I keep walking, following someone I recognize, navigating the corrugated-iron doors of the bazaar I know so well, until I come to the open rear door of an armored vehicle, agape and welcoming, and though I am dizzy I unfurl Cody into the back with the help of men I do not recognize. Doc jumps into the back with Cody, starts working on him again and all of a sudden I'm facing Jason.

He hands me the radio.

Take care of Cody, I tell him.

I will, he says.

And before I know it they are gone.

We are alone. The storm has subsided. The stars protrude from their cloud-cover and offer us tiny sparkles for our efforts.

Ruben puts his hand on my shoulder and offers me a cigarette. I gladly accept.

There's a pile of odds and ends lying on the ground in front of a collection of blue barrels. Leftover metal detectors, a sickle, Cody's torn clothes. Helmets and rifles.

I drag on a Pine and rifle through Cody's blouse and trousers. Attached to a belt loop I find a pair of dented dogtags scored by shrapnel.

Cody Fisher. Protestant.

Alive.

We return to the Hill, three fewer than we left.

15

Visitors

In some wars, getting blown up is as common as brushing your teeth. Not in Afghanistan. Here you almost always survive the morning. You keep performing the mission, whatever that is. And when you do get blown up, you go back to this fucked-up version of normal, even though you're not ready yet. You still rotate the watch. You still leave the base. You still send up patrol cards. You do the same thing you were doing before. The same thing every day. Day in, day out.

Here's one. Security patrol in vicinity of sectors D4X and D4Z in order to meet with local elders, Hajji Nuralee and Hajji Ayatullah. Depart friendly lines at 0500, return at 1100 hours.

Or maybe it's this one. Conduct deliberate vehicle checkpoint in vicinity of Hajji Mohammad in order to interdict contraband and deter the enemy. Depart friendly lines at 1530, return at 1730.

What is the mission? It's a security patrol in the vicinity of sectors D4X and D5A in order to observe nighttime and early-morning patterns of life near the Helmand River and resupply Patrol Base KT-4. Depart at 0300, return at 1000. Big patrol.

Or it's a security patrol in the vicinity of D4X and D4Z in order to meet with Hajji Sailani and provide nighttime security for Hajji Sailani's village. Depart at 1800, return at 2100.

Or it's Operation Gridlock: a deliberate vehicle checkpoint. Depart at 1300, return 1400, go back out at 0120, return 0620.

Security patrol in the vicinity of D4X and D4Z in order to meet with local elders and spread an information operations message in Hajji Khaled Kalay. Depart 1500 and re-enter at 1900.

Or maybe it's a night observation post in the vicinity of Hajji Mohibullah Kalay and Hajji Nuralee Kalay. And maybe you're departing at 0200 and returning at 0600, but instead of walking all the way to Hajji Mohibullah Kalay in the dark you just sit down behind a wall where the GBOSS can't see you. And maybe every once in a while you just call in the position reports of the places you're supposed to be but you aren't until you have to walk back to base. And maybe you do more and more of this as the days and the nights pass without sleep or rest or pur-pose, as the chance of getting your legs blown off increases because you can't see any goddamn indicators in the dark, as the risk outweighs the need to walk five clicks to a village where there are definitely going to be bombs, and where they'll know you're there anyway from the dogs barking, and where the person in charge will lie to your face.

From up the chain of command you get a new task. A census of the local population. Time to figure out who's who and where they live. So you sketch out your villages, grab your pens and your rite-in-the-rain notebook. You join up with another squad and start talking to people. Knocking on doors. Taking down names. Names like Babrak Andar and Mullah Sattar and Hemat Sehab and Juma Khan and Qari Azizullah. Mononymous men with orange fingernails, like Sadar and Zendani and Zemari and Zulmai. Maybe one time you find a huge bag of what looks like liquid heroin, and some pictures of a young man with the Mujahideen, and some Taliban letters. You take the guy in for questioning, thinking maybe this will lead somewhere: actionable intelligence that helps flush out an IED lab, helps stop drug money funneled into explosives used to kill American and Afghan soldiers.

You see the guy you detained walking down the road a week later. Nobody ever tells you why he was released.

And maybe during this most important mission, this census, you take pictures of dwellings. Label them so you can remember.

Compound eighteen. Pallawanakha. Agha Mohammed. Three males, five females. No guns.

Compound four. Qari Khan. Ten people, four men, no guns.

Compound ten. Thirteen people, four men, no guns.

Compound five. Jamal. One bolt-action rifle in dubious firing condition. You take him back to Durzay to register the gun with the Afghan Army because God forbid anyone in this war-torn country has a weapon to protect themselves. But then again, maybe he's Taliban. You almost feel like you're doing something, when all you're really doing is collecting grid squares.

And maybe on one of these missions your men teach an Afghan kid to say "fuck this country." They make him shout it in return for a pen.

And instead of stopping them you laugh along.

The price of a combat action ribbon. Some pay all they've got. Others, not so much. It seems the higher your rank the less you pay. It's no secret that Marines covet this tiny red and blue and yellow piece of cloth. We peek enviously at each other's uniforms when we're all dressed up. Someone comes back from deployment and you ask them: did you get a CAR? How did you get it?

We convince ourselves there are degrees of combat. The most permanent proof of that is the ribbon on your chest in a dress uniform.

You bear witness to immense insecurity in the ranks of the Marine Corps regarding the lack of a CAR. The grunts especially. A deployment goes by without earning a CAR—did you even really do your job? You are the infantry. The fighting front line. Your profession is to create chaos upon the enemy, to sow discord and spring hate from the barrel of a machine gun, or a rifle, or a SMAW.

But when the enemy is invisible, you create chaos only among yourselves. Men fake firefights and say things happened when they didn't. They disregard the immensity and danger of their own deployment. They forget that walking around is dangerous enough.

To bring home a combat action ribbon in Afghanistan often means finding yourself on the receiving end of a bomb you can't shoot back at. When Cody and Russell and Jason earned their combat action ribbons, it came at the cost of one Marine sent home permanently, one shipped to Dwyer and back, and one toughing it out with a concussion up on the Hill. For the others on that patrol, we earned ours through the crushing shockwave of the yellow-bucket IED that cleansed us of the notion of this war being some sort of adventurous summer jaunt south of the Hindu Kush. We earned it running our hands through blood-soaked clothes and cutting off sleeves of FROG-blouses. We earned it carrying the weight of extra weapons and armor. We earned the combat action ribbon on the walk back to the Hill, so dehydrated we could no longer sweat, walking in the pitch-dark and just missing another IED that we found the next day. We earned it without firing a shot.

Those of us who came home without this token of inflated importance did everything expected of a Helmand province grunt. We did the work that nobody else was cut out to do.

Other Marines tried to do our job. Engineers with their hyper-alert 360-degree turns and goggles on their helmets. Light armored reconnaissance. Artillerymen. They managed; we thrived. We were made and molded to endure such things, to be proficient at the tactical application of war. To carry out any mission until we fall from death or starvation. There is honor in that. Even if you did not get a combat action ribbon, there is untold honor in the profession of the infantry.

There is little hope that the Marine Corps will ever change its view on combat action ribbons. You can walk over a bomb, grab at it with a sickle, pull it out with your bare hands and you'll never get one. It must explode. You must endure the cleansing test of fire to gain this yellow-red-and-blue bit of cloth. You must take a test you might not survive.

In the days and weeks after they get hit, I learn which hospitals Cody and Jason are in. We hear about Cody's touch-and-go surgeries. His blood loss and his scarring. I speak with Jason on the phone, a tense conversation only because I'm so unprepared to talk to him. At night I shake and hyperventilate and think about what I'm supposed to say if I ever get to see Cody again. We move into the hottest days of the summer, down two, replaced by two. We walk slower. We take fewer chances.

A few days after the blast I notice Cody's blood on my flak jacket. I do not wash it off. I do not want to forget.

You'd think that being isolated in the countryside would keep visitors away. Instead, the Hill attracts war tourists like flies to trash.

We always know when someone's coming. We see them stumbling in the knee-high grass as they approach. We hear them on the radio. They're required to request permission before they come in. Sometimes they don't request until they're almost on top of us. The other squads in the platoon do this sometimes as well, as if they're trying to catch us doing something naughty.

A platoon of engineers heads out to us. I'm told on the radio that they're coming to determine the feasibility of building a road to the Hill. Construction-type engineers, not the infantry attachments I'm used to. Like Demir, the engineer who came out to the Hill briefly at the beginning of the deployment. A giant of a man. Wizard with a saw and a hammer. He made the plywood table, and the weights, and the pullup bar. He left as fast as he came. Abandoned us for greener pastures. Every time we undertake a project around the Hill, I miss his knowledge and instincts for building. Now I hear he's making bench-press stations at the company combat outpost.

These engineers are disciplined and clean-shaven and alert as they walk the half-mile from their vehicles on the road to the Hill. Never have I seen more 360-degree turns, more heads-on-swivels, more M-frame sunglasses and Marine Corps-issue Nomex gloves. Their plate carriers are dirty, but dirty like a dealership's brand-new car after a test drive in the snow. My body armor is the beater you keep outside year-round, the one that always starts when you need it.

When they clamber up the Hill I'm there to greet them, one hundred and fifty-five pounds of Clif bars and Nescafe. I'm shaking hands with their Staff Sergeant and Lieutenant when they call me by the wrong rank.

"So, Sergeant, how long have you guys been out here?"

It makes me flash a knowing smile at Ruben, who's standing by, listening in. I'm not even wearing chevrons.

The Lieutenant and I tour the Hill and bullshit a little. He comments on the state of the place. Gives some compliments. Tells me he'd love to get a little Caterpillar up here, something to help fill the Hesco and dig out the hooches. A pipe dream. I entertain him.

We're circling around the berthing area when I catch sight of something that makes the hair on the back of my neck stand on end. Something I haven't seen in months.

A ponytail.

There's a woman in the group and she's just taken off her helmet. Though I'm talking to the engineers' leadership, I can't help but shoot guilty sideways glances at her.

Our female companionship on this deployment has been the solitary Playboy magazine we keep in the shitter and gigabytes of pornography on our iPods. There is an implicit understanding that every time you pick up the Playboy in the shitter, you pick up fluids and sweat of every other man on the Hill, but this does not bother you anymore because most things do not bother you anymore.

Now, for the first time, a member of the opposite sex visits the Hill. An engineer. A female Marine. It's impossible to tell if she's attractive. Not that it matters.

I can already sense my men inching closer, trying to get a better look. Nonchalant, like the reason they're all suddenly standing around in groups of three by the berthing area isn't to get a glimpse of a real, live woman, to see a female face not covered by a *burqa*. We are guiltily transfixed. We know that nothing can come of this, and this knowledge only makes our collective, silent longing more painful, a testosterone-induced craving persisting even in the grime and the danger of combat.

The rest of her platoon is male, and as they catch our eyes glancing they huddle closer to her, protectively, instinctively. As if we, the filthy locals, ever had a chance.

All we want, all anyone wants, is to break General Order One, the edict that prohibits sex between military personnel in Afghanistan. We envy the masses of soldiers who violate this order every day at giant Forward Operating Bases, places like Bagram and Kandahar and Dwyer and Bastion, massive bases where men and women work side-by-side, screwing in air-conditioned container houses between trips to Green Bean Coffee. Throughout Afghanistan, soldiers and Marines and airmen and sailors fuck away the loneliness of Their Personal Wars while we, the dirtiest of grunts, jerk off into plastic bags with sweat in our eyes and dirt under our fingernails, our asses chapped by endless walks in bumfuck, Helmand Province, our uniforms black and stiff with grime.

Ours is a fleeting fantasy. There is nothing to be done about it except to allow my men and myself the twenty-minute thrill of vivid imagination, stolen glances and unrepeatable whispers. Things are said by discourteous and lonely twenty-one-year-olds that do not reflect well on anybody. I make sure these things are not said within earshot of the woman or her fellow engineers. The lurid underbelly of the Corps stays hidden in our whispers. In the end, we know this road leads nowhere.

The engineer Lieutenant, his platoon sergeant and I head up to post one to get a better view of the route. I ask what they plan to do. Maybe build a road, they say. Where, I ask. From the route to the south directly to the Hill. Maybe four hundred meters in a straight shot, somehow accounting for the walls. So I show them the path, and we talk about the logistics. Getting a paver and a bulldozer out here. Grading and gravelling. Leveling a couple of structures, here and there. Buying land from the locals.

"Sergeant, if we get a road out here, how much would that help?" asks the Lieutenant.

"A bit," I answer. "And by the way, sir, I'm not a Sergeant."

"Oh, I'm sorry. Corporal?"

"Lance Corporal, sir."

The Lieutenant is mildly bewildered. I feel a moment of idiotic pride, happy to have unintentionally fooled him.

The engineers pack up to leave. They depart the Hill, turning and sweeping, alert and uncomfortable, and as they go we think about the bigger bases and the deployment that never was.

I'm at Durzay and I'm briefing officers from the battalion that will relieve us in a few months. I'm talking to all the company commanders, the executive officer, and various staff officers.

I am shirtless. I am lifting weights when they walk up and I am shirtless and even as they ask me questions I continue to be shirtless. I do not put my shirt back on. Later Two-Bravo chews me out for it. It doesn't matter, because for reasons I cannot explain it is important not to wear a shirt in this moment. I am a Lance Corporal and Cody had a needle stuck between his ribs and into his lung and I helped write Russell's Purple Heart citation and I do not want to put my shirt back on. Not for them. Not for anyone.

I am shirtless, and they ask questions, and I explain how we fight Our Personal War.

We don't leave the wire without a Thor pack, a sickle, two metal detectors and a dog if he's available. Eight guns minimum, that counts Afghans, doesn't count terps. We don't have vehicles, so we walk everywhere. We don't walk on roads. We don't walk on goat paths. We don't walk anywhere that we've walked on the last three or four or five patrols. We don't cross bridges—we go down a bit and cross the canal instead. We get wet. If we have to cross a bridge we'll see if there are civilians crossing it so we know it's safe. We walk with civilians if we can—they know the safe paths, and the Taliban don't want to kill a regular Afghan, just like we don't. If we come up to a place where two roads or paths meet and we have to go through it, we scrape it up with the end of the sickle, little X's, maybe a foot long, overlapping.

If there are wires, the sickle will pull them up. If there's a pressure plate, the sickle will sink down into the ground. When you bury something there's a pocket of dirt, and then the sickle-head gets up underneath it and you can feel it pulling. And the wire will show in the dirt, like a snake, and if you get lucky and you catch a big hole with a big yellow jug in it, you can pull that right up by the handle if you want. We don't do that, though. That's EOD's job.

You can also use the sickle to bust up stacks of poppy stalks, or hay, or wherever you think a bomb might be hidden.

It's war. It's not war. It's a game, it's all just a dangerous little game we play with the Taliban. Pretend you're one of them, pretend you're a Taliban spotter, and you've been watching the patrol all day. You say, where would I put this bomb to kill the Marines? And then you avoid those places, if you can. If you can't, you find the bomb. Or try to.

Avoid paths. Sweep. Sickle. You're always being watched, so you can't walk anywhere you've walked before, except there are only so many places you can walk. So sometimes you'll walk the same places again, and that's where it's dangerous. If you can, walk a little to the left, a little to the right. Stick to the rules. The Taliban won't put a bomb where they can't hit one of us. They always want to hit one of us.

An IED is three things: a container of explosives, an activation method, and a battery pack. The components are either together in one hole or they're split up. The explosive is usually fertilizer in a plastic jug. You can't pick it up with a metal detector. The activation method can be a lot of things. Maybe it's a pressure plate. A pressure plate is usually two wooden planks with some carbon rods between it, and when you step on it, it creates an electrical circuit that goes from the battery pack to the blasting cap and blows the whole thing. You can pick up a battery pack with a metal detector, but usually it's off the path, because they know we can pick it up. But they put the bomb itself where they can hit us, on the path.

Three kinds of activation methods: pressure plates, which anyone can step on and blow up; radio, which they can blow up from far away; and kite string, which they can blow up by pulling on a long activation string. There's also a thing called pressure release, where you move something and it blows up. We've never found one. But they're out there.

If you're near a village, and there are kids and civilians walking down the road, there won't be pressure plates, otherwise anyone could step on it and kill themselves, taking a couple of kids along with them. They'll use a kite string, or a garage door opener, so they can blow it up when we're walking by.

The Taliban know our Thor blocks radio signals, so they'll probably put a kite string in. Those are the most frightening. You know someone's watching you, and there's nothing you can do about it.

Our Personal War is a minefield, devoid of antagonists. Though we want desperately to hold somebody accountable, to shoot and kill, we cannot. There is nobody to fight. There is nobody to kill. Today, and tomorrow, and every day we leave the wire, we have but one purpose: to walk around and try not to die.

One day we're visiting Durzay when I see my old squadmate, Levi. He's come down on a convoy of up-armored MRAP's and MAT-V's, vehicles designed to withstand IED blasts, armed with .50 caliber machine guns and Mk-19 grenade launchers. They are as indicative of the reality of this war as Cody's newly-earned combat action ribbon. A defensive shell. An expectant target. The type of vehicle the military buys for survivability instead of lethality. We are not supposed to kill anybody. No, we are here just to play whack-a-mole with the Taliban. And we are not the mallet.

"How you been? What are you doing out here?"

"Good man, really good. I'm on the battalion jump platoon. I ride around with the battalion commander and visit the different positions."

"You guys out of the big FOB up north?"

"Yep."

"How is it?

"It's great. Really great. Great gym, exchange, chow hall. Frickin' awesome man." Levi rarely swears. Instead he substitutes with words

I stopped using in third grade. Antique terms like heck and frick and darn but spoken honestly, without airs.

"What's the team like?"

"Lot of senior guys. Everybody's really chill, mature. I love it. It's great, man. Really swell."

"How's the BC?"

"He's great. Big on Crossfit. Has this one thing where he always wants a bag of paleo beef jerky under his seat." He shrugs. "No big deal."

Jump platoons are drawn from all over. A collection of odd cats. He's in good company. I feel genuinely happy for him, though throughout our conversation there are sentences that congeal on the back of my teeth but never make it out. Hard sentences, with implications that I'm not really ready to consider. Sentences that indicate a shared suffering that I don't want to acknowledge.

This time's different, isn't it?

Deployment's so much better when you're not a boot.

Look at us now.

I choose not to say these things. I feel as if I lack familiarity with Levi now. My insecurity about our first deployment leads me down the path I always find myself on: imagining that the person I'm talking to doesn't like me, doesn't want anything to do with me. I imagine that Levi has somehow read my mind, as though he knows that I chose not to stand up for him when he was treated poorly, even when standing up would have accomplished nothing. But it's impossible to read minds, and right now he is joyful and exuberant, talking about the chow hall up at battalion, the size of the gym, the relaxed schedule he keeps. He is now, again, the innocent Levi I knew a year ago. The one who taught me about LARP'ing and invited me to visit him in West Virginia. It seems we are still friends.

I tell him about the Hill. He's heard about us getting hit. Says it's big news all over. People are talking about it throughout the AO. I give a restrained smile and don't say much.

When the battalion commander finds me, I bid Levi farewell. The BC and I speak for a few minutes. We take our shirts off. We do ring dips and muscle-ups on the gymnastics rings hanging from Durzay's pullup bar. He tells me I'm doing a good job. Tells me we're all out here doing outstanding work. He hands me a coin. I'd rather have Cody back.

I wave goodbye to Levi as the trucks leave the base, kicking up gravel and moondust.

Two reporters visit the Hill.

The first has a very hard time getting to us. He's old and out of shape and probably doesn't belong in a war zone. Somehow he manages to hop on a short jaunt from Durzay with some General and a Sergeant Major and Two-Actual. Two-Bravo comes out earlier that day and helps us clean up the base. Makes sure we're wearing good uniforms, that we've shaved and our hair is in accordance with the Marine Corps Way: slightly longer and dirtier than garrison. Our good image is his good image.

We watch as the helicopter lands at Durzay, a whirl of sand and rotors and a prime target if any Taliban ever had the initiative to shoot at it.

The detachment plods along from the platoon's home to the bazaar, stops briefly, then humps from the bazaar to us. I'm excited for the General to arrive. I go through the script of what I'm to talk about when he gets here. What should I highlight? How we burn shit next to where we sleep? Or perhaps the bug arena? No, I took that down already.

I wonder: what would a General say if he saw a Lance Corporal running a base out here? Perhaps he'll promote me on the spot. Perhaps he'll give out coins—that precious commodity, a rarity in the Marine Corps, coveted like an academic degree or a war trophy. Given out in lieu of something permanent, like a ribbon. Perhaps he'll tell me the machine guns on post one are dirty.

Perhaps he'll fire me and put a dildozer in charge.

About a hundred yards from the Hill they take a knee. A long pause, then a split into two elements. I watch as ever so slowly the element with the General turns around and heads back to Durzay.

My stomach sinks. My adrenaline washes down through my feet and out into the ground. An opportunity trudges away from the Hill.

"You have got to be fucking kidding me," someone says.

"They're just gonna turn around like that?"

"You mean we cleaned up this whole fucking place for nothing?"

"So if the General's not coming up, who are the other guys?"

"I don't know."

"Why are they turning around?"

"Who's the civilian wearing the old ass gear?" someone asks.

Through the binoculars I see a figure in the middle of the patrol, getting ready to fall out. Even at this distance I make out his red face and his ill-fitted helmet. He looks close to heat stroke.

"I don't know. Reporter, maybe?"

"Did anyone say we were getting a reporter?"

"Nobody told me."

"Staff Sergeant, are we supposed to be getting a reporter?"

"I'm not sure," says Two-Bravo.

"Is he staying here?" Terrance asks.

"He has a daypack," remarks Ruben.

"So he's gonna stay?"

"Maybe, I don't know," I say.

"Who do you think he's a reporter for? Like a newspaper?"

"I don't know, man."

"There's a reporter coming?" asks Russell.

"Listen, boot, you gotta keep up with the situation," says Terrance. "Don't ask stupid fucking questions."

Russ is straight-faced. "So is that a yes?"

Terrance looks up at the sky, the picture of exasperation. "This is old fucking news, man. You gotta catch up on current events, mother-fucker."

Russ shrugs. He eats some expired Reese's Pieces.

"Is the General coming?" he asks.

The whole squad groans and rolls their eyes.

"Get the fuck over here so I can smack the stupid out of you," Terrance says. Russell darts just out of reach.

"Since the General's not coming we'll probably get a motivated speech from the Sergeant Major," Ivan whispers to me, careful not to let Two-Bravo hear.

"Great. I didn't think this day could get any worse."

"Which Sergeant Major is he anyway?"

"I don't know."

"Maybe he'll stay overnight. Then we can have a shitty day tomorrow, too."

"I'll put a dildozer in his sleeping bag if he does."

My green gear squawks. "KT-4, KT-4, this is Two-One Bravo."

"Two-One Bravo, go for KT-4."

"Roger, request permission to enter friendly lines, eight packs, how copy, over."

"Roger, solid copy. Permission granted."

"Roger, out."

We watch the patrol begin the arduous climb up the embankment and arrive at the top. The Sergeant Major, well-muscled and lean in the way career Marines tend to be, unfastens his flak, puts his gear down and pulls out an eight-point cover, like he's standing in formation on the parade deck at the depot. The sweaty maybe-reporter is conspicuously absent.

"Good morning, Sergeant Major," I say, affecting a good mood.

"Mornin' devil," says the Sergeant Major. He is well-fed and sweaty, his uniform clean and soft-looking. He outweighs the heaviest Marine on the Hill by at least twenty-five pounds, and me by probably close to seventy-five.

I hear panting and scuffing feet and I turn to see a red-faced man in his fifties pushing on his knees as he slogs up the hard-packed dirt. He wears a t-shirt with an old tan flak jacket, a green uncovered helmet and brown cargo pants. A camera hangs across his chest like a bandolier. The Marine who stayed with him on his trudge up the hillside throws an exasperated look my way. I just shrug. If this is where he wants to be, then here he is. But I won't babysit him. And he definitely isn't going out on patrol with us, not if the hump from Durzay to the Hill is this difficult for him.

The reporter flops down on Nate's cot like a newly caught fish on the deck of a trawler. I smell laundry detergent.

"Water?" someone asks the reporter. He nods. One of my guys takes a bottle from the cooling pit and hands it to the old man, who chugs it down with speed and intensity. He asks for another one and pours it on his head. The water and the sweat drip onto Nate's rack, soaking it through. The old man takes another bottle and starts drinking again. I look at Terrance. We're going to have to slow this guy down.

We mingle and bullshit with the Durzay Marines, then I talk to the Sergeant Major. Our conversation is like every conversation I have with every higher-up that comes to the Hill. They all blend together, asking the same questions, getting the same answers. I give interchangeable responses to interchangeable queries. After a while they all sound the same. The only thing different about this conversation is the reporter.

I ask the Sergeant Major who the old man writes for. He tells me the name of a military-oriented publication.

"What's he doing up here?"

"I guess he wants to write something about you all."

"How long's he staying, Sergeant Major?"

"Couple days. He heard about you. The IED, all that. He wanted to come down and see what y'all were up to. You all are gonna be famous." He gives me a serious look. "Keep him safe now, oohrah? You do your best to keep him out of trouble."

"He looks like he might have a heat stroke, Sergeant Major."

"Well, then, it's your job to make sure he doesn't."

"Roger that, Sergeant Major."

"Don't you take him out on patrol, either."

"Even if he wanted to, I wouldn't take him. I don't want to pick his body up out of a canal when he has a heart attack."

One unique part, the reporter, and then the conversation is the same as every other, bits and pieces blending together so I can't tell who asks them or when they ask them, imitations of each other, the same body language, the hands on the hips, the raised eyebrows followed by pursed lips and dirt-scuffing the ground. It is the same as every conversation we have with every visitor, with everyone who comes to the Hill, except this time it's with a Sergeant Major, who speaks in Sergeant Major-isms. It goes something like this:

"Place is a shithole," the Sergeant Major remarks. "Where do you sleep?"

"Out here, Sergeant Major. On the cots."

"You don't live in these bunkers?"

"No, Sergeant Major."

"How come?"

"Too hot."

"Even down in there? In the dark?"

"Yes, Sergeant Major. Too hot during the day and at night. Got too hot about three weeks after we came up here."

"Y'all ain't got no air conditioning units you can put in there?"

"Negative, Sergeant Major. And we couldn't run them if we did."

"Why's that?"

"The generator doesn't work."

"Well why the hell doesn't the generator run?"

"It just doesn't work, Sergeant Major."

"Devil dog. What do you mean it doesn't work?"

"It stopped working the day after it came up here."

"Did you try to fix it?"

"Yes, Sergeant Major."

"You ever get another one?"

"This is number three. We had two before this one."

"And all of them broke?"

"Yes, Sergeant Major."

The Sergeant Major puts his hands on his hips, wrinkles his eyebrows close together. He walks to the machine, turns a dial or two. Presses a squishy black fuel thing on the side. Kicks it.

"So you got no electricity?"

"No, Sergeant Major."

"Anyone ever come up here to repair it? Mechanic or something?"

"Yes, Sergeant Major. A gen mech. He couldn't fix it."

"He say what was wrong with it?"

"Yes, Sergeant Major."

He raises his eyebrows at me. "Well?"

"He said it needed a part."

"Did he say he was gonna get that part?"

"He said he would get the part."

"He ever come back?"

"No, Sergeant Major."

"How long ago was that?"

"A while. I'm not sure."

A beat. Two.

"Didn't y'all test it before you brought it up here? Did it work then?"

"Yes, Sergeant Major."

"And now it doesn't work."

"No, Sergeant Major."

"Well why the hell not?" he asks.

"It's just too hot, Sergeant Major," I say.

"It's just too hot," the Sergeant Major repeats. "It's just too damn hot."

Gathered around the berthing area, the Sergeant Major gives a rousing, characteristic morale speech to the squad. The kind filled with vague Marine Corps advice, the key currency of Sergeants Major, things like keep our rifles clean and shave our faces, remember we're Marines first. He reminds us we're fighting the right fight, the good fight, training the Afghan soldiers and protecting the population. And we should make sure to get haircuts regularly. I run my hand through my own hair, long and filled with oil and dirt, standing on its own.

A rousing speech. A characteristic Marine Corps speech. A speech any Sergeant Major would be proud of. I forget it immediately. He departs with the other squad and Two-Bravo.

The reporter stays, and despite my initial skepticism he turns out to be a nice guy. A bit of an oddball, some sort of freelancer who's seen some shit and written about it.

For three days he hangs out around the Hill, hovering on the margins of the squad, occasionally asking questions, drinking our cold water.

The reporter's habit is to strip down to his silk shorts and t-shirt and sit on a rack, panting and looking around through fogged spectacles. Because of this habit we quickly notice he doesn't wear anything underneath his shorts. His testicles, wrinkled like a bulldog's jowls and covered in long white hairs, emerge from the depths of his shorts and sprawl upon the green cot. In the heat his balls stick to the fabric like velcro. He splays his balls for all of us to see, day and night, never seeming to notice that they've emerged from their silk sanctuary. We do not tell him. Instead, we give him an affectionate nickname.

Old Balls.

Old Balls is genuinely interested in the squad, and he seems to enjoy our black humor. He has a grand time huffing and puffing around the camp, inspecting half-finished projects, eating MRE's. When we ask him about his job he expounds at great length. He is well-travelled, having crisscrossed the theater as a war correspondent. He eats dinner with the Marines and the Afghan soldiers, who welcome him as a new face. At any given moment I worry he is going to have a heart attack, yet his obvious enthusiasm for being here shines through and endears him to us.

After three short days of sea stories and cigarettes we escort Old Balls down the Hill and across the fields to Durzay, where he catches a convoy out. Before he leaves he gives us his contact information, an email address and a phone number. He tells me he'll send the article he's going to write about us.

True to his word, a few weeks later I open an email with a link to the story as I'm sitting in the sweltering computer tent at Durzay. It is a good article, painting the squad in a good light, talking about recent events. I send it to my father, who tells me he's proud. I tell him not to send it to Grandma. He asks why.

Isn't it obvious, I say? The story is about us getting blown up.

The other reporter who visits the Hill isn't like most. He's a combat camera Marine. He carries a rifle and wears body armor, but his primary weapon system is a high-definition digital camera. He points and shoots at us all day on two different patrols. He hits us with shutter after shutter, clicking and walking. He is professional and poised.

The Combat Cameraman is there and not there. He walks within the squad but carries nothing extra. He is in shape and keeps up with us just fine, traipsing in front or in back, looking for a shot. When he points the camera at me I am self-conscious. I try not to pose, but I know I do, and despite my affectations he captures me in a way I've never been captured before.

Later, when I see the photographs, I am struck by how war-like they are. How they remind me of the most famous pictures I've seen of Marines. How well-shot they are. Composition, shadows, lighting.

He captures me with my helmet off, seated in Hajji Khalid's village, my hand on my chin, talking to the elder. Jack's picking at grass. You can see the dirt on my Oakley sunglasses. The grease in my hair.

He shoots the moment one of one of my guys strikes a poppy stack with our short sickle, forcing a cloud of dust and dry stalks into the air. The missing antennae on our Thor pack. An eerie snippet of time, captured forever: seconds later, we find an IED in that poppy stack.

Over Tony's camouflaged shoulder he photographs the controlled detonation of the IED. A dust cloud fifty feet high. A calm Marine. A picture that circulates around the internet for years to come. A classic snapshot of war, posted and reposted on social media pages, the identity and context of its subject lost to history.

A Marine of the Hill, seated, extending his hand to a small child. His uniform is soaked at the shoulders and the boots, wet from sweat and ditch-water alike. He smiles, and the boy smiles back.

Pictures of me jumping over a broken ditch-bridge, my rifle in one hand, nothing in the other, looking down at the quickly approaching ground. Terrance giving Doc a hand up coming out of a deep canal; you see Doc from Terrance's perspective. A first-person view. Terrance and I on the radios, calling in the ordinance disposal experts. The whole patrol, laid out before the Hill. Searching an elder with Ruben and the Afghan Army.

After the war I look back at these eighteen photographs and wonder how I got so lucky. Bomb Squad skips the posed, blurry pictures of our forebears, transcending into a living art-piece, a part of the chronicle of the Afghanistan war, Helmand Province, 2011. We are not just in the story, we are the story. Ten guys on a Hill, surrounded by fields and each other, grateful to survive another day. Filmed as we were, not as we wanted to be. Men at war are rarely captured so well. Nothing is posed. The bomb in the poppy stacks is real. The inexperienced, anxious Lance Corporal is really having a conversation with a man who dealt with Russians and cultivates heroin-producing plants.

But the combat cameraman is also a visitor, and so he too leaves. Like the other reporter, he tells us where to find the story. One day, when we are back at Durzay, I go into the computer tent and look at the website he told me to search. The story is similar to the other one. But in this story, there are pictures, good pictures and words, except he's far better with the pictures than the words and so the pictures stand out on the page like exhibits in a museum. And of these pictures there is one that strikes me more than any other.

It is a Marine, silhouetted against the dying sun, head turned to the left, standing on a canal embankment. He is framed by rough plant shoots, taller than him, to his left. His radio antenna leans gently from a pouch under his arm. He is alert, scanning out from his vantage point, his shoulders pulled back like a wrestler's.

He is me. And when I see him I think of Jason and Cody.

I turn the computer off quickly.

16

Lance Corporal of Marines

Nobody tells you how hard it is to lead your friends. I'm a Lance Corporal, they're Lance Corporals, and all I want to do is shoot the shit. Skate. Smoke Pine Lights out by the burn pit. Let somebody else make the decisions.

But on any given day there's a squad up here that needs radio batteries, or water, or ammunition. Ten men and a dog that need feeding. Two daily excursions that need destinations. Disputes that need settling. No matter how underqualified I think I am, it's my problem. It's all my problem.

Since the beginning of the deployment I've lost nearly twenty pounds on a frame that can afford to gain ten. Physically, I'm a jungle cat. Mentally I find my patience and my intellect exhausted beyond anything I've experienced. Every night I stay up to talk to the men on post. I am awakened from sleep in the middle of the night to speak to higher. Long day patrols where I sweat anxiety with every step, frying my adrenal glands. Midnight observation posts where I strain to watch shady farmers dig through night vision monocles.

I feel guilty for feeling sorry for myself, but that doesn't stop me from engaging in unbridled bouts of self-pity. I doubt myself. Many days I wish they would send a Sergeant or a Corporal out here. Someone with qualifications and training. Just let me be a fireteam leader again. One among many. Tell me where we're going and I'll suit up my team and we'll hop to it and you can lead us there, Sergeant. As long as I don't have to make any hard decisions about who goes first or whose turn it is to walk point or who gets to live.

Because the Marine Corps Way insists on perfection, even tasks I delegate need my supervision. If someone takes out a patrol, I check their cards and grids. If logstats get recorded, I double-check for accuracy before they're sent up. The only standard is the Marine Corps standard, even though this slips further and further away as we drive deeper and deeper into the deployment. I don't know how to slow down in my pursuit of it, and it shows in my eyes, my speech, my demeanor. I become involuntarily imperfect. The war makes my neck thin and my shoulders stooped. Each day I survive on an inner fire of insecurity and fear of letting anyone—my men, the Bravo, the Actual, the Marine Corps—down. But it does not come easy. I am not Sergeant Hernandez of my first deployment. I am not superhuman.

I am just a young, scared Marine. I deal with the same things that the other men of the Hill do, and maybe do a worse job of handling them. Food poisoning and pit vipers, coffee running out, tearing the seat of my pants. Higher-ups come to the Hill which means a battle to get the men shaved and in proper uniforms, but it's so hot I let them wear pants and a skivvy shirt. Then all of a sudden someone's upset they got the same crappy shift on post two nights in a row, so I have to tell one friend to switch with another friend, except I can't pull rank and I sure as hell can't intimidate him. I have to persuade him to do it, and even when I'm done he's still not happy because grunts aren't happy.

Or maybe the chopper drops off supplies at the bottom of the Hill and we need to get everything from the bottom to the top, and every man can carry two boxes of MRE's at a time, except some of the men choose not to and only carry one, which slows down the whole operation. So I have to figure out how to get the men to carry two boxes at a time, and to get the ones that are slacking to move faster, and to have someone on overwatch with a machine gun, making sure we don't get smoked. But who's on overwatch? Who's on the working party? Who gets to rest? How do we get all these cases up onto the Hill when it's a hundred and twenty degrees and humid like Tampa? And how do I get them to start moving again, knowing that we have a grueling evening patrol and nobody's going to sleep tonight?

It's everything. It's all the time. I need to persuade my team leaders to fill the Hesco barrier on the exposed north side of the Hill while I'm out making friendly overtures to Hajji Zulmai. The Hesco barrier, normally filled by engineers driving a backhoe, needs to be filled by hand, with entrenching tools and a lone shovel. A monumental task, maybe essential to the survival of the squad if we're ever attacked on that side, maybe pointless because we've never been shot at. Pouring dirt in the square wall seems utterly futile while you're doing it. My men shovel scoop after scoop of dirt into the endlessly deep Hesco, never feeling like they're getting anywhere, asking "why don't we just leave it as-is?" as if that thought doesn't speed through my head every time I look at it. Sometimes I come back from patrol, and nothing's been improved, and nothing's been done, and I am a Lance Corporal in charge of Lance Corporals. I drop flak and work on it myself, waiting for the men to join me. They usually do. They are extraordinary men and they are doing the best they can and I am one of them because I am a Lance Corporal. With rank, perhaps we'd get more done. Perhaps the other squad leaders at Durzay would cut me some slack. Perhaps Bravo and Actual would let me slide more. But without rank, I can play chess and gripe and complain. I don't have to maintain a strict social isolation. I can ask Jason and Terrance their opinion and they'll tell me what they really think.

What they feel, what we all feel, is a growing sense of isolation from the outside world, from the rear echelon Marines at Dwyer, even from our platoon-mates down at Durzay. Festering resentment boiling over. Sometime soon, we're told, we'll need to come down off this Hill, and then we'll be among our peers again. Everything is measured in degrees. Justified or not, we rate our degree of danger, brutality, combat as higher than the ones down at the base just three-quarters of a mile away. Where once we were house animals, wondering when we would be let back in, now we are a pack of wolves, hunting and surviving on our own. The Hill is our home, our source of greatest hardship and misery, but it is also the thing that differentiates us from the rest of the platoon, the company, the battalion. We are the Lost Boys of the First Battalion, Third Marines, cast away on the furthest-flung island in the Helmand sea. Expended and forgotten. Left to fend for ourselves, with only the Marine Corps Way as our guiding code.

And the Way doesn't suit us any more.

17

Bomb Dog

Ivan was a grunt, just a regular rifleman. Sometime between his first stab at war and his second, his platoon sergeant asked if anyone wanted to be a dog handler. He volunteered, because when he was in Marjah he got blown up and didn't want it to happen to anyone else. Being the dog handler was a way of exerting control over one's circumstances. Fighting IED's is mostly futile work, but maybe with a dog you could nudge fate one way or the other.

He went to a school in Hartford, South Carolina, an explosive detection dog handler course that took about a month. It was good training for Afghanistan. Grassy hills, closed-down schools, some scattered urban environments. Plenty of open fields to replicate how Marines patrol in Helmand.

When you get to dog-handler school, the instructors try to pair you up with a dog that fits your personality. The first dog Ivan had didn't work out. His name was Dude, and they were together for only a day. The trainers introduce the dogs to you by watching you, monitoring as you walk them, ask them to sit, stay, react. The instructors can tell right away if you're not a good fit for a dog, or a dog's not a good fit for you. During this introductory period Dude didn't respond well to Ivan, so Dude went to someone else. Instead Ivan got Willie. Willie was a good dog for him. They clicked right away. Ivan did the rest of the training with Willie, from day two all the way through to the end.

When you're in bomb dog training, you're not training the dog—the dog comes pre-trained, a bomb-sniffing package tailor-raised for the military by a contract. No, you are training yourself on how to handle the dog. The dog already knows how to find scents and respond to commands. From the time they're puppies, these dogs live to find things and get a reward.

So Ivan learned how to handle. On-leash, off-leash. Using hand-and-arm signals, tools and voice commands. Learning which commands work, which ones don't. Some dogs respond better to some commands than others.

Hand up means back, hand left or right means go that way. Dropping the arm means come back. Willie was a black lab, smaller and less aggressive than a German Shepherd, but more nimble and better for the harsh Helmand climate.

Some dogs are food-motivated; these working dogs loved the Kong toy. They are trained into it from birth, deprived of it except on special occasions. The trainers who raise them show tough love, keeping the Kong from them so it means something. Willie lived for the Kong toy. It was like crack to him. But it was reserved for special occasions. Willie would have to find something, a real something, to get the Kong.

During training Ivan would mainly use hand-and-arm signals for directional purposes. To get Willie to sniff he'd give a verbal command: *Hey-Hey!* With this attention grabber Willie would look and Ivan would move his arm right or left to search. Together they'd zero in on the target area, and eventually Willie would find what he needed to find.

Sometimes, if Ivan knew there was something around, he'd say *Hunt it up!* and Willie would pay extra attention. There's something here, Willie would think, and it would make him a little bit more active, sniff a little harder, focus more.

Not that Willie needed to pay more attention. He was a good bomb dog, even for bomb dogs, and he could find a homemade explosive wherever it was hidden. At the schoolhouse and in Hawaii and at Camp Dwyer they exposed him to updated scents as the unit received more and more substances. Homemade explosives of the like used in IED's downrange, ammonium nitrate, fertilizer, different combinations of chemicals. Find the scent, get the Kong. Simple. If he was training he got a white bumper toy, which Willie liked, though not as much as the Kong. Sometimes Ivan pulled out the Kong to remind Willie what he was *really* sniffing for. But Willie didn't get it unless he found something real.

When we did our pre-deployment training in Twenty-Nine Palms, the company shipped Willie out to train with Ivan, and then later to Camp Dwyer, Afghanistan. This time together made Willie and Ivan very close. The stronger the bond between dog and handler, the better he finds. Their bond was very strong.

One time, during in-country training, Willie lay down in a place where Ivan and the trainers hadn't hidden anything. Ivan, thinking it was a false hit, brought Willie back and sent him out again. Once more Willie lay down in the same area. So Ivan showed the trainer, walked out to where Willie was relaxing on the dirt, and what do you know: an old plastic bag with a trace amount of homemade explosive still on it, buried a foot deep, maybe years old. Just faint specks of explosive dust clinging to the plastic. Still Willie found it.

Willie was a good dog.

On the Hill the days are hot and long and Ivan tries to take Willie on as many patrols as he can, but the heat is blistering and he can't go out every time. When Willie gets hot he jumps in a canal and swims and cools down. He is young and sturdy. He does not slow the patrol.

If necessary, Ivan can take one of Doc's saline IV solutions and insert it subcutaneously. Squeeze it, drip it under the skin. Let Willie rest in the shade. He can perform basic first aid and canine preventative medicine. He can cover up Willie's feet, protect them from the hot sand, clean anal glands, apply pressure dressings. In emergencies, Ivan can take care of Willie. But the goal is to maximize the dog's utility and avoid emergencies. So Willie can't go on every patrol.

One time a feral dog bites Willie. Ivan carries a nine millimeter Beretta for just this purpose, so he shoots at the feral dog, trying to kill it. He misses. The pistol jams, because it is older than Ivan and the magazine springs are loose and there are no replacements. Before he can bring his rifle around, the dog runs away. We medevac Willie onto a chopper and out to a nearby large base, where the five-hundred-thousand dollar weaponized animal receives rabies shots and Ivan receives an ass chewing for discharging his pistol. He has violated the Marine Corps Way, or maybe just the Idiot's Guide to Counterinsurgency, where someone at a higher echelon of command decided the dogs that Pashtuns leave outside their houses all night and beat with sticks are valued members of the family, and that killing one will gravely damage The Strategy, and we will lose who knows how many weeks or months or years of progress, and that every Afghan dog must be protected and worshipped and paid for if shot.

The EOD guys at Durzay give Ivan the most up-to-date samples to train Willie on. Combinations of homemade explosives in different configurations, each with a different scent, highly distinct to the nose of a trained dog. He spends the cool evenings and mornings running Willie around the Hill, hiding plastic baggies in difficult-to-reach places. When the time comes to find bombs, Willie and Ivan are ready. As far as we can tell, Willie's sniffed out more IED's than any other dog in the battalion.

On one occasion Ivan and Nate and I are clearing a compound, looking for a new spot to put the patrol base. It is a futile search. Nothing we find makes much tactical sense. The compounds are located in strange areas, or full of human shit, or indefensible.

One compound we clear is full of human shit and near a road. Ivan takes Willie through the whole thing, sniffing each corner, clearing it for the rest of us to walk around. Ivan notices one room that isn't connected to any of the others, just a door from the outside that leads to the inside. As they walk toward it Willie's attitude changes.

Hunt it up! Ivan says, and Willie leaps through the window and sits down right on a massive blue jug of homemade explosive with wires coming out of it. Seventy pounds of homemade explosive, hidden for later, to be emplaced on the road, meant to blow up an American vehicle. Willie saves lives that day.

Another time Ivan is walking two-man with a short sickle, hitting haystacks and poppystacks. He always beats the poppystacks, just in case, never knowing what he might find.

He's beating haystacks and using hand and arm signals to send Willie around when he notices another change in behavior—just what you look for in dog handler school. *Hey-hey!* He says, and Willie runs across a road to a poppy stack and lies down. For Ivan this is enough, but for EOD we need two sources of confirmation, so Ivan asks Mario with the Thor to accompany him to the poppystack and beats on it with the sickle. He hits it two, three times and what do you know? A radio antenna, a yellow jug and a quick sprint back to the squad's position in case anyone's watching, or the Thor isn't working.

The bomb is just enough to kill one person nearby. We blow it in place.

When Bomb Squad gets hit on May 25th, when Cody and Jason and Russ are wounded, Ivan watches from the Hill. He hears us scream into our radios and run to the bazaar. For the rest of his life, Ivan thinks about that day. About how Willie would have found that bomb, and the other one nearby, and how Cody's face would have been saved its scarring, and how Jason would have been saved his traumatic brain injury, and how Ivan could have saved even more people than he and Willie would go on to save. But on the Hill, nobody blames Ivan. It's not his fault we got hit. It's nobody's fault. It's my fault. It's just war.

After the war, Ivan gives up the dog. Willie heads back out to combat, while Ivan reenlists and moves on to other assignments. Later Ivan tries to find Willie, to make contact and adopt him, but Willie ends up with someone else. He works for a very long time, a productive career of finding bombs and earning Kong toys and sniffing. He is a good dog. After Afghanistan, Ivan never sees him again.

18

Magic

One evening these two sniper types tell us they're going to provide overwatch from the Hill as we conduct a night patrol. I'm good with it. I have a very specific route to follow. I'm heading out to investigate the area where we recently found an IED, see if anyone comes around to plant another one after dark, catch us where we've walked. At least, that's the plan I send up to higher.

We step off just after sundown. We are practiced and cat-like, agile and avoidant of pitfalls. We pick our way across a series of large canals and park outside the village of Hajji Sailani. We're under no illusions. Plopped on our asses on the side of a canal, half of us have our night vision monocles down while the others adjust their eyes to the darkness. Half of us keep watch while the others relax, just a little. We never see anything on these OP's. I'm sure the Taliban know we're out here, but they're far sneakier than we are, and make far less noise, and look just like everyone else. We'd never catch them if we saw them, and they won't pick a fight in the dark with eight heavily armed and technologically superior Americans. So we sit and we drink Rip Its and we bullshit.

Tonight I've brought some *Magic: The Gathering* cards to play with Nate. It's tough to see the words printed on the card-faces, even in the moonlight, so I turn on my night vision optic. The cards turn green and glow. The writing's still hard to read. With some cards I go by memory. Our playing surface is our laps. Into it we draw seven cards each from two pre-made decks of sixty cards that my dad ordered for us from Amazon. We lay down our land-cards onto our knees, forests and mountains and islands. Tapping for mana and deploying creatures and spells against each other. Taking life. Gaining life. Sorceries and enchantments and turns and tapping and untapping. Drawing cards and putting cards in our graveyards.

It is a moment of sheer absurdity: two Marines playing a fantasy card game through night vision while out on a combat patrol.

Nate attacks, and since I can't block, he deals one damage to me with his Bloodthrone Vampire. I untap and draw a card. I play a plains, tap it for one white mana, and lay down a Silvercoat Lion.

My black radio, near-silent to better keep us hidden, squawks at me. I carefully lay down my hand of cards and bring it up to my ear.

"Say again, last station," I say quietly.

"Roger, this is Skullfire up on the Hill. I said we see movement to your east, about fifty yards."

Nate raises his eyebrow. I shake my head.

"What kind of movement, Skullfire?" I ask the snipers.

"Looks like a guy digging, Two-Three. Putting in an IED."

My eyes roll so far back into my skull I can see my brain.

"Fucking sniper team is out here two days and already they think this is *The Hurt Locker*," I say to Nate, not keying the handset.

"But if we don't go check it out, who knows what they'll do," says Nate.

He has a point. Snipers are always looking for a shot. It's not that they're wrong to do this; it's that we have been indoctrinated with the dogma of not engaging as a first reaction, of ensuring hostile act and hostile intent, both of which I know are hard to discern through a scope in the middle of the night. We have been cautioned against combat, scared straight from taking shots without being shot at. This is not Fallujah in 2004. This is a whole other kind of war. I am worried for the snipers, and for us.

"Roger, Skullfire, it's probably just somebody working on a canal or something, break." Unkey the handset, key it again. "But we'll check it out just in case. Give us a minute to move."

"Roger, Two-Three," comes the reply.

Nate throws up his hands. "I was just about to fuck you up!" he says, flashing a powerful *Magic: The Gathering* card.

"And instead we're going to run down some fucking wild goose chase *bullshit* in the dark," I say, packing up my deck, stuffing it neatly back in its case. "We'll finish later. If we don't take a look, these snipers might do something stupid."

Nate agrees. We all agree. Snipers are an interesting breed. I meet far more Billy Zanes than Tom Berengers. I need a Tom Berenger on the Hill. Someone who will have my back but won't get me in trouble for war crimes. I need a fucking Mark Wahlberg in *Shooter*. What I feel like I have on the Hill is the guy in *Rambo* who shoots at Sylvester Stallone and falls out of a helicopter.

I gather the squad. We start moving east, following the biggest canal we can find.

"Skullfire, this is Two-Three, walk me on to where you saw this guy," I say. The tall shoulders of canals, the bushes and the farm trees obscure our line of sight to the target area. I know there's a village ahead, and maybe a compound or two outside, and I know that the folks in this part of the world like to stand outside after sundown, digging in their fields, hidden from the hot sun by a few hours of night. My socks squelch in my boots as we cross out of a ditch and make it fifty yards or so. I call the snipers again.

"Skullfire, this is Two-Three, I'm about fifty yards from where I was before. Do you see us? I'm shooting IR for you," I say. I wave at Nate to shine his infrared flashlight. "Skullfire, how copy?"

No answer. I lead the men further east, toward the desert sand and Durzay, away from the Helmand River. I send a couple guys to the north and the south, looking for our mystery digger. The snipers take their time answering my calls. Finally the radio burps quiet static waves, the voice of Skullfire, low and jumpy, breathing heavily into my ear, as if he's hiding, as if he's getting ready to tell me a secret.

"Two-Three, the target is actually three hundred meters to your west," he says, and when he does I throw my head back in exasperation. Nate starts to laugh. I jam the handset, annoyed.

"Skullfire, roger, we're returning to base. You can show me what you're looking at when we get up there." I begin to stuff the radio back into my pouch.

"Not only did they ruin our game, now they're wasting our fucking time!" Nate says. The radio comes back to life.

"Negative Two-Three, we're engaging."

Adrenaline-induced paranoia. Fear of consequences.

"Skullfire, are you sure he's—"

Boooooooom

Before I can even finish my question the sky claps, the night air amplifying and pushing a massive booming sonic slap through the atmosphere and into each of the surrounding villages, unmistakably a gunshot from the Hill. The hugeness of it means it's probably a Barrett fifty-caliber sniper rifle, a weapon with a cartridge so large only five fit in the magazine. The bullet snaps as it travels over our heads. I yell at the men to get down, hoping the snipers haven't mistaken us for Taliban. My only comfort is the fact that they're snipers, and snipers are only supposed to shoot once, one bullet per kill, so I pull out my radio, ready to ask for a battle damage assessment, and then

Boooooooom

the sound of a second shot reverberates throughout the countryside. Again the bullet snaps over my head and I think this must be it, two rounds is more than enough but then another *boom* and another snap, and I give up trying to key the radio. Instead I try to figure out where the snipers are shooting. *Boom* again, and again, and then a short break.

I poke my head up over the embankment, looking around in my nightvision, but I see no movement.

Boooooooom

The snipers must have reloaded. They've fired six rounds now, *seven, eight,* and I'm racking my brain to think what could have possibly drawn their ire, *nine,* to shoot this many rounds from a sniper rifle. There are no rounds being fired in return, *ten,* and the night is deadly silent save for the gunshots. I'm being hailed on the radio by Durzay but I don't answer because the shooting starts up again, another reload, *eleven, twelve, thirteen* rounds fired from my Hill. I imagine an Afghan man out there, Taliban maybe but probably just a farmer, scurrying around frantically, still visible in a white-hot thermal scope, darting from cover to cover. I wonder, *fourteen, fifteen,* if the man knows why he's being shot at, and I wonder why the snipers are missing. I am stunned at the inaccuracy, the need to shoot three magazines at one target, an affront to the mantra of one shot, one kill, ready to die but never will. There is no doubt they are missing over and over and over; if they had hit their target the shooting would have stopped. I wonder what the people in the surrounding villages think of the snipers. They must think that we are the ones shooting: us, me, the men of the Hill. Me, the face of the U.S. Marines for six villages, annihilating the silence. They must think us mad. Or maybe they think that we've finally found a real Taliban, a nighttime emplacer and we're just making sure the job is finished. Again the shooting begins, unbelievably, *sixteen, seventeen, eighteen* rounds in the dead of night and then as soon as they begin, the rounds stop, and the sound lingers in the air for a few moments before all is silent again. And I think about how maybe the villagers in the surrounding countryside are ignoring the shooting, gratefully huddled on their ground-lain beds, thanking Allah they are not the targets. Or perhaps they think of their interactions with me, the *chai* we've shared, the promises we've made, and they hear the bullets, imagine the slaughter of Taliban insurgents, and maybe they think: yes, I suppose that young man can protect us. Look at what he does in the middle of the night. Hear how he kills the Taliban.

It occurs to me, sitting under that barrage, half-inch bullets flying over my head, that what happens here is only what you think happened. There are no absolute truths in this place. Tomorrow I can tell the surrounding villagers we killed two Taliban. I can tell them we shot four IED emplacers, catching them in the act, and they will tell their neighbors and their neighbors will tell the shopkeepers and the shopkeepers will tell customers from Safar or from the uncharted wastes south of here and the story will spread, even if we don't kill anyone, even if we shoot at nothing. Right now, I don't know what the assessment will be. I hope desperately to find a variety of bomb-emplacing materials, to discover sure sign that the kill was good.

In my core I want nothing more than to fight back. I want to feel as though we've accomplished something, and I want to keep bombs from being emplaced, and I want the snipers to do their job, and I want to kill the Taliban and win the war but something in my gut does not feel right and I am afraid for the snipers and for myself and for the squad and for the village.

The night is quiet, the shooting ended. My radio buzzes.

No, Durzay, I don't know what's going on. Yes, I'll figure it out.

I radio the Hill. The snipers can't tell me the exact location they shot at, but Ivan and Terrance are back at the Hill so I kick the snipers off the radio and have my guys walk me on. We pick our way through the bramble and the mud to the place Terrance describes, a collection of two compounds a hundred yards away. There we find a deep irrigation ditch, water running into it through a pipe, a shovel discarded in the water. No blood to be seen through our night vision. No dead bodies. No Afghans hiding in the bushes. And thus far no IED's, although we are careful where we step and we'll have to come back tomorrow to make absolutely sure.

We walk to a small building nearby, a type of outdoor rectangular mud house, one blue grated window. Lively sounds emanate from it. Laughter, tinny Afghan or Pakistani music playing through weak speakers. The smell of marijuana. I bang on the door with a tightly clenched fist, hating myself, dreading what I might find out.

The music stops. All is silent for a few moments while the occupants figure out what to do. I wait. Whispers from behind the door. Still no answer. I bang again. This time the whispers are louder. Hushed arguing. Things moving. Scuffling feet, growing nearer the door. It opens.

"*Assalamu a'laikum*," I say to a face. It is red-eyed and scared. He greets me back. I stand in the doorway, feeling dirty. The room is full of men, ten or twelve of them, huddled around a hookah and a radio. They look up at me with wide eyes. No night searches, I remember someone saying during a brief at Dwyer. I'm not searching, I tell myself. I'm just asking questions. Trying to find out if the snipers hit anything so we can take them to the hospital and pay their families, or alternatively catalogue them as Taliban and keep count. I think that warrants a knock in the night.

I use my bad Pashto to ask if the men heard gunshots, if they were the ones shot at. I pantomime a sniper rifle. I make shooting sounds. I pick up dirt and throw it into the air, pretending to shield my face from the blasts.

Did we shoot at any of you just now? I ask in English. I wish Jack were here.

Heads shake no. Hands flip up and down. Red henna palms and forced smiles in response to an absurd line of questioning.

Imagine if someone shot at you while you were drinking beer in your backyard. While you were cleaning your gutters. While you were watering your lawn, thinking about spreadsheets or the Chicago Cubs or who invented cable internet. Imagine someone began shooting at you from a place you couldn't see, and in the ensuing scramble to get inside you lost your beer, and then inside the house your mother and your father and your brother and your cousins who were all over to watch a football game heard the gunshots and saw the ground explode all around you and your face is white with fear and then the gunshots stopped.

What would you do?

You'd tell them all to sit down, pretend it didn't happen and thank God you're alive. And when the armed men who occupy your country came to your door you'd say:

No, sir, I didn't hear a thing.

No, I certainly wasn't running for my life.

Yes, sir, I'm certainly happy you're here. We're all happy.

Because if you do say that you were shot at, what's to stop the men with guns from finishing you off?

So I ask my absurd questions, and I go next door to a dark compound where nobody answers the door, and I thank the stars that we don't find anyone blown to pieces tonight. And I pray that no families show up to Durzay or the Hill in the morning, carrying the body of a farmer who was just digging his ditch at night, when it's cool, like so many other farmers.

Be it luck or something darker, no bodies are found. Nobody comes to the Hill, or to Durzay, bearing gunshot wounds. There are no confirmed kills. I breathe a sigh of relief.

I do not blame the men who tried to kill Taliban that night. We all want to fight. We are all little more than adrenaline and testosterone and the urge to do what we've been trained to do.

I have no doubt the snipers thought they really did see an emplacer out there. But it does not matter. They forgot where we were. What we were doing. How the war was being fought. They forgot that we, as an occupying force, have chosen not to take risks. They have forgotten that there are men who really believe in this counterinsurgency strategy, and that killing here is not only discouraged, but punished.

They thought there was a choice: to stand by and watch, or to fight back. They thought that if, through their experience, training and deductive skills, they believed someone was here to hurt us, someone was trying to emplace a bomb that could kill us, that they could take the shot. They thought that they could make a difference. That they had a choice.

They were wrong. There is no choice. The only choice is not to shoot.

Maybe in ten years they'll look back and think: I just wanted to save lives. I thought it was a good shot. I wanted to do my part. And maybe they'll be right.

But today, they are off the Hill. It is likely they will stand post until we go home. It is likely they will no longer leave the wire. It is likely they will dispense of the illusion that this is a war where we kill the enemy on purpose.

19

BOLO

Three weeks after his wounding Jason comes back to us on the Hill. He has changed, but not overly so. He still grins from ear to ear any time he's nervous, or excited, or unsure, or angry, or happy. He's a few pounds heavier on chow hall food. He shows us his collarbone, where the scarring and holes from ball bearings and rock shrapnel are healing but not all the way healed. He says he's mostly okay. His arm is weak. He missed having his weapon on him while he was gone.

He tells us that after he and Doc and Cody got in the vics at the bazaar they drove to Durzay, where Two-Bravo worked on Cody with Doc and the battalion surgeon. From there Cody and Jason were evacuated to the nearest trauma center, COP Payne, overland, in the same vehicles. As they were driving the air cleared, so midway through the movement a medevac bird was called again, and this one landed and shuttled them away, over the Helmand River, to the west, where they landed at the COP and were moved into the trauma tent. There they cut Jason's clothes off. He lay naked on a table while doctors and nurses worked on him and Cody. Stabilized, Cody went on, back to Germany and the States. Jason went to the huge Forward Operating Base, Camp Dwyer.

He spent a few days in Dwyer, out of place, watching movies and eating steak at the chow hall. They threw away his old fatigues when he was at Payne so they issued him brand-new camouflage utilities, non-FROG, non-combat, with no nametapes and no cover. He walked around Dwyer feeling like a recruit in phase one of bootcamp, before they let you unbutton your blouse all the way down. A First Sergeant stopped him outside the chow hall.

Why don't you have a weapon? he asked. Or a cover? Or nametapes? Or a shave, or a haircut? What the fuck is wrong with you, Marine?

Jason shrugged. I just got blown up, he said.

That almost shut the First Sergeant up. Except for the haircut, which Jason had to go get immediately. The Marine Corps Way can only make so many exceptions.

The First Sergeant was still outside the chow hall when he got back.

One day it's just Jason and his fireteam on the Hill. He's sitting on the edge of post one, looking out at the world, his legs a hundred feet above the earth. He is eating expired Skittles, naked except for silk shorts and Oakleys. Easy to spot from far away, as far as the shimmering river in its sunken banks. Pink and green and carefree, dangling off the side of a cliff. Visible from outer space. He pulls a green candy from the bag, and

snap

the earth between his knees explodes. He falls backward, behind cover. He gathers his rifle and peeks over the edge of the embankment. Through his optic he scans the nearby village of Hajji Zulmai to see if he can spot the shooter. There is no movement. No sign of any sniper. No sign of anything at all. Just a warm, lazy afternoon under the Helmand Sun. He's gone, whoever the shooter is. Jason is chasing ghosts, the same way he did before he was blown up, the same way all of us will chase them for the rest of the deployment and for the rest of our lives.

Jason spends the rest of the day looking through the optic of the TOW missile launcher. He stays well-covered and out of range. He picks Skittles out of the dirt and eats them one by one.

Durzay calls up and tells us there's a BOLO out for a white Toyota sedan heading toward the Helmand River. They say we're supposed to go out and trap it in a quick vehicle checkpoint. Hurry, they say.

This is a problem, I reply. Most of the Afghan soldiers and half of my squad are at Durzay right now with Terrance, loading up on pre-workout and Copenhagen from the PX Truck. Doesn't matter, they say. Needs to be done. Came down from higher. Roger, I say. I don't know who I'm talking to and I don't really care.

I tell Jason to take his team and do the checkpoint, get out on the road and make himself very visible to the GBOSS camera so whoever this is so important to can tell we did it. Three Marines and the last Afghan soldier head out. I watch them with binoculars.

Suddenly I realize I am the last person on the Hill. There is not a single Marine within a hundred yards of me. For the first time this deployment I am completely alone. A sense of overwhelming freedom warms me from the inside out. Privacy, solitude. Freedom from choice and responsibility and the need to tell people what to do. I sink heavily onto the camp stool on post one. I stare at the sandbags. I am alone, and this produces endorphins, yet just as suddenly as my sense of freedom comes to me, a sense of anxiety rushes behind it, stopping me, battering me with waves of nervous apprehension. The thought of being without backup on the Hill ferments a rising panic deep in my stomach. Like heartburn it rises through my esophagus, into my larynx and my throat, seizing me wordless as I try to swallow. I think about blind spots. I don my body armor and grab my rifle with a death grip.

I am alone, and I really am *alone*, just one guy on a Hill, surrounded by ghosts who are trying to end me. I am certain that they would take any opportunity to cut me from navel to nose. We have been attacked with bombs and booby traps, but never up here. It would probably take only a small contingent of Taliban to overrun the position. I am sure someone wants to fight me here, to breach the c-wire and engage me, tear me apart, knife my liver while my body freezes from fear. I do not know if they could kill me, and I do not know if I would even have warning before they did.

On my first deployment we had a final defense plan written in black sharpie on cardboard and hung on the wall of the firebase. It was only half-serious. Fight from outside to inside, it said. Fall back to where the chow's stored. Fight with shovel and fist and knife. Don't give up the ship. Fight to the last man. Destroy the radios.

But for the Hill, that plan could very likely turn into a reality.

The Hill is so vulnerable that all of us sleep with our flak jackets and weapons next to our cots. We are condition one in all conditions. The M203 gunners have belts of high explosive grenades lying on their plate carriers, ready to deploy in an instant. Fragmentation grenades, rockets, machine gun ammunition, MK19 40mm belt-fed grenade ammo staged and prepared for use.

If they breach the wire, I pray my posts are awake. If they come into the berthing area, I hope I can tell them apart from the Afghans. And if I have to fight them with my bare hands, I pray that I am stronger than them, even this emaciated, lean version of me, strong enough to overpower and break their arms with the little martial arts I learned from watching ultimate fighting as a teenager.

But to be effective, this plan needs defenders. And right now the only defender is me. There is nobody watching the entrance. Nobody alert near the Afghan hooch. Never have I felt so vulnerable, so exposed. I need to keep an eye on the radio, so I stay at post one, and as I do I prepare for the Taliban taking advantage of our moment of vulnerability. I tighten my bootlaces and grab the hilt of the KA-BAR knife I've carried on my belt for a hundred combat patrols. I conduct the obsessive rituals I've developed over two trips to war, rituals designed to channel my nervous energy into action. I snap my fingers and stomp my feet against each other. I hear the boot-heels *thump*. I scrape the side of my blackened trousers with my fingernails, pulling off grime. There's a little rip in the crotch of my trousers, one I've been fingering for some time, and now I make it wider and bigger until I force myself to stop. You only get so many medium-regular pants before they run out and issue you a large-long or a small-regular and then it really rips.

I want to check in with the VCP so I finger the button of my black gear, trying to call Jason. The radio doesn't make a sound. I look down and notice it's dead. How long has it been dead for? I turn to grab a battery from the rack and

oh fuck

I am face-to-face with an Afghan child of nine or ten. He startles me so badly I nearly fall backward. I bring my rifle up and point it at the ground in front of him, not because I think the child poses any danger to me, but because I am embarrassed for being caught off guard.

"How the *fuck* did you get in here?" I ask the child.

The child flips his hand.

"I don't know what the fuck that means."

He flips it again.

"What do you want?"

He points to a pack of water bottles, then points south toward the road. He does this several times. I think I am beginning to understand his meaning, but I need to be sure. I replace the black battery on my radio, my hands working while my brain tries to figure out exactly how this kid got into the base. If he got up here, couldn't he show someone else how to get up here? Is it a big secret? How many times has he seen us come and go? Did he move the concertina wire out of the way himself, or did Jason leave it open?

The black radio beeps to life in time to catch a transmission.

"—some water and bring it out here, over," says Jason's voice.

I key the handset. "Say again, Two-Three Bravo."

"Roger, I've been trying to get ahold of you for a while, all good?"

"Yeah, battery died on the radio, over."

"Roger, okay, yeah we're black on water out here, so we sent a little kid to get some, over."

I shake my head. On the one hand, I appreciate the ingenuity. On the other hand, the kid scared the shit out of me. He also exposed a weakness in the concertina wire, my deepest fear and something I'll have to look at. I feel vulnerable and stupid.

"Roger, he's here. I'm sending him back with a case."

"Yeah, roger, could you pay him too? We promised him ten dollars but nobody has cash, over."

Again I shake my head. "Roger, I'll pay him," I say. I give the kid a case of twelve water bottles and a ten-dollar bill and push him gently back out of the gate and down the Hill. I tell myself that when the teams return, we'll go down and re-evaluate the concertina wire. We'll look around the Hill for vulnerabilities, for places where people can get in, and shore it up with another layer of C-Wire, and we'll move the wire out by the burn pit a little further out, and we'll make a gate with a lock on it or something. We'll figure out some way of keeping the bad guys out, of hedging our bets against hand-to-hand combat.

Jason never intercepts any white Toyotas, and Terrance returns with packages of fruit roll-ups and sunflower seeds. When the whole squad is safely inside the wire, the sense of solitude and vulnerability slips away, replaced by responsibility and resignation.

20

Bazaar Day

Daylight. No morning patrol. Early on Sergeant Mike wakes me up and asks if he and Wali, the cook, can borrow a couple rucksacks to grab rice and eggs and sodas from the bazaar. I'm groggy. Sure, I say. Don't lose them. The Corps will have my balls if we lose these rucksacks. I give Sergeant Mike ten bucks for a couple cartons of cigarettes. They head off down the Hill. I can't get back to sleep.

For ten or twenty or thirty minutes I sit with poor posture, spine stretching forward, shirtless, vertebrae poking through the skin on my back. I am lean bordering on malnourished. Every bit of excess fat and muscle stripped away as I burn a thousand calories an hour, hours of patrols a day, days of patrols in a week, weeks of war that add into months that take years from my life. I can pull myself out of a canal, I can carry a man for a mile, but I couldn't bench press my body weight if you paid me.

Remove me from this war. Spirit me away. Let me be anywhere else.

Waves of tortuous monotony. We do the same things every day. Things I ignore. Things I put off until the last minute. Things the men won't do anymore, things we no longer care to do, things I can no longer make them do. I compress ever lower, again feeling the vertebrae of my lower back, little cockroaches pressing against their cage.

Drooped-over, I am statue-still, every fiber of me wishing I were some-place else. I stare at my feet and I think of nothing at all. What is there to think about? What is there to do? The Hill, polluted with dis-carded water bottles and plastic wrappings from rations and the refuse of Marines who have stopped caring. Maybe we should clean it all up today. Maybe I should eat a bullet.

I crack and ache over to the piss tubes and as I walk I hear the rustling of the men as they adjust themselves, trying to stay awake in the morning light, trying to make it to eight o'clock. If they're lucky, if the day is cool, they'll make it to eight-thirty. The sun warms my shirt-less torso as I step out into the light and inhale burning shit from the burn pit and tobacco from post one. The morning air is a better smell than the mid-day air and the mid-day air is a better smell than the af-ternoon air, but nothing compares to the night-time air. It is one of a very few comforting smells, the evening air, the cooling of the fields, the humidity that makes you sweat in the cornfields instead of lightly bathing you in beads of wet. Even though I am miserable, in years to come I will miss the evening air. Right now it is only the morning air, and I suppose I will miss that too.

When I piss, I am granted a view that stretches for miles, and this helps to cheer me up a bit. My morning malaise begins to be replaced by calm resignation. Maybe things aren't that bad. Maybe I just hate wak-ing up.

I can see the furthest villages under my charge in the distance. I can see another hill, far on the horizon, and maybe I can make out a flag or two fluttering from its crest. Close enough that I could shoot it with a TOW missile if I wanted to. Far enough I'll never walk to it. It doesn't matter. Someday it'll all fade away. Far, far away, until I can't recall this piss, or this morning, or last night's patrol. Until I can't recall the names of the Afghan soldiers or the types of batteries I order and carry from Durzay to the Hill. Until I can't remember the names or the faces of the men. Until I can't remember the feeling of Cody's slick gritty torso rubbing against my shoulders. It'll all fade, or I will, and in any case this morning is not the worst morning I've had here on this Hill, so if it's not the worst morning, I can get through it, because I've been through the worst morning. So I'll have breakfast. I do not look forward to much, but I look forward to breakfast.

Hot water from an MRE heater bag, instant coffee my father sent me, a snack bread and some peanut butter. Breakfast makes me feel warm and, if not happy, then at least not depressed. I feel the men moving around me, hear their steps as they scrape the floor. It is a cool morning, but as it gets hotter the men wake and as the men wake we are silent. Not a word passes between us. Not now.

When we were boots, a friend made up a rule that applied only when we were out in the field. It was after our first deployment, when a couple of our seniors were still around but we were largely on our own. We had leeway to be cheeky, and it was a cheeky rule. He made sure everyone knew. He'd tell the platoon sergeant, and the men, and anyone who would listen:

No yelling before morning chow.

We, the platoon, decided this was the new gospel. Every exercise we went to, we enforced the rule. We talked in soft tones on waking. If someone needed to be punished, they were punished after chow. It was a rule for the field only. In garrison, when we ran the swamps or radar hill or down the flightline, we'd yell and be yelled at. Garrison is garrison. But in the field, the rule was the rule was the law was the gospel.

On the Hill we take this idea to its extreme. We never yell before breakfast. We rarely even speak. We sit on our racks, on boxes by the table, in the shitter, by the burn pit, the piss tubes, in post one, lean against water bottles, by the food, on the sandbag wall. We wear no shirts, bandannas around our heads, Crocs on our feet, unshaven and filthy. Grunts. But quiet ones.

This morning, to my great chagrin, someone violates the gospel.

"Kirk! Hey, Kirk!" shouts Nate from post one.

"Yeah," I say back softly, in deference to the rule. The only reason for heresy against the gospel is a bona fide emergency. This had better be an emergency.

"Kirk, you gotta see this!" he shouts again, sounding disturbed or excited.

I get up, not altogether very quickly, and shuffle to post. My sweaty feet slide against the grimy plastic of my Crocs.

"What?" I ask resignedly.

"Look!" Nate points. Immediately I spot the source of his dismay. My heart pumps faster. I grab the binoculars. Cupping the eyepieces to block the sun I stare through the dirt-streaked glass, scanning the field. It takes me only a moment to recognize Sergeant Mike. Like Willem Defoe at the end of the movie *Platoon*, he is running and stumbling as would a shot deer. He is armorless and weaponless. His arms flail as he stumbles, catches his feet on furrows. He is just past the wall, a couple of hundred yards away. I rush to the plywood table, in the middle of the men, rousing them and shouting and getting their attention as I go.

"Up, up, everyone up! Gear on now! Something's happening with the ANA!" I start giving orders. "Jason—take your team and grab Sergeant Mike from the field. He looks hurt. Use the landing zone at the bottom of the Hill, call a medevac if you have to."

Jason knows it's serious and doesn't hesitate. He and Doc and Nate start grabbing medical gear, flak jackets, rifles, the stretcher we finally received, far too late. They're wearing t-shirts and silkies. They do not change. Speed is essential. His team darts down the Hill, a blur of clanking magazine pouches and bare calves.

I'm thinking of the bazaar, of Sergeant Mike and Wali leaving an hour ago with our rucks and gear. I didn't see Wali when I scanned the field, so I assume he has to be around the bazaar, although I can't be sure. I begin to gather equipment for the movement there. Thor, sickle, metal detector, water. Tools for the uncleared distance between the wall and the bazaar, the part we can't see. I take a few extra moments to don my camouflage blouse and my trousers and tie my boots. Today, even though one of my Afghan soldiers is dying somewhere in the fields, or in the bazaar, or in a house, or in a shop, I take the time to blouse my boots and tuck in my shirts. I do it because I am tired of the snide remarks and the glances and the accusations. I do it because even though two Afghan soldiers in my care are wounded, I know that when we reach the bazaar, some other squad might come and meet us there. I do it because years ago, when I was first issued them, I was brainwashed with the idea that if one does not wear one's FROG blouse, and one is struck by an IED, one will suffer terrible burns, because the blouses are fire retardant. I remember distinctly the times we were told, over and over, that with our arms bare, without the godly coverings of Fire-Resistant Organizational Gear, our flesh will melt away like blackened chicken skin. And it is not that I believe this fact that makes me put the blouse on; I've long thought that maybe that kind of melting only happens in vehicles or places where someone can be trapped and set on fire. No, it is that by not putting on the blouse, I am conducting an offense against the Marine Corps Way. It is because wounded men lying in a pool of their own blood on the ground in a bazaar is no excuse not to be in the proper uniform.

I do it because I can be trusted to kill the enemy, evacuate the wounded, and assess the damage afterward. But I cannot be trusted to have an untucked shirt. I do it because the Marine Corps puts the infant in infantry.

And so now, as I'm putting on my helmet, as I'm buckling it, as I'm getting ready to rescue a wounded soldier, I am concerned in large part about what happens if Mario or Terrance or myself are caught without a blouse on in the bazaar. I am thinking about what I might find in the bazaar and I am thinking about how much trouble we will be in if we strike an IED and our skin is crisped to a slightly higher than acceptable degree. I am thinking there is no such thing as a good excuse. I am thinking about Wali and I am actively postponing his rescue because I can't be seen running outside the wire with only a skivvy shirt on.

This is the Marine Corps Way. On the Hill, perhaps, I can ignore it, as long as nobody's watching on the GBOSS. At the base of the Hill, Jason's team can plausibly forget about it, the problem conveniently coming to us. But heading out into the bazaar I can't. All I can do is touch the cards in my left shoulder pocket and hope we're not too late.

I leave my gloves and I don't tuck blouse my boots but still it takes an eternity to leave the wire. I go from nearly naked to battle-ready in a matter of minutes, but still this is perhaps longer than Wali has left. I carry a Thor and a sickle and a metal detector and a rifle. I dart down the incline of the Hill, stumbling, sprinting as I hit the field, charging across the field toward the wall. The gear is awkward. Running is un-comfortable. I listen and feel the *slap-slap-slap* of the Thor on my back.

I know the other Afghan soldiers on the Hill are already in the bazaar. As soon as they saw Sergeant Mike limping through the fields they ran to him. They cradled him, comforting him and vowing revenge. When Doc came down the Hill they handed Sergeant Mike over and sprinted away to find Wali. Now they are somewhere in the bazaar, searching. They are unburdened by worries about FROG blouses and the Marine Corps Way.

As I run I call up to Durzay and update the Lieutenant. Breathlessly I let him know my other three Afghan soldiers have already run out to find Wali, that I am following with a fireteam, that we will be calling in two medevacs. The Actual acknowledges. He tells me that another squad will be out to meet me soon. Fine. The more the merrier. They can confirm I am in the proper uniform.

My sprint turns into a run turns into a jog. I chance a look behind. Ruben is on my heels, followed by Terrance and Mario. My legs burn and my lungs heave embers but still I run because if I don't someone will die and it doesn't matter if I step on a bomb so long as I get to him.

As I near the bazaar I see it's deserted. No shepherds, no flocks of sheep, no bustling crowds of Pashtuns, no doors open, no motorcycles buzzing by. No children sitting on blue fuel barrels, no smiling men wearing *dishdashas*, no *tsinga yay's* or *jorday yay's*. No noise at all, save for some faint moaning coming from the center. I run up a rise into the bazaar proper and emerge from between two buildings. The moaning is louder to my left so I turn the corner and jog to a blue awning, where I find two of my three remaining Afghan soldiers crouching by Wali on the ground. The third is furiously pacing, as if trying to draw a culprit from thin air. I part the two soldiers and there's Wali bleeding from a wound in his groin.

"No good," he grimaces. "Double no good."

I pat his leg. His pants are pulled down to his ankles, his grime-stained briefs soaked with blood. I crouch beside him and begin to triage, but it takes effort to inspect the wound closely. I am afraid of what I might see. I am always afraid of what I might see.

I am saved when Ruben appears with a medical bag. He pulls on a pair of sterile gloves and begins poking around and as he examines and moves things around Wali cries out and Ruben discovers he's been shot in the scrotum. The bullet has exposed cords and skin and flesh inside, a mess of colors and shapes, lines and circles and hair and blood and Wali's stoic grimacing grunts. I can't tell if the testicles are destroyed and I can't look for long before I turn away, too afraid to commit the image too firmly to memory.

Ruben's combat medical skills rival those of a Corpsman. His steady hands work the wound, prodding and triaging as he reassures Wali it'll be okay. He cuts and he stuffs and he wraps with practiced, relaxed ease, a grunt who can take lives and save lives just the same. As Ruben works on Wali he reveals a clean shot through the scrotum and the leg and out the upper thigh. He pushes and he wraps and he fills the wounds with gauze.

The green radio glued to my cheek, I speak with a squad from another platoon. They're on the way, just now leaving Durzay. I hear a stupendous roar and look up to see two Ford "danger" Rangers filled to the brim with Afghan soldiers pull into the bazaar, a flurry of dust and arms and tires and AK-47's. As they disembark their vehicles they shout and run and pound on doors and kick things over. They disperse to every corner of the bazaar, looking around with my ANA, searching shops.

On black gear I talk to Jason, still seeing to Sergeant Mike at the bottom of the Hill. I decide it's best to do a single medevac for the two men. I send the lines for the two patients, with a grid from Jason and a grid nearby for the two landing zones. I tell Durzay I'll talk to the bird as it comes around, have it go to two different smoke positions.

Where the bazaar was just deserted it is now full of Afghan soldiers, and the Afghan soldiers have found Afghan men, pulled them from hiding places, or maybe just found curious passers-by, or maybe dragged them from the closest compounds in the vicinity. They have dug up these bewildered, sometimes indignant men from God Knows Where and now they're slapping the men, berating them, removing their caps, screaming in their faces. Are they enraged at the insult to the Government of Afghanistan, that someone had the nerve to fire at its representatives in broad daylight? Perhaps it is the anger of impotence, of illegitimacy, of a tired group of men with the same mission as I. Tired men drawing disappearing pictures on a beach, day after day, month after month, scrawling in the sand until one of the artists is pulled away by a rogue wave.

One of Durzay's ANA kneels over Wali and gets the story from him, telling it to me in interrupted but passable English. Wali, conscious but in pain, speaks in short sentences.

He tells me that Wali and Sergeant Mike had been sitting in the satellite phone shop, making calls. They were squatting when two men on a motorcycle approached and shot them both. Somehow Sergeant Mike managed to wrestle a gun from one of the attackers and run away. Wali had not been so fortunate. He had fallen onto his back after being shot. But the attackers were gone as quickly as they had arrived, scurrying away on one of the ubiquitous motorbikes of Helmand. Wali had crawled out to the middle of the bazaar and collapsed underneath the awning where he now lay.

As I wait for the bird—ten minutes out now—the squad from Durzay appears in the bazaar. I shake the squad leader's hand and update him on the situation. We decide that since he has a full patrol's worth of men, he will take over security of the landing zone while I walk the birds on and investigate the scene with the Afghans. While we wait, Terrance and I take a look inside the phone shop. As I approach the stall, with blue barrels on either side and a red painted sign over the entrance, I hold my rifle at my shoulder, instinctively, ready to shoot, knowing the men are probably long gone but hopeful as I imagine confronting a real-life Taliban. I find nothing alive in the shop.

What I find instead is a rectangular garage stall behind a blue corrugated iron door, twenty feet deep and seven feet high. It is carpeted and littered with wires and power outlets and boxes of sim cards and pillows and cell phones and on the roof are a bundle of satellite dishes with wires connected to a generator, which sits outside.

The interior is a murder scene from a television police procedural. I am the detective. I stoop to look at brass casings. Pistol rounds, judging by the size. Makarov probably, several of them. Blood streaks and drops leading out of the door. Toward the back of the shop I find my borrowed rucksack, a helmet, a flak jacket. No weapons. No ammunition, no magazines, no grenades or smoke or flares. The men who did the shooting were here long enough to steal weapons, or maybe they came back for them, but either way I'm glad to have my rucksack. Had I not found it I'd probably get an ass chewing and have to pay for it.

On the back of the wall and on the floor are several bullet holes. Misses. I conclude that the ANA had probably been unarmed, un-armored. They were shot sitting down. They had been in the white, oblivious and unaware, maybe even high. Their guard had been down and they had paid the price for it.

Two Blackhawk helicopters approach the bazaar from the south. The gunship breaks off and circles overhead. The other, a white and red cross painted on the side, lands in the purple smoke at the bottom of the Hill and picks up Sergeant Mike. As it rises and approaches, I throw a smoke and call the time. The pilot radioes back to me the color. Green. I confirm.

The bird lands. We carry Wali on a stretcher to the helicopter, where we are met by two Air Force Pararescuemen who wear expensive-looking lightweight body armor and Salomon boots. They take our casualty onto the belly of the bird. Before the doors close, Wali clutches my hand.

"You'll be okay," I tell him.

In days to come I learn Wali and Sergeant Mike survive, but I do not see them again. I hear a rumor that Sergeant Mike ended up in a decrepit prison somewhere near Kabul for unspecified crimes. I don't give this scuttlebutt much credence, but it wouldn't surprise me. Sometimes I think of Sergeant Mike and imagine another future for him, one where he stood and walked away from his hospital bed, one where he went home and never came back, one where he no longer had to survive on austere Hills and partner with foreigners with no understanding of what it meant to live the war instead of visiting it. I like to pretend Sergeant Mike finally decided that His Personal War had concluded, and now it was Somebody Else's War, and that he was living somewhere in a village up north by Mazar-e-Sharif, raising children, socializing with Wali every Friday at mosque, and changing the radio station whenever it mentioned Helmand Province.

The bird takes off. Terrance and Mario and Ruben and I join the Afghan soldiers in their search of the bazaar. Our goal is to find lost gear, but as we begin looking we watch it turn into something less than this, something baser and darker. A platoon of Afghan soldiers, furious at the wounding of their comrades, furious at other recent Afghan Army deaths, deaths on nearby roads, deaths in nearby villages, begin opening doors and pulling clothing off of shelves and taking things and breaking things. They whip into a frenzy when they find, inexplicably, a flak jacket in one shop and a helmet in another, and in their minds this means the shopkeepers are somehow in on the whole thing. The shopkeepers very well might be.

We have no water, having run down the Hill without any, and I am thirsty, so I pull a Fanta from a refrigerator, promising in my mind to pay it back. Others begin to take Fantas and Afghans who have joined us for the search grab a Fanta and pretty soon everyone has a Fanta. I make a pledge to pay these shopkeepers back for the drinks, even look around for someone to pay, but the shopkeeper is nowhere to be found. I leave some money underneath a stack of headscarves but quickly gather it back up as I realize the shopkeeper might never find it.

The Afghan soldiers stay angry. There is no accounting for the Afghans. Someone breaks glass and enters a drug store. I advise them against taking anything from there, but they are Afghan soldiers and do not listen to me.

From somewhere the Afghans produce five or six military-aged men and make them kneel in front of the sat-phone shop. They are rough with the civilians, who shout objections. The Afghan soldiers shout back accusations. We watch. It becomes very clear to me that this is not our fight. Perhaps this is not even our war. This divide which exists between the angry Afghan soldiers and the angry Pashtuns of Garmsir, who let the Taliban walk among them and drive motorcycles into bazaars and shoot soldiers, who know where the bombs are and do nothing about them, this is maybe not something we can solve with presence patrols and wheat seed and compensation for shot dogs and soccer balls and hand-cranked radios and chocolate and pens and key leader engagements.

A pair of bolt cutters appears and yet more shops are searched. We try to limit the damage as we rifle through stacks of loosely-organized head scarves and pajamas, searching for hidden meaning. My mouth sticks with soda and lack of water, but this does not keep me from smoking. A Pine hangs from the corner of my mouth as I wander the rows of shops, looking in barrels and picking up tarpaulins, scanning for weapons and boogeymen. The Afghan soldiers are less careful. The shops they touch are left disheveled at best. I watch a unibrowed soldier rake his hand along a row of potato chip bags, knocking them onto the floor. He dislodges cigarette cartons and spices and picture frames and the shopkeeper's desk and ledger. He smashes a tailor's sewing machine. Another Afghan soldier shoots a few rounds from his AK-47 into a shop. One more unloads a burst from a machinegun into a row of goods, spraying from the hip. I meander.

Sergeant Mike is gone, I muse. We'll have to get our own rice now. And I'm sure we'll have to pay the shopkeepers for anything the Afghan Army breaks today. They certainly don't have the money to fix it.

The Afghan soldiers knock over motorcycles and toss boxes in the canal. They march the captured men around, showing them bloodstains, locations where their compatriots had been shot, emphasizing each point with a kick or a slap. The locals don't plead or cry; rather, they argue and debate. Some of them say nothing, a solemn display of indifference.

I catch sight of a Marine smoking, a man I know, a man who doesn't smoke, has never smoked. I ask him why he's decided that now is the time to start.

"It's impossible not to," he says.

21

Shura

The shopkeepers are upset.

The rest of the platoon is doing a helicopter operation across the Helmand River, so I'm asked to come down to Durzay as the lead Marine in a short-notice *shura*. I'm to sit alongside the ANA lieutenant down there, the commander of the unit that Sergeant Mike and Wali belonged to, and ask store owners how two Afghan soldiers were nearly murdered in their shops. I do not know what to expect. We arrive at Durzay to a mob of middle-aged Afghan men murmuring quietly among themselves outside the base. We check them for weapons and explosives and bring them into the meeting area.

A boot from another squad, also staying back from the helo op, takes notes for me:

Shopkeepers are disappointed in the destruction of their shops and they are angry at the shootings on bazaar day. One of the shopkeepers' shop was broken up and shot. Someone stole new boots from one of them and money. He said he had names of them but lost it. One of the shopkeepers admitted to seeing the soldiers in the shops and they did not steal anything. One shopkeeper said he lost 1,500 rubies in phones and cameras and said his shop was destroyed. Jamal said he was paid back for his shop being destroyed. Kirk assured them there will be payments for the shops and told them they found some ANA gear in the shops and had to search them thoroughly. A shopkeeper asked why they broke his door and mixed tea together. Kirk assured them the Marines are committed to helping them out but that ANA getting shot in their shops after we have been helping them so much was like a smack in the face. Jamal said he is thankful for the Marines and ANA because he used to get robbed and had to carry things to his shops. Kirk told them the shop will be fixed, but they should be mad that Taliban attacked us in their bazaar. The commander told them that two children told him there was Taliban with guns who passed through the bazaar and no one else told him. ANA commander asked why the shop-keepers came. Their response was to complain against the destruction of their shops. They said they don't care about ANA being shot, they think that if their shop is shot today what's stopping him getting shot tomorrow. Kirk assured we will patrol in the bazaar still and make sure it reopens and still will buy from them. ANA commander told them that if they try to help them they will bring security. Kirk told them to try to open the shops and they will get a list of what's broken and they will try to fix and reimburse them of all damages but they have to realize they have to help us help them and we will bring the se-curity to the bazaar. They said they can't reopen because their doors are open. Kirk told them they need to start fixing the shops then Marines will help them. They said they can't go back to the bazaar because it's broken. Kirk told them he will come down today and advise what needs to be done but they will have to go there and fix some stuff today and he is not making a list just looking around but will take notes of the bigger things destroyed and they need to let us know when Taliban is there so we can help them and they need to secure their things they still have so no one steals them at night. Kirk said he wants to be able to walk through the bazaar and know it's as safe for Marines as it is for the locals. Kirk told them that if they are not there while Marines aren't there they can't help them. ANA commander told them we are military and can't guarantee a time to come to the bazaar.

After the shura I try to pay one of the shopkeepers for the Fanta I took. I find a candidate who may or may not be the right shopkeeper and give him some money. I take some Rip Its from the Durzay refrigerator and ruck back to the Hill.

On a clear day we find a barrel of homemade explosive in a compound by the bazaar, one which none of the shopkeepers ever tells us about. It's hooked up to a pressure plate, but there's no battery pack. Me and the EOD Sergeant tie a rope to it and pull it up and out of its location. It's big and heavy and takes some time to break free, but when it does we pull it into a nearby field, away from the bazaar and houses. We cannot move it much further without putting other houses in danger, so the tech decides to blow it here. We clear the bazaar and post guards at the entrances so nobody walks through. He sets the charge and we take cover behind a wall. When it goes, the shockwave purges me, a final goodbye to the young man I used to be. A nearby herd of goats witnesses my transformation. They are unfazed.

22

The Warrior

The Afghan Army soldiers always want our packets of chicken. We tell them to buy their own. They steal our chicken. I give them chicken so they stop stealing it. We don't have any more chicken.

Before he got hit, Sergeant Mike would always complain how we used his men as pack mules. We did, and we do. But we don't want to. We want to train them to take our places, but it seems as if they intentionally refuse to learn. Perhaps, they think, if they cannot fight on their own, the Americans will have to stay. But that is not The Strategy. The Strategy calls for an Afghan transition, but the Afghan Army soldiers rarely stand one shift of post without falling asleep. Our Hill is vulnerable. It has many blind spots. The prospect of waking up to a Taliban fighter standing over me with an AK-47 pointed at my head haunts me, disturbs my sleep.

I do not want to die, so my men stand post with the Afghans.

Higher-ups talk about "getting them ready." Ready to go out on their own. Ready to sweep. Ready to react to contact. Ready to call in their own reinforcements. But no matter how many times we tell them not to walk on paths or drive on the roads, they jump back on, eventually paying the same price we paid. The lessons do not stick.

Our ANA do not have any night vision. No medical gear. No air support.

They barely even have any food. They buy rice and beans in the bazaar. They check in with their platoon headquarters using an antique radio. Every day they request things from God Knows Where, but nothing ever shows up.

That is, Sergeant Mike used to tell me he would check in. I don't know. I never knew what he was saying on the radio, or who he was talking to. But it is my best guess that when we leave, the Afghan Army will lose every single position. They will all die. All of Garmsir will go back to the Taliban. I do not want to see this happen, but there is little I can do. So I train the Afghan soldiers, and hope for the best.

There was this guy in the School of Infantry who grabbed my flak jacket. A giant of a man. Huge fists, like anvils welded to pistons. I was a "squad leader," a position that meant nothing, except it was my job to make sure everyone got to formation on time with the proper equipment and a close shave. Everyone hated me, for good reason. They resented me for trying. They loathed that I cared. If I were on the other side, I would have hated me too. When you're going through basic training and SOI, you think it means something to be in charge of the other trainees. It does not. All you get from it is resentment and disdain. Your peers hate you, your instructors hate you. You end up hating yourself.

I don't even remember how it started. His name was Harris, or Harrington, something like that. When he grabs my flak, we are on a live-fire range, getting ready to shoot machine guns, maybe the M240, maybe the fifty-cal. I tell him to stop doing whatever it is he's doing, and instead of complying he wraps his sausage fingers, swollen with muscle, underneath the right shoulder of my flak jacket. I use one hand to try and remove it, unsuccessfully. His grip is far too strong, his hold too deep. I realize half the platoon is looking at me. Waiting to see what I do. So I stop resisting and speak to him with what I hope is a calm voice, although I'm shaking like a leaf.

"Get your hand off me, Harris."

"Or what?"

"Get it off."

"What the fuck are you gonna do about it?"

Nothing. I'm going to do nothing.

I'm saved by an instructor walking up on us to see what the problem is. Harris lets me go. What happened? Nothing, I tell the instructor. He leaves. On Harris' lips, a wicked smile. He could have killed me. Smashed me into the dirt, held me down and pounded my face until I could only be identified by dental records. And there's nothing I would have been able to do about it.

Another time we're in the squad bay, cleaning the shitters and mopping the floor and organizing our wall lockers. It's called a field day, and if you finish up with your own area you're supposed to clean up the common areas, the bathrooms and the quarterdeck and the showers. I notice a guy just standing by his locker, looking into it, not doing much. I walk over to him and politely ask him to participate. He politely tells me to fuck off. In an instant I find myself with one hand on his throat, Terminator-style, squeezing, not knowing why I'm doing it, not really, only that I've heard too many Drill Instructors threatened to choke recruits, too many Marines intimidate trainees and recruits with threats of violence. I've watched too many action movies. The choke is uncomfortable, but not so uncomfortable that he can't put his own right hand on *my* throat, thereby restricting air to *my* brain. We stand there in the middle of the squad bay, watched by a circle of boots, the two of us clutching each others' throats in an idiotic moment of ego and hubris, neither of us wanting to let go, but neither of us wanting to punch the other one and get in a real fight and get in trouble. I have no idea how to fight. I am sure the boot across from me, this carbon copy of me, this Midwestern white kid with a high and tight and glasses, also does not know how to fight, or else he surely would have thrown my hand aside and broken my nose in three places.

For a long moment we stare at each other and squirm until we both release our hands at the same time. We are no worse for wear except for nail marks on our necks and bruised egos.

"Fucking retards," someone remarks loudly. I slink away. I don't last long as a fake squad leader.

Our days on the Hill are long. Merely moving from one's cot to dispose of a water bottle becomes an arduous task. Why bother? I am in charge but I am nobody's master. We are wild men. We recognize no lords, no titles. Still, someone must try to lead.

When you're in charge it helps to have an ordainment. A piece of paper that says *I'm better than you.* You need rank. And if you do not have it you lead only by force of will.

I do not sleep. It is the heat, and it is the worry of the day's duties and it is the worry of conflict. But most of all it is the heat and the night patrols and waking up to check on the men as they smoke cigarettes and stare off into the distance with their night-vision monocles up, not looking at anything. Most of all it is the heat.

When I do sleep, I see a man without skin.

The men. The men argue more now. They argue with me. They argue with their team leaders and with each other. With the Afghans and with the villagers. With the sun and the cots and the food and the wind. They argue with themselves and with the imagined specter of the Bravo or the Actual or maybe of me. When we have the energy it ends in a confrontation. Like the time one of them tells me to fuck off as I'm leading a patrol out. I can't turn back around and walk into the Hill. The Lieutenant would ask why the delay. So I tell the man I'll be back. I'll handle it later.

When I return, I tell him clearly his actions are unacceptable. He bucks up to me. I stand chest-to-chest with him. I think I would probably lose the fight if it came to blows. I tell him I'll send him off the Hill tomorrow. He can go fill sandbags at Durzay. That seems to bring him down. The thought of losing his spot on the Hill appears to worry him. I am nothing compared to what the Bravo would do to him, and he knows it. So he quiets down. He is one of us again.

Our driving purpose becomes surviving long enough to go home.

Some nights I feel like a failure. As though I have done a piss-poor job of keeping my men from harm. No other squad suffered thirty percent casualties in one day. No other squad has a man back in the states, undergoing surgeries every other week. No other squad has been targeted for destruction like we have.

Other nights I think we've succeeded. How many bombs have we found? How many bombs have we avoided finding, by the routes we pick and the paths we don't walk? We are at the furthest razor-sharp edge of influence in the battalion's area of operations. We are the edge of the empire.

The narrative I've created for myself tells me that I've done a good job. I've kept the base running, haven't I? I've seen the men fed and I've sent up the patrol cards to the Lieutenant and I've done the census circus. I've done the job, haven't I? The job of the Marine? The grunt? The warrior?

No. I am no warrior.

The story of the warrior is an anecdote told to soldiers and Marines and sailors. It goes like this: in ancient Greece, or Sparta, or Macedonia, or Rome, or among the Vikings, or wherever the teller of the story decides it happened, there was a man who was wise and old. And he said that on every battlefield, out of one hundred men, ten shouldn't be there at all. Eighty are just cannon fodder. Nine are good men, fighters, and we're lucky to have them because they make the battle. Ah, but one—one is the warrior. He is the one who will bring the others back.

You spend your whole time in the Corps hoping you're the warrior. But statistically you're just a target. And none of us should be here.

After a while, things stop making sense. You realize there's not a lot of point to walking around at night, unable to see wires or fresh dirt or anything at all. You realize you've been in purgatory, trapped in a tiny base being beaten around by dust and eaten by flies, and you're going to be there for who knows how much longer, and you realize that you're setting patterns, and those patterns are going to get you killed. So you change your patterns but you end up setting new patterns without meaning to. And you fall into canals in the middle of the night and you climb your way out of them and as you do you rip the crotch of your pants and the elder you meet in the next village can see the outline of your dick when he shakes your hand. And when you get back to the patrol base you spend endless hours counting things and moving things and sitting on things. You clean your face just to maul it with a razor blade. You use a microfiber towel to wipe your balls or your chest or your sunglasses but it becomes so grimy and thick with muck that you end up transferring dirt to yourself rather than from yourself and pretty soon you give up and you hope another towel comes in the mail. And when you go to civilization, to a bigger base, higher forces you to do training you don't need on systems you don't use, or even worse on systems you use every day, in classes taught by people who haven't used those systems half as much as you have. Some Gunny tries to teach you how to use a sickle. When you tell him he's wrong, he tells you you're wrong, and he's right because he's an E-7 and you're an E-3 so you say Aye Gunny, stop listening and color your notebook with a red pen.

When you're doing all of this you think about Vietnam and Iraq and you wonder what people will think of this war. You wonder which war they'll compare it to, which war they'll liken it to the most. Probably Iraq. They'll be wrong.

I ride my first motorcycle on the outskirts of a village near the Helmand River. It's a little red 125cc *Hilmand* and the shifting part confuses me. I try what I've seen in motorcycle magazines. I am lucky the clutch is very forgiving. I make it down the road a bit, using my legs to balance as I nearly fall.

Against all logic, I take my helmet off to ride. Too afraid of bombs and bullets to walk the countryside without a Kevlar crown, too stupid and young to wear one on a motorcycle. No wonder Marines die on these things.

23

Cujo

One of my guys finds a puppy on patrol. It follows him back to the Hill. He can't get rid of it.

It's a mangy, dirty thing. Flies circling its nose, matted fur, all orange and brown. It smells of shit and burning trash.

Here's what probably happened: the dog walked up to him in Hajji Sailani's village as he was sitting against a wall, his feet in a dry ditch, surrounded by candy wrappers. He was tired and hot. He was eating a chocolate bar.

He probably didn't even notice the dog until he felt a warm gritty tongue on his thumb. And maybe at first he just looked down and didn't feel anything for it. Just a dog. Another dumb Afghanistan thing. IED's and night patrols and a stray dog eating half-melted chocolate out of your hand in a ditch. A ditch filled with human shit.

"Stop," he might have said. The dog kept licking his fingers.

"Cut it out," he might have said, a little firmer, but not much.

Maybe the dog kept licking his hand, and maybe he took the pound cake wrapper and pulled it away, and maybe he tried to show as much disapproval as he could muster, hoping the dog could read his expression, and maybe the dog knew some words, or maybe it could read his mind by looking at his face, and he could say words that the dog would understand by the way he said it. But then again if it's an Afghan dog, maybe nothing he said or did would make sense.

"Listen, I don't think you're supposed to eat chocolate," he might have told the dog.

The dog might have licked his arm, probably for the salt. The Drill Instructors in bootcamp always said that you need salt when you're hot because it all comes in your sweat. The more you sweat, the more salt you lose. Eventually, depending on whether or not you're acclimated to the environment, and how good of shape you're in, and how hydrated you are, there'll be no salt left at all. Eventually, the water will go into you and out of you and pretty soon water won't do anything for you and you'll go into heat exhaustion and then heat stroke. Maybe that happens to dogs, too.

"Listen, man. I don't think you're supposed to eat chocolate. I'm pretty sure you'll die," he might have said.

Here's what definitely happened: the puppy did not die from any chocolate bar. Nor did it die from the other things it might have eaten, the jalapeno cheese spread, the lemon pound cake, the crackers, the veggie omelette.

It did not die on the way back to the Hill, after following the patrol for miles. It did not die when the patrol passed by the crucial walls that separated the area that was safe and visible from that which was filled with IED's. The puppy, panting, hopped along.

Back in the wire, I have a conversation with the man who found it.

"Cute puppy," I say.

"Look, I know we're not supposed to have them up here, but it followed me."

"I know. There's no way to stop them following you sometimes. But we can't keep it."

"I know."

"They have fleas. It's a battalion thing. We couldn't have dogs on the last deployment either."

"Roger."

"Also since that video went out on YouTube a few years ago they're really iffy on dogs at patrol bases."

"Yeah, I know."

"He can stay the night. We'll drop him off on the patrol tomorrow."

"Roger."

I start to get up.

"Can I give him a bath?" asks the man who found him.

"Sure."

He sets about his task with vigor. He wears gloves and hot water bottles from the shower area to spray the dirt off of the puppy. He lathers the dog with Old Spice body wash, pulls hair with a thick-toothed comb. The dog does not bite or squirm or fight back. It seems happy. It returns all of his affection and then some.

When he's done, the dog won't stop following him around. The squad loves it. Everyone knows we can't keep it, but a dog's a dog anywhere.

"What are you gonna name it?"

"Cujo," he says.

I try my best to get rid of that dog. I really do. Maybe I should have tried harder. But it just keeps coming back to us. One time, we drop it off several kilometers away. Tie it to a tree. It breaks free and comes back that night.

That's when I give in. I let the squad keep it.

The dog becomes our mascot.

"Fuckin' Cujo."

"Cujo! Come here, Cujo!"

"Kill, Cujo, kill!"

Why Marines feel the need to make things so aggressive, so masculine, so killer-y, I don't understand. Life in the Marine Corps is a competition to see who's the most hardcore, the roughest, the least capable of human emotion. Steely-eyed killers, all of you, said the Drill Instructor upon graduation. You are now part of the brotherhood. What do Marines do? Kill.

Brotherhood of killers. Always masculine, always aggressive. The dog never stood a chance of having a normal name. Surrounded by men who sing cadences about killing, who dream about killing, who wish to kill, the dog is destined to be called a homicidal name from a Stephen King novel. They make us repeat in bootcamp: we're born to kill, ready to die but never will.

Here's a favorite of the infantry. My seniors taught it to me when I was a boot:

I went to the playground...
Where all the kiddies play...
I pulled out my 240...
And I began to spray!
Singing left right left right left right kill!
Left right left right—you know I will!

Cujo was his name.

Are you going to help fight off the Taliban, the boys would ask, with grave expressions.

Wherever we went, it went, sometimes stuffed into the dump pouch of a flak jacket.

A dog with a name like Cujo had to live up to expectations. It needed the taste of flesh, so the guys could be sure it would kill Taliban.

We fed it stringy goat's meat. Dried-out chicken. Succulent beef patty mixture.

We played with it—but only to build rapport. When the killing started, Cujo would know the bad guys from the good.

It got along well with Ivan's bomb dog. They played together a little bit, but Ivan would break them up if they were getting too buddy-buddy. Security concerns. Willie had a job to do.

I went to the market...
Where all the ladies shop...

I pulled out my machete...
And I began to chop!
Singing left right left right left right kill!
Left right left right—you know I will!

Some higher-ups visit the Hill a couple of weeks after Cujo starts residing there full time. Most of them don't seem too concerned about the dog. Their questions are routine.

You know you're not supposed to keep dogs here, right?

Yes, but it won't go away. We've tried everything.

Does it have fleas?

I don't think so. We cleaned it up with soap and water. We take care of it.

Just make sure it doesn't bite anyone. Rabies is nine shots in the stomach.

Roger that.

So what's this I hear about you all not wearing shirts?

One hot day, while we sat around under the camouflage netting, the squad played a game. It was an old, traditional game, one most every Marine has played. The game was a test of manhood through daring feats.

No Balls, we called it.

Man, I could eat a chocolate dairyshake without any water. No Balls. So there goes one of us, choking on the fine grains of an MRE milkshake, unable to breathe until we intervene and give him water.

I'll eat a scorpion, said another man, and maybe he did, one of the gladiators, a tiny white specimen. Eat it with the stinger attached, someone told him—No Balls, motherfucker—so maybe, holding it by its deadly, translucent stinger, he bit into the head. And maybe he stared straight into the other man's eyes while he did it.

Any mundane or idiotic or imaginary act could become a No Balls event. Complain about patrol. Kick him in the nuts. Jump the canal. Walk up to the IED. Shoot it with a flare. Shoot a rocket at the Helmand River. Kill yourself. Eat with the Afghans. Patrol without water. Rip It challenge—drink one, two, three, five in a row. Tell your wife you want a divorce. Say "fuck" on the radio. Shoot the wall. Kill yourself. Throw a grenade in the burn pit. Fuck a goat. Fuck two goats. Give me your sister's phone number. Send First Sergeant a friend request on Facebook. Steal a watermelon from the patch next to the Hill. Destroy all the watermelons. Steal from the Durzay refrigerator. Throw your night vision in the burn pit. Kill yourself.

Most of the acts we called No Balls for could never happen. It was just a thing to say, when there was nothing to say. Every day we said it. Every day we didn't mean it.

One man, a replacement who came to the Hill after Cody was blown up, loved No Balls more than any of us. He would do or pretend to do just about anything to be the Most Ballsy. One time it got a little out of hand.

Name it, he said.

I don't know, said someone. Go get Cujo, bring him over here.

Then what?

I don't know, I haven't gotten that far. No Balls.

So the man creeps over to where Cujo's keeper lies on his cot, half-asleep, sweating in the June heat. Cujo's on the ground next to him. The dog is picked up. It makes a small, happy yelping sound, as if it is pleased to be picked up and cradled. By the time the man on the cot is awake, the dog is halfway to post one, its carrier laughing hysterically

"What the fuck are you doing?" says Cujo's keeper, annoyed, barely awake.

The squad's laughing, having a good time. Cheap entertainment. Perfect for a hot, bored day in Helmand Province.

The man who found Cujo eases off his rack and trudges to post one. The two men face each other, one of them dancing like a court jester, legs pumping up and down while he holds the puppy in front of him.

"It's mine now!"

"Give me back the fucking dog."

"You won't keep the dog away from him! No Balls!" someone says. Everyone's still laughing.

"He'll give it back," someone says.

"He's going to get his fucking ass kicked."

"Maybe. But it's funny either way."

The two men grow closer to the edge of the post. The man on watch removes himself from between the two of them.

There is a precipice and a long drop. They edge toward the cliff. The man holding the puppy throws a look at the squad. It's a joke. Just another joke. Nothing to worry about.

He thrusts the puppy out toward the cliff's edge, one hand on its neck fur, one hand on its belly. Its legs dangle a hundred feet in the air. The laughter lessens considerably, like a lock closing on a river, smaller and smaller until the laughter is gone altogether, replaced by a nervous kind of tittling, nobody knowing how far to push the joke.

"Should I do it?" he yells. The man who found Cujo can't do a thing. It's all just a game. If he throws a punch, then it's his fault. He'll be the one who can't take a joke. Just a game. Just a dark, funny game.

"No balls..." someone says quietly. Still joking. Everything's a joke. It has to be a joke. What is he going to do?

Just a dark joke. Combat humor.

The man holding Cujo smiles. He brings the dog back in to his chest. He begins to hand the dog back. The game's over now. Everyone gives a collective sigh of relief.

Just a joke. A stupid game we play out here, in Afghanistan, in combat.

A combat joke. Nothing to worry about.

And then the man throws Cujo off the Hill.

"No Balls," he shouts.

24

Penance

I remember the dog. I remember watching it disappear and I remember I was stunned, my mouth was open and I was aghast. And I remember my guts wrenching and I remember the men going to the bottom to find it still alive. And I remember them picking it up and cradling it and bringing it back to the top. And I remember it wasn't alive for long before it faded away and I remember very clearly there was nothing we could do. And I remember meeting the eyes of the man who threw it, who thought it was all part of the joke, and I remember being furious. I remember the squad's disbelief, our outrage, our anger and incredulity. Most of all I remember a great sadness. We all felt it.

I remember thinking: why does this dog matter so much to me? Maybe it was the stories I'd heard about other deployments. The bad: a guy who tortured kittens to death, three of them, throwing them in the air over and over until lungs collapsed and bones broke, then tossing them over a Hesco barrier. Guys tying 550 cord to chickens and swinging them around their heads, dousing them with diesel fuel and lighting them on fire, whirling and burning. A guy who hung ham in concertina wire to attract and shoot dog after dog after dog, throwing the bodies in the burn pit. The building smell of death.

The good: a dog that followed my squad around in Nawa on my first deployment, defending us, fighting off other dogs who tried to attack us, then sleeping at my feet when I stood post. Hand-feeding macaroni to orange kittens who chased mice around sandbags while I stood post.

Whatever the reason, I remember knowing instantly that what happened with Cujo was not acceptable. That we were not lost. That this was not something I could just let go. That there would be consequences for the man who broke our code. I remember giving him a choice: to stay here and face my justice, or to leave the Hill forever and tell our leaders why. He chose to stay.

He chose to pay his penance. He worked, and he sweated, and he did these things by himself and in armor and in the hottest part of the day. I sat with him and we spoke, and I asked him why he did what he did. He apologized, again and again, even though he admitted it didn't feel nearly as bad to him as it did to me. I told him why these things were wrong, how he hurt the squad. He told me about his upbringing. I learned of the cruelty of circumstances he had endured growing up, a childhood and adolescence so different from mine that I did not know what to make of it. We talked for a long time.

I remember being overwhelmed and conflicted. I remember thinking that not everyone grows up with the same sense of morality. I remember thinking that he was one of us, and at the same time that there must be a clear right and a clear wrong, even when things are always so gray, and maybe it is my job to enforce it. I remember the stories Iraq Marines would tell about shooting every dog they saw as they drove around in armored vehicles. How they purged strays with rifles and machine guns not only because they were ordered to, but because they wanted to, because they enjoyed it. I remember thinking that if I had been in Iraq, I would have done the same, and maybe I would have enjoyed it too. I remember thinking a dog is one step away from a person, one step toward darkness, and I remember thinking that loyalty means nothing unless you give someone a second chance. That the squad's failure was my failure, and this particular failure was certainly and unequivocally my own. I thought about the idea, drilled into my head since day one: handle things at the lowest level, and if you can't, you shouldn't be in charge.

I remember not knowing what to do.

I remember thinking that we were at war. I remember remembering Cujo, licking my hand. I remember thinking I needed hands to carry weapons and backs to carry the Thor and souls to carry the danger we all shared. I remember guilt, and shame, and a deep sense of sorrow, and that no amount of rationalizing could assuage the sick feeling in my stomach. I remember thinking long and hard about the squad and the burden losing one member would put on the rest of us.

A moment in time, before that day: the man who thought it was all a joke, next to a canal, carrying a Thor. A radio-controlled bomb. The Thor, with only three or four working antennae out of eight. The man, a few feet away, nonplussed, neck burning. The Thor buzzing, and clicking, and clicking, and clicking, and clicking, and clicking. A bomb that didn't explode. A day that nobody died.

25

Coming Down the Mountain

As the summer turns to early fall we're pulled off the Hill while the platoon searches for a new home. KT-4 becomes a four-man observation post. We turn it over to another platoon, and then we live at Durzay for a short time. After Durzay we head south. We are already very far south, but even further, patrolling the border with Pakistan, is a Light Armored Reconnaissance Battalion. These men hold an infantry designator but ride in armored vehicles. Mobile by nature. They occupy Firebase Zero-Zero, which our platoon takes over and where we spend the remainder of the deployment.

I arrive ahead of the rest of the platoon for a leader's reconnaissance. I spend a few days living with the LAR Marines, getting to know their area of operations. The country they roam is only a few miles from the Hill and looks much the same. Maybe it is greener. It feels subtly foreign. Two covers of the same old song. The Marines themselves are so dissimilar to us as to be nearly unrecognizable. There are valleys and rivers and worlds between us.

I learn about their tactics. How they patrol. Who their village elders are. I become familiar with the dwellings nearby, the houses and the camels and the shops.

What I learn scares me. These men do not know the risks they are taking. Like cows in a minefield they stroll along roads without worry, their chins held high. They do not sweep. They do not use the sickle. They walk in tactical columns. The road outside Zero-Zero turns and disappears behind a thick wall of brush, canals on either side, invisible to the small GBOSS camera, and since I think like a Taliban to survive the Taliban, I think this is a perfect place to put a bomb. Yet as we walk it the men still do not sweep. Their metal detectors stay slung upon their backs, as if they are waiting to be told to use them. They are glued to roads. They do not keep their Thor in the middle of the patrol. I want to scream at them: *this is how you die!*

I am confined, claustrophobic and constricted, more afraid than I have ever been in Afghanistan. These Marines must have a death wish. No—not that. They have not heard the Gospel of the Holley stick. They have not learned the Good Word of the Ranger File. They have not felt the Holy Spirit of the metal detector, been preached to about the Counter-IED Commandments. They have been fighting Their Own War five kilometers away. At first I wonder how the enemy has not picked up on the difference in their tactics. Why have they targeted my squad, when these Marines present an easier target? I squash this thought. Any day a Marine survives is a good day. Even if it is seemingly pure luck.

When my squad arrives and the LAR Marines leave, I breathe a sigh of relief, but not for myself.

At Zero-Zero we are with the rest of the platoon. At first we do not integrate well. We do not want to integrate. It is, as always, a matter of degrees. We think ourselves a degree or two of suffering beyond the ones who stayed in the valley. We are the isolated hill-people. Our uniforms are filthy. Our weapons condition one. Beholden only to ourselves, we are the wheat and everyone else is the chaff. We are an irregular unit, operating on our own set of codes and procedures and morality and justice. It can be a harsh justice. We are wild, but we are not wicked or evil. We enforce our own morality.

Now, when we come down from the Hill, we are withdrawn. In some ways we are uncivilized and unwilling to be civilized. We have forgotten much of the Way and we do not wish to re-learn it. We must be coaxed back to it, or pressed into it. Our leadership wants us to re-claim our membership cards in the Good Marines Club. We want to resist.

We want only what we've always wanted: to be left alone. To stay up on that Hill, that fucked-up, godforsaken Hill, that cursed Hill, the Hill where we stuck our flag and staked our claim. Where we discarded our illusions about winning the war and embraced survival. Where we found and fought and lost and eventually won against darkness.

We may have left the Hill, but it has not left us.

Friction with other squads. Squabbles over things we've never had: weights, grills, cold water, air conditioning. Eventually, grudging acceptance of the new status quo. Two-Bravo tells me to make sure the men don't keep high explosive grenades on their flaks. Tells me it's dangerous and men have died. Orders that we keep it in a special area near the entrance to the base with the rest of the high explosive. Regulations, order, protocol, rules. I am a Lance Corporal. Nobody tells me what to do. Everybody tells me what to do.

On the Hill, we slept with rounds in the chamber, charged and ready. Grenades in their pouches, quick to throw. Though the order is important to Two-Bravo, to me it is a nuisance and an inconvenience. Still, grudgingly, I comply. I tell the men, but the men are my peers and resent nitpicking. The Bravo finds high explosive in our kit again. I tell the men again.

Paranoia. A heightened sense of susceptibility to danger. I trade a laptop for an Afghan Army uniform. I am the keeper of Sergeant Mike's belt buckle, with its Soviet hammer and sickle, a token he gave me before he flew into the sun.

I fail to sleep. There is no enemy. The platoon is my enemy. The other squad leaders are my enemy. I alternate between bouts of prowling, adrenaline-induced mania and abject, depressive lethargy. It is all decided. It was already decided.

It is a few weeks ago, before Zero-Zero, and I am leading scouting patrols, searching for a new home for the Bomb Squad. In one candidate we find a seventy-pound jug of homemade explosive, alone, unrigged. No detonator. Next to the main road, which means it was probably put there to be used on a vehicle. We blow it in place. The shockwaves rattle my teeth.

Another day, another long hump. We spot a likely candidate in a heavily foliaged area. An inland compound next to a fast-running canal. The water is only a little milky, almost clear. We sweep and scan the house and its rooms. We see the windows, and the parapets and the rooftops we can shoot from, the close shrubbery that could hide attackers. Fields of fire blocked by trees. Blind spots and defilade. If used it would be a small outpost, large enough for one squad, maybe two. There is ample greenery and shade, large and small fronds, trees and an adjoining field. Small vehicles could get here without a problem. We entertain the fantasy of moving. But it is only a fantasy. And we have only the afternoon to enjoy it.

Sitting on the embankment, we are drawn to the water. We speak in hushed tones, as if we've stumbled upon a magic place, something out of a fantasy novel, where the trees and the leaves and the grass and the rocks all speak to each other. The house itself knows it will not welcome us here, in the same way that we all know this cannot be our new home. It is over. One last bout of imagination before we assimilate.

One by one, pulled as if by some otherworldly force, we discard our armor and tiptoe tentatively into the canal. We wade into the cold water. Our blouses are black, pure black, stiff as bark. Our backs and fronts riddled with heat rash from shoulder to sacrum, from collarbone to navel. Red and angry. I sink into the water. I taste dirt and grasp weeds and dirt comes out of my hair, hair that has had no problem standing on its own for months. There is peace in the ditch. I submerge and re-emerge. Things come to me, things wash away. The men take turns, some of us watching the road, some of us inhaling Reds and Milds and Pines, some of us blowing bubbles, floating, waiting for the war to end.

When we leave, we find a bomb in a stack of poppy stalks adjacent to the road. We blow it in place, damaging more than the canal.

In short time we become like the rest of the platoon. A little less disciplined, a little more stubborn. This band of misfits acclimates and shakes hands and dines with the rest of the grunts. The men who were once our friends become our friends again. We do not forget the Eye of Sauron, and the degrees, and the rest of it, but we put it aside for now. The bonds we had before readjust and right themselves. Being together at Zero-Zero forces our re-integration. We still fail to tuck our shirts in, and we have to be told to shave, and we forget about the high explosives in our flak jackets, but we come to realize we have left one war for another. We have left the Hill, and it is slowly leaving us, even as we wish it wouldn't.

Near the middle of the month a well-liked squad leader from another platoon dies. He is killed driving a John Deere Gator to a small patrol base, much like the Hill, on the only paths he can take. The enemy plants two bombs, the Gator as the target, and like the leader he is, he is selflessly driving it. I listen to the medevac on the radio. The carnage. I remember Bomb Squad's worst day. I am impotent. There is nothing I can do but listen to Someone Else's War.

The company gives a memorial service for him at the combat outpost. Most of us go, tucked uncomfortably into up-armored seven-ton trucks. We ride down roads and I cringe as I think about how vulnerable we are, how we're travelling down these roads with the expectation, the certainty, that at some point a bomb planted underneath will detonate and kill somebody. There is no way to avoid it. We just hope it won't happen to us. And if it does, we make sure we don't ask why. Asking why would make it worse.

The service goes in accordance with the Marine Corps Way.

First Sergeant calls the roll. There is nothing like it in the entire world. The gravitas. The emotion. The seriousness of a senior Marine reading names for the fallen, his piercing voice a gritty bridge to another world.

"Sergeant Anderson!" he cries.

"Present!" cries the Sergeant.

"Corporal Rodriguez!" he shouts.

"Present!" yells the Corporal.

"Lance Corporal Bryant!" announces the First Sergeant.

"Present!" comes the reply.

"Corporal Ott!"

Silence. He raises his voice.

"Corporal Nicholas Ott!"

Silence again. He builds up intensity in the final call, rising to an impassioned crescendo, and with every fiber he screams, stopping on each word:

"Corporal *Nicholas. S. Ott!*"

There is no reply. We stand erect with silent tears.

One night a guy standing post shoots himself in the leg. He's given a routine medevac because it's intentional. He wanted to go home. We are short, and there is little danger, but still he wanted to go home.

I'm woken up by voices yelling at him for being a coward. For forcing a medical evacuation. For not being able to last the dwindling number of days until we all go home.

I'm sorry, he cries. I'm sorry, over and over and over, even as they yell and berate him for his lack of resolve, shouting even as they carry him to the bird. I fall back asleep, no longer sympathetic to either side.

In the morning we forget him. I see him once, months later, back in the States. He walks bow-legged.

Two-Bravo sends a runner for me. I am sitting in the hooch, thinking about nothing. The runner tells me where to find him. I grab my rifle and shuffle to the command operations center.

On the walk, a tingling sensation emanates from the deepest part of my stomach and works its way outwards, from my core to my chest to my shoulders to my biceps and my forearms, landing in my fingertips and my toes and the tips of my ears and my nostrils. In my ears there is a pounding like a piston in an engine. I am suddenly thirsty, though my throat would not drink even if I offered it water.

I open the plywood door, into the heart of the operations center. Two-Bravo is alone. His arms are crossed. He is staring at me, and then words come out, words about high explosives he found on my squad's gear again early that morning, and words about other things, shortcomings, events I never thought important, but to someone with a higher understanding of the Way, someone for whom the world is not just one squad on one Hill, are. Words that sting pride. Words of a staff noncommissioned officer.

Even before he speaks, I know it's over. Two-Bravo relieves me as squad leader. Someone else takes the Bomb Squad. I leave the operation center a self-declared failure, a burden removed unwillingly from tired shoulders, carrying only my guilt and my rifle.

The remainder of the deployment passes quickly. The autumn sun colors poppy fields orange and red and brown. I stand shifts in the ops center and play volleyball with the Afghan soldiers on the other side of the outpost. Though I'm no longer a squad leader I am still asked to go along on patrols, to make sure new Corporals have a chance to gain some experience, to take over if something goes wrong.

On the last patrol of the deployment we bring along a newly arrived platoon from our sister battalion. We depart shortly before sunset. We are supposed to walk to several villages, hit a few checkpoints along the way. Cover ground. Gain experience.

We do none of that. The new Corporal and I walk a few hundred meters from the base and sit on a small rise. We smoke cigarettes in silence. We have more than enough experience. No reason to risk anyone's death, now that we are so close to the rest of our lives. If there ever was a reason.

Coming home is just going to war in reverse. We hold our breath as our massive airplane gets closer and closer and closer to the blue water of Kaneohe Bay, landing just at the edge of the cliff, the runway almost too short for it. We cheer. A great American flag waits for us in the hanger of the airfield. We disembark and move through the crowd.

The Corporal from the last patrol and I make our way to a parking lot, where we stand by somebody's pickup truck. We wear Hawaiian leis and masks, showing the emotions we think people want to see. Seniors and family and friends are waiting for us, but there is no rush to find them. The new Corporal and I share an Anchor Steam beer, and the silence. Three years later I attend his funeral.

Part Three

"Let's drop the war."
"It's very hard. There's no place to drop it."
"Let's drop it anyway."

— A Farewell to Arms

26

Our War

Denver, Colorado

It's like this: someone tries to get into your apartment in the middle of the night, some guy who lives a floor up, same apartment, and he's drunk but you don't know that, and as this guy is opening the door, you sense it somehow and you surge back to earth. Your dream state fades away and you surface, fully alert, heart pounding and drenched in sweat, adrenaline coursing through your veins as you activate those simmering, sub-surface protective systems you keep on low power now that you're out. Instantly you are awake, as awake as you were when they used to wake you up for firewatch, and you're moving before you even know what or why or who. You grab the baseball bat you keep next to your bed, leaning in the corner. You cross the distance in a single step and in a brutal burst of controlled violence you kick the door back into his face, hard, hard enough for him to scream an apology. He pushes back and you kick the door again and you stand there, hand high on the hilt of the bat, and he's on the other side saying he's sorry and you're confused. Through your hyperactive haze he explains and you realize it was all just a mistake. Nobody is trying to get into your apartment on purpose. Nobody is trying to kill you. He lives one floor up, he's sorry and you're sorry and you don't know what to do so you crumple to the floor. The pounding of your heartbeat against the inside of your skull makes your ears hurt. You pant and heave and realize how close you were to maybe finally killing someone. And even though when he stepped over that threshold it would have been legal and justified under the law it would have been the most brutal kind of tragedy. The weight of this hits you all at once. You drop the bat and it clatters to the floor next to your bed. Sleep eludes you. It takes a day to come down.

Or sometimes it's like this: you're standing in the kitchen of your suburban Colorado single-family home with detached garage, long driveway and fenced backyard. You're looking at the firepit you just built. You're proud of yourself for finishing something. You found your courage, and this sustained you throughout the building process. You focused. You planned. You went and bought rocks, put them in the back of your buddy's pickup truck. You poured the rocks and the gravel yourself, shoveling it out one heavy scoop at a time. You cut the branches all by yourself, making sure you could start a great big fire without lighting up the overhanging tree. You dug furrows for the border stones and planted them, little red-brick waves that keep the dirt from your backyard path, and you laid paper that keeps weeds from growing out of the ground and into the rocks. What a pain in the ass, but you did it. You should be proud. You haven't been able to care about anything long enough to finish in quite some time. A year or more. Ever since you got out.

So you're watching the firepit, drinking coffee, when you hear it: a high-pitched scream. A terrible, advancing, shrill sound, aching toward you, ready to burst, to explode in the yard or in the driveway or on top of the house. You start to shake and tremble and you throw your beer at the fire. The noise continues, rises, closer and closer now. The sound of death, artillery rounds falling onto your open backyard. Here they come, you think as you shoulder your way into your kitchen. Closer and closer. The trees shake and the garage shakes and the floor shakes as you open the trapdoor to your cellar and close it behind you. There is no light and no sound except for the screaming of the rounds, piercing through the darkness. Closer and closer. You huddle in the corner and wrap your knees around your legs and scream. You scream and you scream and you scream and even when the noise is gone you scream,

oh god oh god oh god oh god

but there's nothing you can do but sit and wait for it to go away.

In a minute or so it registers that what you are hearing is not an artillery round. It is not going to hit you. It is not going to kill you.

It is just a jet. It is a jet and it is flying overhead and it recedes into the distance but you don't move for a long while, not until you feel spiders crawling on your legs. You climb the step-ladder out of your cellar to find your dog lying on the tile floor, panting, waiting for you, again.

When we got back from Garmsir I lived with an alcoholic roommate in Mackie Hall, the most degenerate barracks on Marine Corps Base Hawaii. My roommate's ritual for Saturday afternoons was to drink thirty Coors Lights and take an Ambien. By eight or so he'd be leaning heavily over the third-floor railing, threatening to flatten himself on the ground below. I'd have to bring him back into the room and lock the door from the outside or he'd kill himself, not out of any desire to stop living, but out of sheer stupidity. The Corps let him reenlist.

I made Corporal a couple of weeks after we arrived at the island. By becoming a noncommissioned officer I was able to get out of details like the gate guard duty Jason got stuck with. They even made me an instructor in a fireteam leader's course. Five days a week I was teaching boots and peers how to coordinate rocket shots, write patrol orders and lead fire and movement. I still felt like a failure. Two-Bravo taking away my squad in Garmsir was fresh in my mind, and every time I stood in front of the class I felt like I had something to be ashamed of. The edge of that shame took many years to dull. It cuts deeply even in later years, as I grow older and more removed from it, even when I tell myself I was twenty-one and stupid and proud and doing the best I could, because my best wasn't good enough. And even though I kept the playing cards from my shoulder pocket, the two of spades and three of clubs that saw me through so much misery, I feel distant from the squad I once led.

One night, a few months after coming home, after putting my roommate to bed, I grabbed a hat from my wall-locker and walked over to a party in an adjoining barracks, where men I knew were drinking Jack Daniel's and playing rowdy music. I don't remember exactly who was there. Maybe Jason. Maybe Tony. Maybe Russell. Maybe none of them. The only person I remember for certain was Cody. I remember this because it was the first time I had seen him after his injury.

Cody looked like a shadow of his former self. Where before he was burly and thick, he was now thin and gaunt. Where his teeth had been white and straight, some were missing. His face was pockmarked and discolored. His clothes fit loosely on his frame. He walked with a limp. At the sight of him, my overriding urge was to run away. Our eyes met and without thinking I fled, turning right around and walking out the same way I came in. Before I could help myself I was standing over white catwalk railing, trying to hold it together, breathing deeply through my nose to keep from sobbing. Cody walked up and leaned over the railing by my side.

"I'm sorry," was all I could choke out.

"It's okay," he replied.

We stood silent for a long moment. Then we talked. I asked him about the Wounded Warrior Battalion. He told me about his injuries. We reminisced about the Hill, the short time we had before everything changed. The time he left his night vision on post. How he concocted an excuse that made me laugh. How I couldn't even bring myself to be mad at him about it. As we spoke I kept the guilt to myself. I think he knew.

As we spoke, I pulled a hat out of my back pocket and handed it to him.

Kentucky, read the brim. He still has that hat.

It's Memorial Day in Denver. I don't remember the year. So many of the years have felt the same since giving up a part of myself in exchange for freedom.

On this Memorial Day I am sitting on a high-backed chair in a local dive bar. Before me are a couple of coins and three napkins. On those napkins I write the names of three men. Three men I used to know. Three men I want to remember. I buy three beers, all at once. I tell the bartender, and he brings them for me, a little perplexed, then less so when he sees the coins and the names.

Jason sits across from me. He came to Denver not long after we put the Corps in our rearview mirrors. He moved across the country because some things needed forgetting. He is here in the bar with me because some things need remembering.

We sit at a table in the corner of the dive bar, drinking to the men on the napkins. This is not an original ritual. I first saw it on the internet somewhere. I latched on to it. I don't want anyone to think I'm doing things I saw on the internet, so I keep the napkins close and don't advertise what I'm doing. Despite finding it online I feel that as far as tributes go it is good and honest. I don't want attention for myself. It is the men whom I drink to that could use some attention. It is the never-ending war that could use some attention. As I set the beers on the napkins I imagine, somewhat arrogantly, that nobody in the bar knows anything of this war except for what they see in movies, what they read in books with tridents on the cover.

I do not relate to these books and movies. Even if they are about the Afghanistan War, they aren't about My War. Our War. The men on the napkins' War. Nobody seems to know about this particular war. Cody's War. Terrance's War. Doc's War and Russell's War and Nate's War. Nobody seems to know about the trudging and the misery and the canals. Nobody seems to know about the men on the napkins and they don't seem to know anything about chasing ghosts in Helmand Province and they don't know about the endless fields of brown and red and purple and green.

In the coming years the number of names on the napkins grows. I come to know more men who passed away when they got home than died in the war. Men who died before they were thirty years old. Young men who stayed young forever while old men grew older. It is the tragic cycle of war and post-war.

It is jarring to hear that a young man you knew died. Your own mortality is at stake. You think: if him, why not me? Wasn't it just a couple of years ago you saw him? If he's gone, is he even real anymore? These men were real, and then they became memories, and you fear now that's all they'll ever be. They will exist solely in the neurons of your brain, and those neurons will fade over your lifetime. As the neurons fade so will the men.

Until they're on the napkin. It sounds so stupid when you say it out loud, but a napkin in a dirty bar becomes your link to them. When you are twenty-four and the Corps is still fresh in your mind these things matter to you. They are not cliché. You write the names of men on the napkin not so you can show other people, but so you can show yourself. Then they are tangible and real and you can talk to them again. I can talk to them, and sitting here now I can talk to Jason about them. We talk, and then we're silent.

Two in the morning, sometime in December and you've just left a pub in Cap Hill. You're pretty far gone but you can't go home yet. Something keeps you up, keeps you moving through silent snow-covered streets. You leave solitary footprints. You are awake.

You walk. North on Grant Street, past the 10th Avenue street-sign, past the fat man walking his bulldog, up so late, past the modern-looking orange and grey 1000 Grant Street building with its fifteen-hundred-dollar studio apartments, past the brownstone government building with its diagonal parking spaces with ominous "no parking" signs. Past the sloping concrete and desert-brown weeds in the cracks, the gentrified trees, the wizard-spired old house made of red brick and fenced off, past a row of seven-year-old cars, past the yellow fire hydrant and the funky looking building with the turquoise arches and the hill you cruise down on the way to school, past the part where the street narrows and congests and the heads-down couple who stop talking as you walk by and the back of your old building on Logan Street, past the Chinese takeout place and the Domino's Pizza and the Buffalo Exchange and the first-ever Quizno's, and the bar you've never been to and the Corepower Yoga where someone you know teaches college students how to backbend, past the homeless couple on a corner, shouting at each other, past the rideshare parking lot, past the conglomerate-rock office, past the green pedestrian barriers where it gets dangerous and the sidewalk is always slimy, the shitty old apartment building and the Pub on Penn, which never changes, and Pablo's Coffee, where a girl with a huge disk earring always ignores you until you order, and where you always put a tip in the jar anyway; past Beauty Bar, with its disco nights and man buns, past the Kirkland Museum of Art you've never been in, past the bicycle-sharing station that never has any bikes, past the Capitol Hill Convenience store that never has a sober clerk, the hip breakfast spot with the two hour wait, the boutique smoke shops and the boutique coffee shops and the boutique boutiques; past Wax Trax and Kilgore Comics and the idea of reading, past the red bricks, again, and the green barriers on the road, and the school and the over-bridge and the graffiti-filled basketball courts and Washington and Clarkson and Ogden streets, all the way until you reach the Downing street sign, where you stop.

You pull the collar of your peacoat up against the cold and light a cigarette. You walk into the middle of the street without looking. Nobody's on the road. You stare west, toward the city. Nothing moves. You send a text. You get a reply.

You follow your footprints out of the street. You walk out of the cold and into someplace warm, someplace maybe the war can't follow you.

27

Pruntytown

Blue Ridge Parkway, Virginia

Stillness in the campground, fog above the grass, pain along my spine. When I wake I am for a moment on the Hill again, savoring the coolness of the early morning, dreading the inevitable heat. Having grown used to the comfort of a queen-sized bed in the years since leaving the Marines, I am now sore in muscles I don't remember having. Overnight my arm went numb, trapped beneath my body. I let it sting while the blood flows through relieved veins like a Pashtun farmer opening canal waters into a poppy field.

Packing is a chore and by the time I'm done the sky is bright blue. Middle-aged couples, perennial residents of the campground, tenants of semi-permanent recreational vehicles, meander under their awnings, drinking coffee. They wave at me as I pass slowly on the heavily laden motorcycle, weaving my way off the gravel and back onto the highway.

It's four hours of riding to Pruntytown, West Virginia. A good day on a motorcycle is long in time but short in distance. It is winding and devoid of traffic. A good day takes you onto roads that curve like camel-humps, serpentine and smooth. Two-lane highways or semi-highways with thirty-five or forty-five or fifty-five mile per hour speed limits. Roads that abut rural ranches and houses, roads that twist their way through national forests and state parks. On a bike like mine you can take the curves comfortably at one and a half times the recommended speed limit. If you're daring, you can double it. One hand on the accelerator, I relax through my four hours, in awe of the scenery. I pass through small towns with names like Shady Spring and Oak Hill and Muddlety. Methodist churches, dollar stores, empty brick garages, lonely gas stations. West Virginia is nothing but green.

In years to come I ride around Europe a bit. The roads there are perfunctory things, perfectly acquitted to their tasks, but the surroundings are always shaped by humans. I ride Germany and Switzerland and Italy and Austria and as I do I often find myself disquieted. There is something unsettling about riding in Europe that I can't quite put my finger on. Is it the rest stops where you pay to use the toilet? The cars passing by at absurd speeds? The lack of back roads and alternative routes? Is it the constant stoplights, or the lack of space? Perhaps it's all of these things.

The most distinctly unique quality of riding in America, in West Virginia, Utah, Northern New Mexico—most importantly, as important as anything can be—is the feeling that we are visitors in the surroundings. We are fleeting life forms zipping through. We are transient and the land is ancient. Not so for the Germans or the Austrians or the French. People have been to every corner of Europe. They have shaped it and carved paths through it and made it accessible and trashed it and cut it down and blown it to pieces and made it beautiful again.

The highest reaches of the Alps have little huts where you can buy a beer or a Schnitzel. The hiking paths are so well-worn you can wear tennis shoes. And the masses and masses of Europeans who move through the land do not treat nature the way that we treat it. They think they are in charge of it. They carve it, manipulate it, change it

THE HILL | 257

to their liking, and even in the places where they want to keep nature natural you can tell it isn't quite. You can spot the straight lines that God didn't make and you can see the poles and the quaint houses and the paths that are all made of gravel and don't go very far. And in some ways it is better but in many ways it is worse. In America we keep things wild, whether by choice or because we have no choice. Perhaps what makes America worth sacrificing for are the wild mountains of Colorado or Idaho or Wyoming or even parts of West Virginia, where you can ride miles and miles without a stoplight, seeing only a few buildings along the way, not slowing down for them.

If you grew up as a boy in West Virginia in a certain era, your parents might have told you that they'd send you to Pruntytown if you were bad enough. Men in vans would snatch you up and you'd be whisked away to the West Virginia Industrial Home for Boys, left to rot in a jail of your own childish imagination. Then that institution closed, and in its place rose a prison. Pruntytown now is just a smattering of houses, an elementary school, the Correctional Center. It is working class. And it, along with the nearby town of Grafton, is home to the West Virginia National Cemetery.

As I pull into the parking lot I am all but shaking. I hop off my bike, put my helmet on the pegs and take my jacket off. In the visitor center there's a kindly woman who asks if she can help me.

"How do I find a grave?" I ask. She points to a touch-screen. It's simple, easy to use. Entering a last name sends a frightening burst of adrenaline into my head which seems to blow my eardrums apart from the inside. My throat is a blocked dam, my esophagus fills with bile and I'm panting, breathing heavily, trying to calm myself. My eyes well up but I keep them from overflowing for now. It's not time. I write down the section, row and number the computer feeds me.

The walk to section five takes seven or eight minutes. I stroll through beautiful rows of grave markers, neatly arranged, deeply etched. A few flowers, here and there. An elderly man standing over a grave, looking through it. I bow my head as I pass.

Section five looks like all of the other sections except that it's the newest, on the furthest hill. There's a work crew there, manning a backhoe, digging graves. The workers with their white safety helmets, four or five of them, joke among themselves. Suddenly I become very self-conscious. Except for these men, I am the only person in this section. Focusing on the directions I have written down, I reach the marker I am looking for.

It is a solemn thing, the marker. Twenty-four inches high, four inches thick, thirteen inches wide. Two hundred and thirty pounds of marble. Standard-issue, like the men and women it denotes. If only they knew how un-standard the person this one marked had been.

I approach, slower now, and as I get to the marker I take a knee and try to hold myself together. I touch the headstone. The day is hot but the marker is cool, like a stone you might have just pulled out of a river. The sounds coming from the backhoe have stopped, and just as I am unable to hold back my emotions any longer I hear a kind voice.

"Sir, would you like us to stop and give you some time?"

I look up at an orange vest and a yellow helmet and a goatee.

"Don't you need to work?" I am barely able to ask.

"It's okay," he says. "We can take a break. Take as long as you need."

I am embarrassed but grateful. He leads the men away. I can still see them, but they are far enough away that I feel some privacy. I turn to the headstone. I read the name and as it registers I am unable to stop myself. I begin to sob, big, gasping breaths, one hand on the headstone and then the other, and then I'm sitting down, clutching the marble as if it were a person. Yes, I say to myself, this is a person. This is Levi. He is a person.

Levi died at night on a motorcycle here on the winding roads of his home, West Virginia. He was buried a year before I came to the cemetery. I missed his funeral because I didn't know about it. I'd spent so much time after I left the Marines intentionally isolating myself, trying to forget some things, trying to hold on to others, and because of this

I missed the passing of someone who made some of my enlistment less miserable. I missed the chance to meet his family, to tell them his stories, stories of things he'd done that they'd never hear from anyone else. Memories they couldn't get anywhere else.

He was buried by his family, whom he always told me had little idea about war or the military, though they were proud of him. As I look at his grave marker, I see what he meant. Under his name is his Marine Corps rank, and under his rank are the words *Persian Gulf*, an incorrect denomination for the time and place of the war he fought. It strikes me that he would have thought this misnomer hilarious, even preferred this, because that was who he was. An absurdist. A happy oddity. A "crazyman extraordinaire," says the etching on his headstone.

I stare at the gravestone and sob and I cannot think of anything but to say I am sorry. I am sorry to Levi in particular because I let him bear the brunt of our seniors' ire. Because I did not stand up to them, stand up for him, like I should have. Because I gave in to social pressure instead of following my own conscience. I'm sorry, I say, again and again. I'm sorry.

I'm sorry. I am apologizing to Levi, and I'm apologizing for him, but as I start to say sorry the emotions come up from the pit of my stomach where they hide and wrench me and cause me anxiety and tear at me and raise my blood pressure and keep me from sleeping and keep me from focusing day after day after day. As I say *I'm sorry* for the hundredth time, I know my apologies are not just for Levi, but for Cody and Cujo and Jason and Terrance and Ivan and Nate and the Hill and the Bomb Squad and Hajji Ismail and the snipers and Sergeant Mike and Wali and Jack and the Actual and the Bravo and all those who believed in me and the ones I let down and the darkness we all went through and finally myself, who I let down most of all.

It is a cathartic release of emotion, a cliché scene in a cliché war movie. I become self-conscious again. I stop crying. I turn and slump, my back against the gravestone, plucking at grass, talking to Levi.

I tell him about the video games I've been playing. About the *Magic: The Gathering* cards I've collected. The Live-Action Roleplaying festival in Germany that I'm thinking of going to when I get there. It's the largest in the world. I think you'd like that, Levi.

I spend fifteen or twenty minutes there, my tears drying in the midday sun. I tell Levi things I've never told anyone. Things that need saying, things I wish I would have told him when he was alive. After a while a sense of calm washes over me. An odd, sad thought pokes its way into my head.

Was Levi ever really my friend? At times I shared a foxhole or a tent or a barracks floor or a post with him. We endured some things together, and we hung out socially, but not often, and we messaged each other on Facebook after the Corps, but not regularly. We were not overly close, not in the way you would think someone who comes to visit a grave should be. He had his circle, and I had mine. And yet here I am, releasing my emotions at his graveside, hurting deeply that he is gone. Surely that means something.

Lying against the marble, I decide that it doesn't matter if we were good friends, or best friends, or just friends. All that matters is that we knew each other. We went to war together. We fought the war we were given, the way we were expected to fight it, together. All that matters is that I am here, for him, for no other reason than to see him, and to talk to him about what happened, and to let him know I am sorry. That I remember. That I will always remember. I think he would have appreciated that, just as I would, if he were lying on the tombstone, our fates reversed.

Acknowledgments

Thanks to—

My father and stepmother. The friends who read and gave valuable feedback on the many versions of this book over the years. My publisher, editor, cover artist, designer and the rest of the Second Mission team. The veteran literary community on social media. And my love, who helped me find my words, and myself, after the war.

Above all, the men of The Hill, most of whom read this before it went to print. Your endorsements meant the world to me.

About the Author

Aaron Kirk deployed twice to Helmand Province, Afghanistan as an infantry Marine, where he participated in Operation Moshtarak and conducted counterinsurgency operations in Nawa, Marjah and Garmsir. His work has been featured in several outlets and anthologized in the poetry collection *War...& After*. *The Hill* is his first full-length book. He can be found on social media at @memoirsofagrunt and on the web at memoirsofagrunt.com.

Printed in the USA
CPSIA information can be obtained
at www.ICGtesting.com
LVHW050850110124
768548LV00049B/1437/J